Databases in theory and practice

Book belongs to :

Mpundu Mukanga (JR)

Databases in theory and practice

Second edition

John Jones

and

Simon Monk

INTERNATIONAL THOMSON COMPUTER PRESS
I(T)P™ An International Thomson Publishing Company

London • Bonn • Boston • Johannesburg • Madrid • Melbourne • Mexico City • New York • Paris
Singapore • Tokyo • Toronto • Albany, NY • Belmont, CA • Cincinnati, OH • Detroit, MI

Databases in Theory and Practice, Second Edition

Copyright © 1997 International Thomson Computer Press

I(T)P A division of International Thomson Publishing Inc.
The ITP logo is a trademark under licence.

For more information, contact:

International Thomson Computer Press
Berkshire House
168–173 High Holborn
London WC1V 7AA
UK

International Thomson Computer Press
20 Park Plaza 13th Floor
Boston, MA 02116
US

Imprints of International Thomson Publishing

International Thomson Publishing GmbH
Königswinterer Straße 418
53227 Bonn
Germany

International Thomson Publishing Asia
60 Albert Street # 15-01
Albert Comple
Singapore 189969

Thomas Nelson Australia
102 Dodds Street
South Melbourne, 3205
Victoria
Australia

International Thomson Publishing Japan
Hirakawacho Kyowa Building, 3F
2-2-1 Hirakawacho
Chiyoda-ku, 102 Tokyo
Japan

Nelson Canada
1120 Birchmount Road
Scarborough, Ontario
Canada M1K 5G4

International Thomson Editores
Seneca, 53
Colonia Polanco
11560 Mexico D. F. Mexico

International Thomson Publishing South Africa
PO Box 2459
Halfway House
1685 South Africa

International Thomson Publishing France
Tours Maine-Montparnasse
33 avenue du Maine
75755 Paris Cedex 15
France

British Library Cataloguing-in-Publication Data
A catalogue record for this book is available from the British Library

Library of Congress Cataloging-in-Publication Data
A catalog record for this book is available from the Library of Congress

First printed 1997

ISBN 1-85032-288-0

Set by Columns Design Ltd, Reading
Printed in the UK by the Alden Press, Oxford

Contents

Preface

The first edition of this book, published in 1986, started as follows.

> The term 'database' has become one of the most used and abused computing phrases of modern times. From its first coinage in 1963 to a few years ago the term was synonymous with 'a large collection of data, usually on a mainframe computer'. With the development of personal computers, however, the definition has changed subtly to include any collection of related data bound under a controlling piece of software. At the other extreme to the initial definition, certain TV programmes have referred to the *basic read* statement with an associated *data* statement as being a database.

It also stated that the majority of 'current' research was being undertaken on relational databases. Since then the usage of databases has changed considerably, particularly as a result of the downward spiralling costs of hardware and the availability of database packages on an unprecedented scale. The database type with the highest usage at present is relational because of the huge increase in small business users. Relational databases are available in many forms although certain companies dominate the market-place when it comes to larger multi-user models.

At the same time there is now a distinct move towards object orientation in both traditional programming areas and database systems, and this book now looks towards the future trends by including more theory and practice of relational models, and then moving on to the object-oriented models.

The misuse of the term 'database' still abounds and one frequently hears of 'building a customer database' to mean having a single file of customer information. Database technology will still aid this user of a single file by allowing easy-to-use but complex search and retrieval methods, but this book is concerned with the analysis, design and implementation of multiple file/table systems. Moreover, it is still very true that a well analysed and designed system will stand the test of time whatever the database system.

This book is in four parts:

- Part One, in which the need for a database approach is looked at and the principal features of a database system are outlined (Chapters 1–6);
- Part Two, in which the work of the database administration in creating and maintaining a database is looked at and, at the same time, the general database features are developed more fully (Chapters 7–9);
- Part Three, which looks at various existing database systems, how their common

elements are identified and how each tackles the problems outlined in Chapter 1 (Chapters 10–13);

- Part Four, in which future trends in database technology (particularly the OODB) are explored (Chapters 14–17).

To be able to follow a large proportion of this book, we have had to assume some knowledge of both basic data processing and, because many of the larger institutions still use it, even if only as a host language for embedding relational languages, COBOL. In many cases the record definitions have been changed to a more general format using NUMBER and CHAR. Those who have a reasonable knowledge may now go to Chapter 1. For the others, read on.

A *bit*, which is synonymous with binary digit, is the smallest unit of data storage, and is able to store 1 or 0. A *byte* is defined as eight bits and, generally, is used as the storage requirement of a single character; 1 Mb is 1 million bytes and 1 Gb is 1000 million bytes: these are used extensively to describe the capacity of storage devices.

A computer file consists of a number of records each of which contains the same number of data items: for example, all customer data would form a file, the data pertaining to each individual customer would comprise a record, and each piece of data (e.g. name, address) would be a data item.

The difference between data and information is an important one. Data are raw numbers or characters, such as 68.42, which on their own have no meaning. They become information when we give them meaning. Thus, 'Mr Smith has 68.42 in his account' is information. For obvious reasons of storage efficiency, the computer only stores data.

It is the task of the application software (or database management system here) to be able to interpret this data in a way relevant to the user's requirements (i.e. as information). Where the record sizes have been used to calculate storage requirements, our numbers may at first seem wrong. This is attributable (we hope) to the fact that where the record contains numeric data, we have allowed for the packing of data (a facility available on most machines whereby a numeric digit can be stored in half a byte instead of the usual one byte). On a similar note, many database systems allow compaction of character items: thus, if only 35 characters of a 200-character field are used then only 35 are stored. All character fields in this book are shown as being their maximum length.

The database language definitions, where shown, are usually lacking in punctuation. The reason for this is that punctuation varies considerably from system to system. (Even with CODASYL databases, where the constructs are common, the punctuation varies from manufacturer to manufacturer.)

Part One
Database Analysis and Design

1

Traditional approaches to data management

1.1 Introduction

One of the problems of the educational system, particularly germane to the computer world, is the problem of scale. Because of time and resource restrictions, students tend to work on data sets of limited size and this can lead them to believe that if their programs or databases work for 20 records then they will work just as well for a thousand, 50 thousand or half a million records. For low volumes of data, design and efficiency considerations can become irrelevant since any computer can process almost anything with this volume of data almost instantaneously.

Much of the students' work also relates to a single-user environment in which the user can recover errors, back up data or change data structures when needed, without any further analysis, design or consideration of the effect on other users. This will be acceptable if they gain employment installing single-user database systems for small businesses, but the considerations of volume add an extra (and very important) dimension to databases in practice.

On this basis, we offer no apologies for maintaining the example of the banking system from the first edition. The problems are amplified, particularly with the non-database approaches of this chapter, but the database approach, dealt with throughout the rest of the book, can be shown to be just as strong whatever the size of business.

1.2 An example

An expanding banking business has approximately 1 000 000 customers, 750 000 investment accounts, 100 000 mortgage accounts, 200 branches plus associated insurances, agents, etc. A transaction occurs if a customer pays money into his/her account or draws money out (in the real world there are many other types but they need not concern us here). Customers average 30 transactions per year on an investment account though individual values can range from one (yearly interest which also counts as a transaction) to several hundred. The mortgage accounts are usually 14 per year (12 monthly repayments plus an interest transaction plus one building insurance premium). It is also possible to pay weekly, so the theoretical maximum is 54.

An investment account may be owned by up to four customers (though most are singly or joint owned). There is no limit on the number of investment accounts that a single customer can be named on. A mortgage account is generally owned by two customers (husband and wife) though never by more than two. Second and subsequent mortgages are possible but need not concern us here. Most mortgage account holders are also investment account holders (though this need not be the case).

At year-end all accounts are capitalized (have interest added) and the transactions are microfiched and then deleted from the system. Thus at the start of the year all accounts have no associated transactions on file.

That brief description of the workings of a bank will suffice for the present. Now let us look at the problems.

The directors of the bank are very interested in introducing a branch network system with all 200 branches connected to a single computer. In addition a 24-hour cash-point service is felt to be highly desirable for the bank to be competitive. They wish a feasibility study to be carried out as to whether to go database or not. Whatever is to be the end result, they want it fully operational within a year and the end product must also be:

- fast,
- efficient,
- secure,
- flexible,
- expandable,
- reliable.

During the feasibility stage the following points are likely to emerge, and need to be discussed, before a recommendation can be made.

1.3 Inherent problems

As with many other businesses, the bank's raw data are decentralized because the business is decentralized. Customers perform their transactions at branches scattered around the country and, because the business revolves around the customer, most of the remaining business is performed at branch level. Now if every customer could be made to transact at only their local branch then these in turn could become autonomous with each having its own set of data. Unfortunately this is not the case and for customers to be able to transact wherever they choose, the information relating to their accounts should, ideally, be available at all branches. This implies a centralized storing of data with networked access from the various branches (nodes). The alternative distributed information system is discussed later (Chapter 14).

In most larger businesses the higher management, who are ultimately responsible for major decision-making, are sited at a head office (they may be regionalized but the effect is the same). They also need access to the information in order to be able to make decisions and guide company policy. In the past this has been done through summaries and reports gathered at the local sites and collated centrally. So that the business may be profitable and run smoothly, their own information and processing requirements also need considering at an early stage of system development.

If, at present, we assume a centralized storing of data with networked access to all users then the next consideration is a comparison of traditional data storage and retrieval mechanisms with a database approach to see which would be more suitable.

1.4 The large-record approach

Most business-oriented computers do not allow variable-length records, and those that do do not allow variable-length occurrences of repeating groups of data within a record. (Those database systems that do often only allow 'long' fields of text which can be stored in a compacted form.) This means that the record must cater for the maximum number of occurrences of a repeating group. Since there is a business need to store information about investment transactions and their associated customers, the file might look something like that in Figure 1.1.

Within this record the investment details would contain the account number (probable key), balances, account type, and so on. Investment customer details would contain the names and addresses of the four (maximum) named customers, and investment transactions details would contain date, amount and transaction-type details for each transaction up to the maximum of 300.

It is apparent that from this record we can obtain all information relating to an account with a single record access which means that any programs reading the data will have minimum I/O time, but the price is in disc storage. This record is 3300 bytes long (see Preface) which, if allocated to every investment record, would produce a file requiring 2.5 Gb of disc storage. This is an excessive amount because disc space is utilized poorly. Most records will use space for only one or two customers and only 30 of the transactions (at maximum storage time at year-end). This in itself represents a wastage of 2900 bytes per record (or 88%).

We also have problems of data duplication, for if a customer owns more than one account then their name and address will appear on each. Can we guarantee that each occurrence of the logically same name and address will be identical? Clearly not without some complicated piece of cross-checking software, and if the customer moves then all occurrences will need updating.

Due to the large size of the file, taking security copies (backup) will take a long time (several hours) on a tape streamer device, but would be considerably quicker using an optical storage device. For that reason any form of recovery that involves reloading old files will be slow (see Section 1.6). More problems arise when we look at the mortgage file definition as shown in Figure 1.2.

The problems are similar to those of the investment account (but on a lesser scale when looking at storage requirements because the maximum number of customers is only 2 and the maximum number of transactions is only 54. However, since most

```
INVESTMENT RECORD
    INV DETAILS          NUMBER(40)
    INV CUST DETAILS     CHAR(70) OCCURS 4
    INV TRANS DETAILS    NUMBER(20) OCCURS 300
```

Figure 1.1 An investment record catering for maximum occurrences

```
MORTGAGE RECORD
    MORTGAGE DETAILS   NUMBER(40)
    MTG CUST DETAILS   CHAR(70) OCCURS 2
    MTG TRANS DETAILS NUMBER(20) OCCURS 54
```

Figure 1.2 A mortgage record catering for maximum occurrences

mortgage account holders will also have investment accounts then their names and addresses will now appear on both, giving rise to more potential inconsistency.

There may indeed be a business need to link a mortgage record to the investment record (or perhaps to all of several). Similarly there may be a need to link all investment records owned by one customer. This logical linking of associated records cannot be readily done by most non-database software and, if required, would need to be supported by some complex index system. An alternative might be to store all other related account numbers on each account, but the maximum number of occurrences is not definable so more space would be wasted through catering for the largest.

The normal 'flat file' approach to data management finds it extremely difficult to represent the relationships between associated records and files that are meaningful to the business, or even to check that data are consistent. If these linkages cannot be done then each record will have to be located independently and the efficiency of the system will suffer.

An easy solution to these problems of data access and data duplication might be to construct one large consolidated file containing both investment and mortgage information as shown in Figure 1.3. Now the customer data are stored only once, but what if a customer owns more than one investment account? What of the insurance record associated with the mortgage? We could allow for these in the record structure shown in Figure 1.4.

Already the record size is getting out of hand (31 000 bytes) and if we extend the arguments to consider the associated endowment policies (if there are any), deeds details, and so on, then, clearly, the situation is getting ridiculous. In addition, what would be the key to such a record? Most filing systems insist on a single key based on a unique identifier (i.e. the account number) and then allow a number of secondary keys that need not be unique. The identifier cannot be a part of a repeating group (i.e. in an OCCURS clause), so which of the account numbers should we choose? Whichever we choose we would have to maintain it even if the account is closed, because other accounts or the mortgage might be kept open. Would such a number still be meaningful to the business? Or to the customer? The mortgage number is

```
ACCOUNT RECORD
    INV DETAILS         NUMBER(40)
    INV TRANSACTIONS    NUMBER(20)   OCCURS 300
    MTG DETAILS         NUMBER(40)
    MTG TRANSACTIONS    NUMBER(20)   OCCURS 54
    CUSTOMER DETAILS    CHAR(70) OCCURS 4
```

Figure 1.3 A consolidated file

```
ACCOUNT RECORD
    INVESTMENTS              OCCURS 10
        INV DETAILS          NUMBER(40)
        INV TRANSACTIONS     NUMBER(20) OCCURS 300
    MTG DETAILS              NUMBER(40)
    MTG TRANSACTIONS         NUMBER(20) OCCURS 54
    INSURANCE DETAILS        CHAR(70) OCCURS 3
    CUSTOMER DETAILS         CHAR(70) OCCURS 4
```

Figure 1.4 The consolidated file approach taken to extremes

clearly a non-starter because 650 000 investment account holders do not have mortgages.

Demonstrably, the large-record approach removes some problems, mainly that of access times, but it creates a lot more that cannot be overcome.

1.5 The small-record approach

A solution to many of the problems highlighted in the last section might be to have several smaller files as shown in Figure 1.5, each with its own unique identifier.

This view has drastically reduced the storage requirements, to a maximum of only 225 Mb, because we now only need to create a new transaction record when we need one instead of pre-allocating large amounts. Unfortunately we now need the investment account number on every transaction plus a transaction number to uniquely identify it (this was not required before because the transaction numbering was inherent in the OCCURS clause). Similarly for the mortgage account.

However, there are still problems with the customer record. Unless we have separate customer records for investments and mortgages we need both account numbers as primary keys. This does not cater for customers having more than one investment account and, in addition, it implies that the user will have to know which key to use to access the record (i.e. they would need to know whether the customer has either an investment account or a mortgage account or both).

The only solution to this would be to invent a unique customer number for each customer. Such a number could be stored on the investment file (in an OCCURS 4) and on the mortgage record (in an OCCURS 2), facilitating access to the customer information from those two files. It would not, however, solve the problem if there were a business requirement to access the accounts from the customer file, because the account numbers would have to be stored in OCCURS clauses on the customer record. Also, such a customer number would have no meaning to either the business or the customer.

If such problems can be lived with or overcome, we still have the serious problem of disc accessing. In the large-file approach we may have used a lot of disc storage but at least we could access all the information with a single I/O. With the small-file approach the investment and mortgage transactions will be stored on disc as and when they occur, which means that they will effectively be scattered across the file in chronological order. In general, if there are n of them then n I/Os will be required to

```
            INVESTMENT RECORD
               INV NUMBER           NUMBER(10)
               INV DETAILS          NUMBER(30).

            INV TRANSACTION
               INV NUMBER           NUMBER(10)
               INV TRAN NO          NUMBER(3)
               INV TRAN DETAILS     NUMBER(20)

            MORTGAGE RECORD
               MTG NUMBER           NUMBER(10)
               MTG DETAILS          NUMBER(30)

            MTG TRANSACTION
               MTG NUMBER           NUMBER(10)
               MTG TRAN NO          NUMBER(2)
               MTG TRAN DETAILS     NUMBER(20)

            CUSTOMER RECORD
               INV ACCOUNT NO       NUMBER(10)
               MTG ACCOUNT NO       NUMBER(10)
               CUSTOMER DETAILS     CHAR(70)
```

Figure 1.5 Example record layouts of the small-file approach

access all of them. Therefore, to read all the related data for a single investment account halfway through the year will take 17 physical I/Os (1 for the investment, 1 for the customer and 15 for the transactions). Indeed this figure will be increased if we have to read indexes and so on.

This may be tolerable for online random processing because all the information will still be available in under a second, but what of sequential processing?

Allowing for an average of 10 ms per disc access, to read through the single large file will take a maximum of 2 h I/O (less if the file is presorted and blocked). With the small-file approach the transaction records are too random for blocking to have significant benefits, although sorting would still be useful but rather time-consuming. Without sorting, the comparable I/O time is 34 h – far too long if daily reports are needed. Thus, run-of-the-mill statistical jobs will become major problems and the managers who need the statistics for their decision making will suffer.

In this way the small-file approach is not wholly suitable either. A compromising halfway solution will still contain both problems to a certain degree because of the trade-off between disc storage and access speed.

1.6 Backup and recovery

Whatever the system, whatever the hardware, it will not maintain its viability for very long unless security (backup) copies of the data are taken regularly, and some mechanisms are available to recover from hardware or software failure.

Here again are problems with the large-file approach simply because the length of time needed to dump the file to tape, disc or optical media will discourage frequent copying, particularly as backups need to be taken when no one is using the data (clearly in a single-user environment this is a lot simpler).

What are the prospects in the event of some sort of computer failure? With most non-database systems the options are simple: reload the last backup copy of the data and reprocess everything since then. In general, if 12 h work has been done since the last backup then 12 h work needs to be repeated.

It is, unfortunately, not practical to repeat online work because timing may be critical. Suppose a customer had £10 in their account and deposited a further £50 in the morning. After lunch they realize they haven't enough cash so they draw £30 out, the cashier being different. The system goes down and the cashiers are asked to re-input their transactions. The cashier from the morning is slower or has the afternoon off and the afternoon transaction gets reprocessed first. The customer is now overdrawn! Even with various safeguards there are no guarantees that the data will be the same after reprocessing as it was prior to the failure.

A further problem is that programs rarely access a single file. If they did and file F was corrupted then it would be a simple matter to reload F and rerun programs 1, 2 and 5 which had since updated it. In practice the situation is usually far less clear and any form of recovery involves the reloading of many files and the rerunning of many programs because of the interrelations between them. This in itself gives scope for a multitude of possible errors: reloading one file too few or rerunning the wrong programs or rerunning the right ones but in the wrong order. Such errors are relatively easy to make but will probably not be detected for some time, by which time corrupted data will have corrupted other data in exponential fashion. In the meantime the integrity of the system will have been lost.

1.7 Concurrency

If the system is such that only one user ever updates the files then none of the problems described in this section occur, but this is not very practical for a medium-to-large organization. To allow two or more people to update does promote problems because if each tries to update the same record at the same time then each will get their own copy of the data and the last to commit their update will overwrite the other's updates, instantly losing the integrity of the system.

To prevent this happening most systems will have some sort of locking mechanism whereby the first user will lock out any others until they have finished. Unfortunately the locking is often done at the file level such that if an online program is run then no other programs can run that access the same files. This could cause major problems to, say, our bank because the investment and the mortgage departments both want to share the customer file (to avoid duplication) but they cannot both have online programs accessing and updating the customer information at the same time. The only solutions to this would be:

- for all user updates to be performed by a single program;
- to have one department updating in, say, the morning and the other in the afternoon while the first logs all its afternoon updates and then batch-processes them overnight.

Both these solutions rather negate the advantages of an online system. The first option might be seen to be more practical but there may be problems of data privacy if both departments have access to all the same data (see Section 1.9). Also how could a single program cope with input from 200+ users?

1.8 Ability to change

It would certainly be unusual if an organization's data requirements remained rigid and unchanging. Specifically, markets are bound to change, or government policy may force changes on the way in which the business is run, or new products may be developed, or, hopefully, the volume of data will increase as the customer base grows. The problem lies with the ease with which it can be changed.

The general mode of changing data structures is to:

1 Write a special program to dump all of the existing data to tape or another disc. Usually this is not a simple backup copy because we may wish to reload the data to file in a more efficient ordering.
2 Create a new version of the file.
3 Load the data back to the new file in the new format by running a specially written load program.
4 Change and recompile all affected programs.

This whole process is likely to be time-consuming if the files are large, and all programs will require thorough testing before the system goes live again.

The problem here is with the last stage. Programs will need recompiling and testing even if they do not directly use any of the affected data. If they are not then the effect could be catastrophic. Let us consider an example where a program thinks that the account number has 10 digits, the account type has 1 digit and the current balance has 6 digits. Thus it reads the data of a single record as

    1234567890 1 000050 (spaces inserted for readability)

The business already has nine different account types when the directors decide to introduce a tenth. This will involve changing the account-type field to two digits. Stages 1 to 3 are completed but the program is missed and the record format is not corrected. It now reads the data as before except that it will now read:

    1234567890 0 100005

Clearly if it is an update program we have problems. The system will not detect that such an error has occurred.

This problem is exacerbated because in a large organization there may be no cross-reference as to which programs use which files so our program, if it is one of many, may easily be missed. Even with careful documentation there are no guarantees that such documentation is complete and/or up to date.

```
        INV RECORD
            INV NUMBER    NUMBER(10)
            INV ACC TYPE  NUMBER(2)
            INV BALANCE   NUMBER(8,2)
            INV CUST NO   NUMBER(6)


        True definition of the investments file

        INV RECORD
            INV NUMBER    NUMBER(10)
            INV ACC TYPE  NUMBER(1)
            INV BALANCE   NUMBER(8,2)
            INV CUST NO   NUMBER(6)

        Program's wrong view of the data
```

Figure 1.6 Incorrect file view of an unchanged program following a file structure change

1.9 Privacy

The normal quantity of information that an organization needs will almost certainly contain various items/files to which access should be restricted. Whether this concerns wages, personnel details or financial information is immaterial: there will be a few people within the organization who are allowed to view such data and, at the same time, many who should be denied access. Whatever the situation, once a privacy decision has been made it should be enforceable whether the data are to be stored on the computer or in a filing cabinet.

In the early days of computers the problem was relatively simple. All work carried out on the computer was done via inputs and outputs in the computer room itself. Thus if you restricted access (physically) there then you only need worry about who saw the various printouts. Today, with data passing along lines external to the computer room or being sent via satellite links the control of privacy is a cause of major national and international concern.

In general terms, a conventional computer system can be written such that the user must have knowledge of a relevant user code (access identifier) and its related password. However, many systems have all related data in a single user area for convenience. Thus if the password gets into the wrong hands the security of the whole system disappears. Especially sensitive data, such as those concerning personnel or wages, normally have to be kept separately but again are usually only protected by a single password.

A potential solution is to give each file a different password, though because programs may access many files, the valid user will find it tedious keying in all the different passwords before the program can begin. In addition this does not solve all problems. In the banking example it may be permissible for most staff to access customer account information, but those accounts belonging to other staff may be more restricted. Similarly staff working in the wages department may be allowed to see salary details for employees up to a certain level of management but no further.

The only practical solution is to hive off the sensitive records and put them in a separate file with a separate password. Such an action is clearly inefficient because the processing of those records will be identical to the others, resulting in the need for programs to be run twice. Thus the system is degraded because it cannot cope with privacy decisions at the record level.

The situation is worse if there exist data items within records that have differing privacy levels. For example, in the personnel system, the general data relating to staff may be available to anyone in the personnel department, but certain items relating to perhaps an employee's promotional prospects or time-keeping should only be viewable by personnel management. Again the decision would have to be to split such items away into another file because the system cannot cope with privacy decisions at the data item level.

These are the reasons why some companies still run two payroll systems (one for management and one for everybody else) or deny access to the system to potential users who would legitimately benefit from access, simply because they are not allowed to see a single data item. The net result of this all-or-nothing approach is illustrated in the next section.

1.10   Application views

If there is a single common fault with many computerized systems within organizations it is that they tend to be a hotchpotch of subsystems that have been developed independently at different times, rather than a single integrated system supplying the data needs of all. The reason for this is simply that each department was computerized according to its own needs. If this was successful then the next was done and so on, resulting in autonomous subsystems. They are autonomous because, for example, there might be a bad-debts item on the mortgage customer information that the investment department is not allowed to see, so the investment department is given its own customer file.

The ins and outs of this piecewise development are clear – two 'ins', inconsistencies and inefficiencies.

1.11   Summary

In this chapter the problems facing an organization adopting the conventional file management system have been studied. Many existing installations still do employ such systems and most suffer from the problems outlined here to a greater or lesser extent.

With a smaller organization than the bank, the problems will be reduced proportionally in most cases, but they will still be there. In particular the problems of recovery, privacy and inconsistency are, generally, very much in evidence.

The major problem areas identified have been the following.

Large files or slow access

We can either have large files with:

- large storage requirements,
- difficulties in coping with deviations from the norm,
- large backup overheads with corresponding slow recovery times,
- problems of restructuring files,
- high memory overheads,
- data duplication and inconsistencies,
- relatively quick access times;

or alternatively we can have smaller files with:

- many accesses required to obtain all related data,
- extra items required to identify each record uniquely,
- difficulty in linking related records,
- data duplication and inconsistency.

Slow recovery

The only practical method available for recovery after any type of failure is to reload the last backup copy and reprocess, which is both time-consuming and error-prone.

Poor backup facilities

Backup is both slow and costly in as much as it must be performed offline when no programs are running.

Poor restructuring facilities

Changing the structure of files is both slow and error-prone because of its dependence on often incomplete or out-of-date information concerning which programs access which files. In general, all programs that access a file will need changing and recompiling even if the changes are to data items not used by those programs. This is due to the all-or-nothing record access mechanisms.

No concurrency

Because only one program is allowed to access for update at any one time, many advantages of an online system are lost.

Privacy

Access to files on an all-or-nothing basis, which means that privacy decisions can only be enforced at the file level, results in the hiving-off of sensitive data, in turn resulting in inefficiency.

Application views

Largely because of the way in which organizations are computerized, application by application, and also because of the organization's privacy requirements, the system becomes a mass of unrelated-but-should-be-related duplicated application-oriented files and programs providing an overall increase in workload and decrease in efficiency.

It would be rather blasé (and, indeed, not always true) to say that database systems solve all of these problems. Database systems vary enormously in their effectiveness. The better ones will solve (or at least avoid) most of the problems described, but the database approach as outlined in the next five chapters will certainly help to develop a system to the best of its efficiency capabilities.

2

General concepts

2.1 Introduction

Having determined the need for solutions to the problems posed in the first chapter, we now need to define broad outlines as to an ideal database model. What will it consist of in terms of recognized existing hardware and software constructs? How will it interface with the operating system? How can it be used by our application programmers (or, indeed, by any other users)?

Although CODASYL databases are now in their declining years the concepts put forward by the CODASYL committees are extremely important across all database systems in terms of what such a system should involve. Nearly all the CODASYL terminology and concepts have been passed on to the new generation of relational databases.

2.2 CODASYL: historical background

Much of the credit for rationalization of early views and concepts concerning databases must be given to the CODASYL (Conference On DAta SYstems Languages) committee that, when founded in 1959, was responsible for the introduction of COBOL which, for all its reported disadvantages, is still the world's premier business language.

In 1965 CODASYL formed a List Processing Task Force which soon became the Data Base Task Group (the actual phrase 'database' was first used by the US military in 1963 during a symposium entitled *Development and Management of a Computer-Centered Data Base*'. Incidentally, this symposium also coined the first definition of a database, which was:

1 a database is a set of files;
2 a file is an ordered collection of entries;
3 an entry consists of a key or keys and data.
    (And perhaps no better definition exists today!)

The Data Base Task Group produced two reports: one in 1969 and a more significant one in 1971. By the end of that year the group had become a committee in its own right, the Data Description Language Committee, producing its own *Journal of Development* (one being published in 1973 and another in 1978).

Since then many other CODASYL committees have been formed, each producing its own journals and reports. However, the aims of all have been the same: to collect together ideas via representatives from computer manufacturers, software houses, users, academics, and so on and then to standardize these ideas into unified reports to act as guidelines for any current or future database development.

How this has been achieved with regard to CODASYL database products is described more fully in Chapter 10. It has been mentioned here merely to show that much thought and discussion has been put into database development, the result being that many traditional database architectures have common roots and principles.

2.3 General definitions of an ideal architecture

In the example of the bank most of the data relevant to the business could be kept permanently on a database (it may be decided to split the data across several, but such matters are considered in later chapters).

The software that will allow one (or more) users to access the data will hereafter be referred to as the database management system (DBMS). In this role, the DBMS acts as an interpreter for the application program, translating raw data as stored on the computer into the user's business-minded view (i.e. as information). This should, in effect, mean that the physical attributes of the computer's data, in other words where they are stored and how they are accessed, are invisible to the user or application programmer. Thus in its simplest terms we have the situation shown in Figure 2.1.

Alternatively, because the physical storage is in binary digits and because the user wants an abstracted view of that data, we require the DBMS to translate the data into the required information. Thus, 00011001000001111001011 becomes a six-digit date, 190797, which the user possibly sees as 19 July 1997. In this way the user's view (or **conceptual view**) is derived from the physical storage by the DBMS (Figure 2.2). This idea is very important because the corollary, that the physical database is an implementation of the conceptual database model, is the keystone for the database analysis and design stages (Part Two of this book).

The conceptual database must, of necessity, contain items and concepts that are meaningful to the user and, indeed, to the business as a whole. Thus the conceptual database of our example will contain different logical areas of information (e.g.

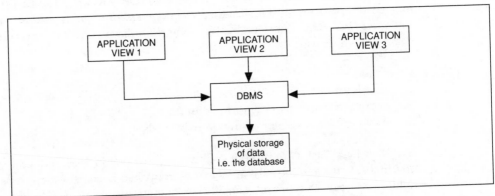

Figure 2.1 Application views of the stored data

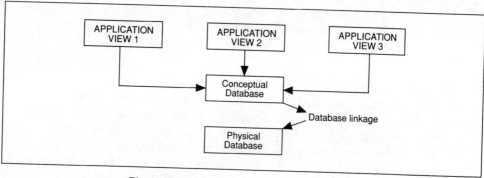

Figure 2.2 Conceptual view of the stored data

investments, mortgages, customers, etc.), each of which will in itself contain items of data (e.g. account numbers, names, addresses, etc.) plus information describing the real-world interrelations between items (e.g. that a customer has an investment account, that an investment account will have associated transactions). This global view of the organization's data needs is referred to as the **schema.**

An application's view of the data will probably form a subset of the whole. (Note that this is not necessarily so, because the application's view may be derivable from the whole but not contained within it. For example, the investment department will wish to know how long a particular account has been open, for purposes of calculating interest accrued, but it is unlikely that this piece of information will be kept in any conceptual model because it changes every day. However, the item is derivable from the date the account was opened which would be a part of the conceptual model.)

In the example, an application may only wish to see the investments. Following our schema definition it is therefore desirable to refer to an application's view as a **subschema.**

We have stated now that a user should only be interested in his or her own abstracted information but that the data are stored physically in binary digits. We now need to look for an interface between the two. First, the conceptual database is rationalized and defined by using its own language: the **data definition language** or DDL. We have also stated that the user is interested only in the conceptual database. Need this necessarily be the same as the one implemented? The answer is 'no'. For example, the user wishes only to relate to a customer's address as, perhaps, three lines of information giving the number and street, the town and the county, plus a postcode. When physically stored on the computer it would be very inconvenient (and indeed illegal on most systems) to describe these items in the conceptual way, namely:

1 number and street of the customer's address
2 town of the customer's address
3 county of the customer's address
4 address code of the customer.

(Note that the customer's address part is necessary to distinguish it from a mortgage address or an insurance company's address, etc.)

It is far more likely that this item would be implemented in a similar manner to:

```
CUST-ADD-1 CHAR(30)
CUST-ADD-2 CHAR(20)
CUST-ADD-3 CHAR(20)
CUST-POST-CODE CHAR(8)
```

(Note also that our implementation of the conceptual view, in most systems, will also force us to define items as having a certain type and length; again this is radically different from the conceptual view where we would not really mind how long the address was or whether, indeed, it took four lines instead of three.)

We therefore need to differentiate between the real-world conceptual model and the implemented conceptual model. The latter will therefore be referred to as the **logical model**.

2.4   Database architecture

To understand the workings of a computer fully, the student must study its architecture. In similar fashion, to comprehend the function of a database system, we must look at its architecture.

The ideal architecture, as originally proposed by the CODASYL committee, is one of four distinct views or models, each of which is defined in terms of its own language and each of which is disjoint from the others except inasmuch as they are all bound together by the DBMS. For this reason the conceptual model (as defined previously) does not form a part of the architecture (although it appears very prominently in the data-analysis sections) purely because it does not form a part of the implemented database system. With this in mind we can define the four existing parts which are the:

- **device model**, where the data actually resides in terms of which discs, blocks, pages, etc.;
- **storage model**, how the data are stored on the data device model in terms of access mechanisms;
- **logical model**, implementation of the entire conceptual (global) model in terms of what the data mean, how they are structured, how they relate to other data items, etc.;
- **logical submodel**, the subset of the logical model relating to a particular application's viewpoint.

In general terms, each of the four components will be described in its own language. The device model will need to interface with the operating system since in all cases it is this that deals with the allocation and usage of system hardware resources. On the other hand, the logical submodel may need to interface with an application program, generally written in a high-level language such as COBOL or C. This latter interface must also be able to cater for the possibility of more than one high-level language being used.

The overall system then, appears diagrammatically as in Figure 2.3. From the diagram the importance of the DBMS in binding the whole thing together is shown. As

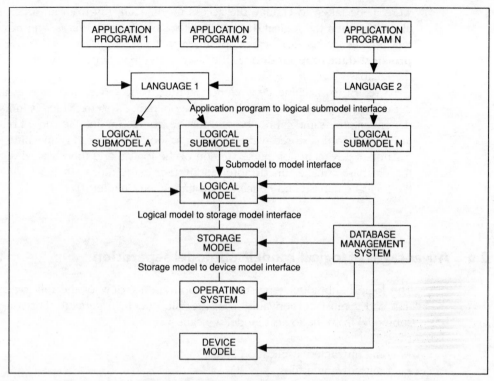

Figure 2.3 A generalized database architecture

the actual interfacing between components *is* carried out by a piece of software, in future this process will be referred to as a **mapping**.

The device and storage models are often referred to jointly as the **physical database** and the logical model and submodel are referred to as the **logical database.** The difference between the two is important: for a single item of data there will only be one logical representation (e.g. customer name = Williams). However, the physical representation of this item of data will be machine/device-dependent (i.e. whether it is stored in eight bytes, two four-byte words, two six-byte words, etc.).

Similarly, we may say that the investment record can be identified uniquely by the account number:

```
INVESTMENT RECORD KEY IS ACCOUNT-NUMBER
    ACCOUNT-NUMBER NUMBER(12).
```

and so on. This shows the logical representation of the record and its unique key. How the key is implemented in terms of indexes, hashing functions and so on is left to the physical database; the user does not want to know.

2.5   Advantages of logical/physical database separation

At the end of the last section it was stated that how the key is implemented should be a part of the physical database. With this distinction it can be seen that if the decision were to be taken to change the access mechanism, say from an index to a hashing algorithm, then the logical database will not be affected, that is, will not need changing, and hence the application program will not be affected. This is referred to as **physical data independence**; the user is independent of any physical changes to the database.

To return to machine dependence, although the device model is clearly machine-dependent because it is controlled by the operating system, which is in itself machine-dependent, the same cannot be said for the storage model. We should be able to refer to how a record is stored without having to look at what sort of machine is available.

Another advantage of the separation of the logical and the physical database is that the database can be tuned more readily (i.e. made more efficient) without affecting the logical database and hence the program (see Chapter 8).

2.6 Advantages of logical model/submodel separation

The logical submodel represents an application's view of the full logical model. To that end it must be derivable from the full model. In general, therefore, to derive a submodel from the logical model we can:

- omit unwanted application areas,
- omit unwanted files,
- omit unwanted records,
- omit unwanted data items,
- change the ordering of items within a record,
- change data types,
- derive data items that are not in the full model from those that are.

The importance of this is that **logical data independence** can be achieved because a program can be protected from any changes to data items or records or files, other than those that it uses, simply because it does not see them and will therefore not be affected if they change. In other words, if program A uses a subschema containing

```
INVESTMENTS-RECORD
    INV-ACC-NO NUMBER(10)
    INV-OPEN-BALANCE NUMBER(7,2)
    INV-CLOSE-BALANCE NUMBER(7,2)
```

if any fields within the investment record other than the three defined above need physically altering then program A will not be affected (note the difference between this and the situation shown in Chapter 1).

As a corollary, whereas the logical data model will be described using its own language, in a program-independent way, the logical submodels will be, of necessity, program-dependent. This implies that they will be defined by using a high-level programming language, as is indeed the case (hence the similarity between the submodel definition above and COBOL). Thus for every high-level language supported by the database system, there will be one for defining associated data submodels. At present this generally involves support for COBOL and FORTRAN in particular, though other languages such as C are supported by some systems. It must be stressed that the logical data submodels are not themselves written in the languages that they support, but rather in similar languages with similar constructs.

There are similar concepts with relational databases. Although these can be accessed through predefined and purpose-built relational languages such as SQL, they are also accessed in larger environments via embedded SQL statements in host languages such as COBOL and C (see Chapter 11).

2.7 Data-manipulation languages

Having defined a logical data submodel for a particular application's viewpoint, we must now define a set of constructs by which our application programmer can access that submodel.

A moment's thought will show that there are two distinct possibilities here.

- The first is to write a whole new language, specifically for interfacing with the database, perhaps with similar attributes to an existing language; such a language would take years to develop, but would have the advantage of being highly efficient.
- The second would be to enhance existing languages, such as COBOL, by adding extra verbs and constructs with the sole purpose of providing an interface with the submodel; such an approach would be less efficient, but would be available in a much shorter time.

It is now history that most manufacturers originally adopted the second approach, now referred to as the **host language** approach, though mention must be made here of the special 'fourth-generation' languages developed for the sole purpose of database interrogation (query languages, Chapter 8) or for the complete task of data manipulation with relational databases (see Chapter 11) and object-oriented databases (Chapter 17). Indeed, query languages are very end-user-oriented inasmuch as they, to a large extent, bridge the gap between conceptual and logical databases by allowing the user without programming skills to access the database using very English-like words and sentences.

The extent of the additions to the host language has varied. With respect to the CODASYL approach COBOL has been enhanced considerably but FORTRAN, with the CODASYL approach, has not been touched because all interfacing is performed via CALL procedures. It is interesting to note that a similar approach has now been adopted for OODBs (object-oriented databases).

2.8 Mappings

As defined in Section 2.4 each of the four models is independent but the database management system binds them all together by using mappings between adjacent pairs (see Figure 2.3). The term 'mapping' may seem a strange one to non-mathematicians but it simply means, in this context, a piece of software acting as a bridge between two models. How this is actually achieved is of no importance at this juncture.

2.9 Logical model to submodel mapping

The mappings between the logical model and the various submodels define how flexible the database is in terms of logical data independence. In general, the more complex they are the more flexible the database. The problem remains as to how complex we want them to be. To illustrate this, consider the three tables of data with reference to the bank example as shown in Figure 2.4.

Consider a database system that only allows the inclusion of whole records from the data model into the submodel for an investment application that requires investment records and their associated customer records. This would be a straightforward mapping of two files into one submodel. However, there is little logical data independence. If either the investment or customer records change in any way at all, the submodel must also be changed, and hence any programs that use them.

Now consider what happens in a database system that allows the investment application to access a submodel containing only the investment account number, the investment closing balance, the customer's name and the mortgage account number if the paid-off flag is set to 1. Clearly, this is a fairly complex mapping since it involves selection, testing and comparison of items. Nevertheless, the degree of logical data independence is maximized: the application program will only see what it wants to see and hence only needs changing if one of the four items is changed.

I-ACC-NO	I-CUST-NO	I-OPEN-BAL	I-CLOSE-BAL
103862409	32938	29.42	55.61
284369103	12311	287.61	93.28
273861008	29943	407.94	409.23
202664310	13887	239.42	21.68

Investment records

M-ACC-NO	M-CUST-NO	M-BAL	M-ARRS	M-PAID-OFF
829562201	1274	15428.82	0.00	0
838219906	4289	23914.21	-38.83	0
839535804	10368	6423.94	26.31	0
877674302	12311	0.00	0.00	1

Mortage records

CUST NO	CUST-NAME	CUST-ADDRESS
1274	BENSON	78 LYTHAM DRIVE, BOLTON
4289	GILMOUR	4 LONDON RD, BLACKPOOL
10368	WILLIAMS	14 THE CAUSEWAY, SOUTHPORT
12311	DENNISON	20 PENNINE WAY, BURNLEY
13887	EVANS	1 MOOR LANE, PRESTON
29943	KING	42 WEST ST, SOUTHAMPTON
32938	FARRER	62 SOUTH VIEW, LEEDS

Associated customer records

Figure 2.4 Sets of data relating to the bank example

Clearly, what we gain in simplicity of run-time operation we lose whenever the database changes. The trade-off between the two is one of the more important aspects of the creation of a database system.

Whatever the nature of the mapping, it must be described to, and be available for use by, the DBMS. Thus, whenever an application requests a particular set of data, the DBMS can look to the associated mapping and execute the relevant piece of code.

When and where this **binding** of the DBMS to the access code occurs is a further point to consider. There are two alternatives:

- It is made at application-program run time (in other words, the access code is a part of the DBMS that the application program uses whenever it is run). This approach is expensive in terms of software (the DBMS becomes large through having many embedded access routines that must always be present), but it does allow a high degree of logical data independence because, if the logical data model is changed and affects the submodel, then only the access routines need changing, and not the program itself.
- The access routines are bound into the application program at compilation time. This means that the access routines and any associated look-up tables need only be present at compilation time, thus saving processor time at program execution time, but any changes to the logical data model now require recompilation of the programs.

The second of these alternatives is the one most commonly found in use.

2.10 Logical model to physical model mapping

Again, this mapping could be very simple: for example, putting the whole database on disc A starting at track 4. Alternatively, the mapping could be far more complex.

Consider our investment transactions. They must be readily accessible throughout the current year, but after a year-end they are no longer regarded as current data because the account will have been balanced up, capitalized and audited at year-end. However, they may be required for reference purposes or for the odd statistical job. There may therefore be a business need to split investment transactions into 'live' and 'historical' data, the former being stored on a fast device for instant access and the latter being on a much slower device. Likewise, it may be desirable to split the investment record itself into frequently accessed and infrequently accessed portions.

A similar consideration might be that the investment record and its associated current transactions are accessed together so frequently that it may be highly advantageous to store them together on the same area of disc. Note that this is different from the concept in Chapter 1 of storing them together as a single record, but would have the same advantage of being accessible through a single physical I/O.

Clearly, then, the mapping can be quite complex and the degree of complexity will govern both the efficiency of the database and the amount of physical data independence. Again, whatever the nature of the logical model to physical model mapping, it will need to be defined, and be available, to the DBMS. The choice remains as to whether this binding is performed at run time or at compilation time with similar considerations to those outlined in the previous section.

2.11 Summary

In this chapter we have defined a general desirable database architecture in terms of its four separate components and have also looked at some of the major functions that we would wish a DBMS to perform. In short these are:

1 to control and manage the database generally,
2 to be able to comprehend the four languages of its four component parts,
   (a) the storage data model definition language (SDDL),
   (b) the logical data model definition language (DDL),
   (c) the logical data submodel definition language(s) (of similar structure to the high-level programming language(s) that it supports),
   (d) the special (query) language or additions to existing (host) languages (DML);
3 the ability to interface between the languages outlined above by means of mappings.

Overall, the system will perform in a fashion as shown in Figure 2.5:

1 the application program requests data as described within its own logical data submodel via its DML,
2 the DBMS picks up this request and maps it onto the logical data model,
3 the DBMS checks the mapping between logical data model and storage data model to see how the data are to be accessed,
4 the DBMS can now check whether the required data are extant in the system buffers in main memory (if they are then we can proceed to 9),
5 the DBMS passes a request to the operating system for a physical access to the required device on the device model,
6 the operating system goes to the relevant piece of hardware,
7 the data are returned,

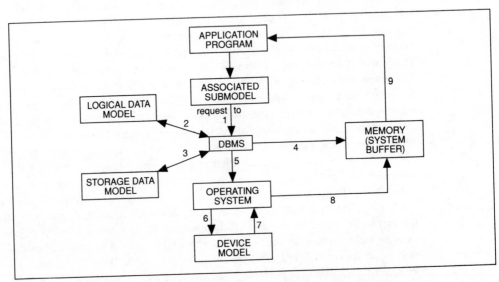

Figure 2.5 Generalized operation of a database management system

8   the data are placed in the system buffers in main memory,
9   the data are copied into the application program's work area and become usable by that program.

If, of course, any errors occur at any time along this path then it is another function of the DBMS to report suitable error messages back to the application program.

Having declared what we would like, the actual construction and implementation of a database with as many of the desired features as possible, and the trade-offs that usually occur, are discussed in the next chapter.

3
Conceptual view: theory

3.1 Introduction

In the last chapter we distinguished the conceptual database (that seen by the user) from the logical database implementation of the conceptual model. In this chapter and the next we shall look at how the conceptual model is derived; Chapters 5 and 6 describe how it is used to implement a logical and then a physical database. At the moment it suffices to state that, within an organization, this forms an essential part of the work carried out by database administration and it will be left until Chapter 9 before we look at who performs this administration and give an overview of their complete functional role.

3.2 Database analysis vs systems analysis

It is essential to note that whereas systems analysis traditionally deals with a particular functional area of a business (e.g. investments or mortgages) database analysis must involve the study of the global requirements of the organization covering all applications but from a non-application viewpoint. This is simply because any areas or items omitted (either accidentally or deliberately) at this early stage will, in general, be difficult to include later. For this reason alone the database-analysis stage forms the most important part of the creation of a database. A simple analogy would be the construction of a pyramid. If every brick is not put in place carefully at the ground level then there is a danger of the entire structure crumbling later on. Thus, of the total time available between the decision to have a database and the running of a live version, some 70% should be spent on the analysis stage, 20% on design, and most of the rest on testing. The theory here is identical to that of the writing of a program: if little thought is given to the planning out and analysis of a problem, a far greater time is needed to implement and maintain the finished product.

3.3 Traditional systems analysis

In the normal situation the systems analyst will go to the relevant users and extract as much information as possible from them on their requirements for:

- data,
- access types,
- frequency of access,
- security,
- output (reports, etc.),
- data sources.

From this information the analyst can eventually produce a systems definition: a report with the system overview gathered together and summarized. If this is acceptable to the user, and is feasible as a cost-effective system, then the files can be designed and the various program specifications produced, the programs written and tested, and, finally, the systems tested (Figure 3.1).

Here the systems definition can be broken down into four areas.

Inputs to the system

1 Origin of the inputs (e.g. counter, personnel office).
2 Layout of the items on the input document/screen.
3 Contents of each input in terms of the size, type and length of the individual data items.
4 Relationship between an input and any other input or set of inputs; for example, whether it is the first part of a multistage input: an 'open a new account' input would be related to a 'transaction for that account' input.
5 Timing of the input. When does it occur? When is it most likely to occur? Are there peak periods?
6 Volume of the input. How much per given time period?
7 Security – who is allowed to input data.

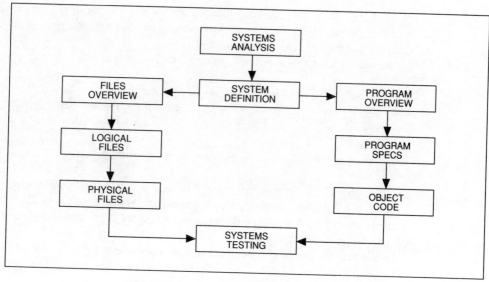

Figure 3.1 Work involved with systems analysis

Outputs from the system

1 Destination of the outputs. Who wants to see the output?
2 Security. Who is allowed to see the output?
3 Layout of the items on the printout/screen.
4 Contents of each output in terms of the size, type and length of the individual data items included in it.
5 Timing of the response. When is the printout required? Is it regular or a one-off report? What are critical response times for screened outputs?
6 Are any other outputs related? (e.g. the payslips and the wage analysis).

Data requirements

1 Combination of the input data and output data with any intermediate items (which are perhaps only input once or occasionally such as interest rates); in other words, the total sum of data items needed for processing.
2 Natural groupings of these items; these will often come directly from the system inputs, although sometimes several inputs will be required to make up a single grouping.
3 Key data items within these groupings that can be used to identify the grouping uniquely (e.g. account number or customer name and address).
4 Type, size, length, range, origin and units for each data item.

Process requirements

1 Inputs, outputs and data items required by each process.
2 Timing of the process. Must they be run within certain time scales? Are they instigated by other processes? How are they related to other processes?
3 What does the process set out to do?

The work of the systems analyst has been detailed because it is also an integral part of the function of the database analyst. However, it must again be stressed that this involves covering the four areas just mentioned not simply for a particular application, but for the organization as a whole.

The outcome of this seemingly herculean task should be:

- a set of all the processes carried out by the organization and their frequency,
- a set of conceptual records (or groupings of data of the same type),
- a set of data items making up each conceptual record with any associated key items,
- a set of relationships between various conceptual records.

These together will form some kind of primitive conceptual database model.

We can now give a preliminary diagrammatic representation of the construction of a database (Figure 3.2). Some of the terms have not been defined yet but it is of interest to compare it with Figure 3.1.

(Note that testing in the diagram is only equivalent to the system testing of Figure 3.1 if we define the whole thing – the database plus the application programs – to be the system.)

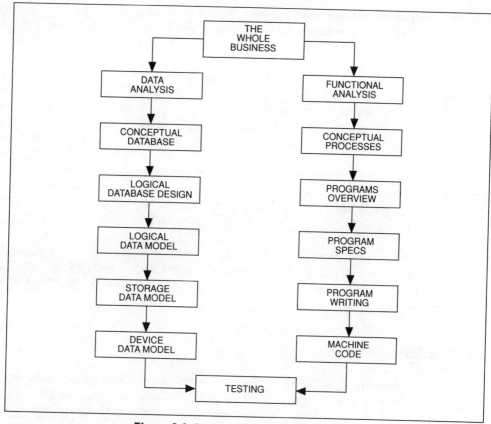

Figure 3.2 Steps in the creation of a database

The natural groupings arrived at in our conceptual model will be used eventually to create conceptual files and records. As will be seen later some of the processes may also fall into natural groupings and these will eventually form the basis of a conceptual process model from which should emerge a program's overview and individual program specifications.

Thus, as with the traditional systems analysis model, we have two distinct paths in the overall design being developed in parallel. Eventually, when we arrive on both paths at the physical machine implementation, the two will merge to form one complete system. This is certainly not to say that the two arms of the diagram (Figure 3.2) are completely distinct; throughout the development there must be a very close linkage between the two to ensure convergence rather than divergence and, in particular, linkage between the logical database design and the program overview stages (i.e. at the assignment of logical data submodels to the various applications).

3.4 Creation of the conceptual model

As stated previously, the conceptual model is the end product of the data analysis and consists of an implementation-free global view of the organization's data requirements.

The term 'implementation-free' implies that the data analysis can in theory be performed before the computer is chosen and purchased. Such a view should be jargon-free and understandable to any member of the organization who is not a computer specialist.

To perform data analysis correctly all areas of the organization should be studied even if they will obviously never be computerized, the reason being that only after such a study can the analyst be sure that all complexities of interdepartmental data and function relationships have been considered.

By the conclusion, then, there will be three clear options for each piece of data:

- to keep it as part of a (possibly already existing) manual system,
- to implement it as part of a conventional file (as often happens with work files and other transient data that are not suitable for inclusion in a database),
- to implement it as part of a database system.

The most commonly accepted method of constructing a conceptual model lies in the use of entities, attributes and relationships, each of which is defined and explained here separately, and is known as the **entity–relationship** or ER model.

3.5 Entities

An **entity** is an object or concept that is meaningful in itself to the organization and about which there is a need to record information, for example, investment, mortgage, insurance, branch. Diagrammatically, these can be represented in a variety of ways, the usual being a box:

```
┌─────────────────┐
│    MORTGAGE     │
└─────────────────┘
```

When the data-analysis stage is complete, there should exist a list of all possible entities. Each should be documented with regard to:

1 an organization-oriented description of what the entity actually is;
2 any pseudonyms for the entity, such as CUSTOMER = ACCOUNT OWNER;
3 names of the data items (or attributes as defined below) which make up the entity;
4 any attributes that identify the entity uniquely (which will act as keys);
5 approximate number of occurrences of the entity, e.g. 100 000 mortgages;
6 growth rate of the number of occurrences (Is it constant? Is it varying by a constant percentage? Exponentially? Does the number fluctuate widely over a given period of time?);
7 people within the organization who are concerned with the entity (Who is allowed to read it, update, create or delete it?).

It is usual for the database analyst to have a purpose-designed form for documentation. Figure 3.3 represents a form for entities.

```
ENTITY NAME – insurance        PSEUDONYMS – None
OCURRENCES – 175 000


READ ACCESS RIGHTS – Insurance and mortgage personnel
UPDATE ACCESS RIGHTS – Insurance personnel
CREATE ACCESS RIGHTS – Insurance manager
DELETE ACCESS RIGHTS –        Ditto


KEY ATTRIBUTES – Mortgage account number + Insurance type
OTHER ATTRIBUTES – Insurance company code, company
name and address, amount of cover, monthly payments
```

Figure 3.3 Example form for maintenance of entity information

3.6 Attributes

An **attribute** is a subset of an entity that is meaningful to an organization in its own right and about which there is a need to store information. Note that at this stage it is sufficient to show the customer's address as a single attribute rather than line 1, line 2 and line 3 as on a mailing address label. However, it may be of significance to the organization to maintain the address code as a separate attribute. Only at the design stage will the address itself be broken down into constituent parts and, similarly, only then will it be assigned a computerized data name (e.g. CUST–ADD). Until then it will be the customer's address.

The information that needs to be recorded for each attribute is:

1 an organization-oriented description of the attribute;
2 pseudonyms by which the attribute is otherwise known (to the business), such as investment customer number = mortgage customer number;
3 entities in which the attribute lies (we are not restricted to one entity per attribute at this stage – indeed, it would be most unlikely for all attributes to be uniquely associated with a single entity);
4 source of the attribute, such as where within the organization the customer number is generated;
5 format of the attribute, that is, its size, type and length;
6 any range of values and units for the attribute;
7 people within the organization who are allowed to access the attribute subdivided into those who can read, update, create or delete it.

Again, a special form is useful for the documentation of this information. Figure 3.4 represents such a form.

As can be imagined, for large organizations there might, easily, be upwards of a thousand separate attributes discovered in the data-analysis exercise. This represents quite a lot of paper! Sometimes it is desirable therefore to combine the forms for entity and attribute documentation, giving something similar to that shown in Figure 3.5.

ATTRIBUTE – Insurance type   PSEUDONYMS – None
ENTITIES – Insurance, mortgage

READ ACCESS RIGHTS – Insurance and mortgage personnel
UPDATE ACCESS RIGHTS – Never updated once created
CREATE ACCESS RIGHTS – Insurance personnel
DELETE ACCESS RIGHTS – Insurance personnel

SOURCE – Customer requesting buildings, contents or all risks cover
ALPHA/NUMERIC – Numeric   LENGTH – 1
RANGE OF VALUES – 1, 2 or 3   UNITS – None

Figure 3.4 Example form for maintenance of attribute information

ENTITY NAME – Insurance   PSEUDONYMS – None
OCCURRENCES – 175 000
KEYS – Mortgage account number + Insurance type

ATTRIBUTE PSEUDONYMS	LENGTH	RANGE TYPE	UNITS	ACCESS RIGHTS READ	UPDATE	CREATE	DELETE
Acc number	10	–					
none		num.	–	I&M	–	M	M
Ins. type	1	1,2,3					
none		num.	–	I&M	–	I	I
Co. code	4	–					
none		num.	–	I&M	–	I	I

Figure 3.5 Single form for entities and attributes

(Note that many of the names on this form have been shortened because of the width of the page. This is not the norm in practice – all names and identifiers should be understandable to anyone not involved in the data-analysis process.)

If this approach is used then two important points must be noted:

- There is now no single list of all the entities to which an attribute belongs. This would have to be created, if required, by searching through each entity chart manually. This in itself may cause problems at the design stage.
- This approach assumes that the access rights for the entity are the sum of the access rights to all of the constituent attributes. This may be the case, but exceptions are possible, such as when a cashier in a branch finds that the customer's account on the computer does not match up with their passbook. Suppose that there exists an entity of outstanding transactions (i.e. those that have not been processed yet against the accounts for one reason or another). All the cashier wants to know is whether the customer has an outstanding transaction to account for the discrepancy. They therefore need access rights for the existence of the

entity 'outstanding transaction' without needing to look at its constituent attributes. Such an access right would not show up on the form in the figure.

3.7 Relationships

A **relationship** is an association between entities that is meaningful to the organization and about which there is a need to maintain information; for example, an investment account has many transactions. Before defining what information needs recording about relationships, we really need to look at all the various possible types and show how they are normally represented diagrammatically.

One-to-one

Entities are related one-to-one if a single occurrence of one is associated with a single occurrence of the other:

One branch has a single branch manager and each branch manager is manager of a single branch.

One-to-many

An example should suffice:

One branch has many associated accounts (hence the double arrow at the account end of the connecting line), whereas each account is associated solely with a single branch. (Note that account is singular, the plurality being shown by the double arrow.)

Many-to-one

This is the reverse of the above. The accounts are related to the branch at a many-to-one level:

Many-to-many

An investment account can be owned by many customers (up to four in our example). Each customer can own many accounts.

Notes

1   There is some divergence in the usage of diagrammatic representation of relationships. The two other common usages are

   (a) that of the 'crows' foot' which instead of having the double arrow shown above (the 'many' part) has nothing at the 'one' end,

   (b) that of the 'diamond' situated between the entities which names the relationship.

Throughout this book we have adhered to the notation shown in the diagrams above.

2   The relationships may not necessarily be between distinct entities. For example, an area branch office might itself be a branch that supervises other branches in the area, but each sub-branch would only be supervised by a single area branch office:

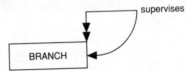

Note that for clarification it is always permissible to write the name of the relationship along the connecting line.

3   Many of the relationships at the data-analysis stage are generalizations that are used to avoid confusion. For example, it might be that one particular branch manager manages two branches because the other manager has just left or is on a course. In most cases such temporary relationships, if they occur frequently, can be shown by the methods described below.

Existence

A relationship may be mandatory, contingent or optional. The difference between them is shown below.

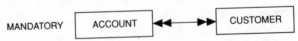

An account must be owned by at least one customer. A customer must own an account (be it mortgage or investment), otherwise they would not be a customer!

The mortgage account must be owned by a customer, but a customer need not necessarily have a mortgage account.

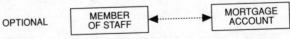

A member of staff may have a mortgage account and a mortgage account may be owned by a member of staff.

Exclusivity

One type of relationship may exclude another: for example, the mortgage will relate to a house, flat or maisonette, but to only one of the three.

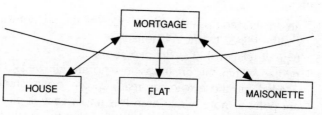

Inclusivity

One relationship may imply another:

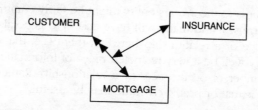

You cannot obtain a mortgage without also obtaining a buildings insurance policy.

Permanence

This defines how long a relationship might last, though it is not, generally, shown diagrammatically. Also consideration needs to be made of what can happen to the relationship over the course of its lifetime. In particular it may be one of the following:

- **Fixed:** once created it is a permanent relationship, such as that between an account and its transactions.
- **Transferable:** once the relationship is created then an occurrence of that relationship must always exist between the entities, but not necessarily the original relationship; for example, a branch should always have a branch manager, but not always the same one. In other words, the relationship between branch and a particular member of staff is not fixed.
- **Transient:** once one particular occurrence of the relationship has been created then one (or both) of the entities can be removed from all occurrences of the relationship permanently; for example, a member of staff may be a branch manager.

He may then be promoted to accounts manager and no longer be a part of this relationship (or the branch may close).

Relationship documentation

Now the various types of relationship have been defined, we can look at the documentation requirements:

1. an organization-oriented description of the relationship;
2. entities joined by the relationship;
3. type of relationship as defined above;
4. people within the organization who are allowed to access the relationship subdivided into those who can read, update, create and delete it. There is an important point to note here. Often less importance is given to privacy of relationships at the design stage in the false belief that the securing of the entities at each end of the relationship is sufficient. However, consider the following:

Access to the arrears entity might be fairly commonplace, particularly for accounts purposes, and many will have access to general customer information, but knowledge of a relationship between them (i.e. that a specific customer is in arrears) may well be a very restricted piece of information;

5. number of occurrences of a relationship. Rather than just saying many-to-many, an actual or predicted value may be useful.

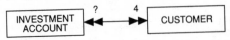

An investment account may be owned by a maximum of four customers. The number of accounts that a customer may have is more indeterminate.

As before, a special form on which to record this information is desirable. An example might be that shown in Figure 3.6.

3.8 Data model diagrams

Following the production of the reams of paper concerning the entities, attributes and relationships, it would be useful to be able to show all the interconnections on a diagram. To show all attribute connections would make the diagram very complex indeed, but it is quite normal to show all entities and relationships using a **Bachman diagram** or **entity–relationship diagram** (named after C. W. Bachman who was a leading light in the CODASYL developments). Such a diagram is especially useful because it gives a global picture of the organization (i.e. the conceptual model), revealing all the interrelations between people and departments and functions.

A very simplified Bachman diagram for our bank might appear similar to that shown in Figure 3.7. (A truer representation would fill many pages.) The points of note to be mentioned here are that a data model diagram will nearly always end up as highly debatable. For example, in Figure 3.7 should the customer be connected to the insurance record, to the agent, to the branch? Should the mortgage-offer entity be

DESCRIPTION OF RELATIONSHIP – A mortgage owns transactions
NO. OF OCCURRENCES – 100 000 (every account has transactions)

ENTITIES JOINED – Mortgage and mortgage transaction
DEGREE – One to many (1–14 on average)
EXISTENCE – Mandatory
PERMANENCE – Fixed
OTHER RELATIONSHIPS EXCLUDED – None
OTHER RELATIONSHIPS IMPLIED – An insurance record
    (one of the transactions will be a buildings insurance payment)

READ ACCESS RIGHTS – Mortgage and insurance personnel
UPDATE ACCESS RIGHTS – Mortgage and insurance personnel
CREATE ACCESS RIGHTS – Mortgage and insurance personnel

Figure 3.6 Example form for maintenance of relationship information

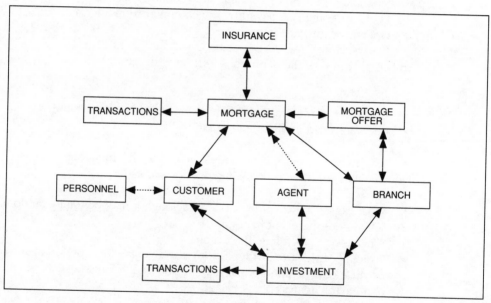

Figure 3.7 Entity–relationship (Bachman) diagram

shown as it cannot exist at the same time as the mortgage record?

Suffice it to say that the data model diagram is not the ultimate goal of data analysis; it is merely a diagrammatic representation that can show the relations between entities and that may be useful as a tool at the design stage. However, it can show useful features at the global level. For example, in Figure 3.7 the personnel entity is barely related to the rest of the model (and only by the fact that some customers will be members of staff). It therefore looks a reasonable candidate for being implemented as a separate database.

3.9 Functional analysis

We have now looked at the tools needed to perform the data-analysis side of the model shown in Figure 3.2, but what of the other side which is equally as important?

Functional analysis is the study of how a particular area of an organization performs or functions. To do this the organization is split into obvious functional areas, such as investment department, mortgage department and personnel, and then each is analysed in terms of what functions it performs. First, again, we must define appropriate tools for the job.

3.10 Operations and events

An **operation** is defined as a task that is performed as a direct result of an event. An **event** is defined as something that triggers off an operation. If this does not sound altogether clear then a few examples should clarify matters.

1   Event: a customer comes in to open an account.
    Operation: process of opening an account is initiated.
2   Event: message is received by the computer from a terminal.
    Operation: message is processed.

In fact we can take the definitions further by declaring:

- operations can cause events,
- operations can often be broken down into simpler operations,
- operations can imply other operations.

As with the data-analysis methodology, when the functional analysis is performed, documentation needs to be maintained for events:

1   What causes the event to happen? (Though it may be totally random.)
2   When does the event happen?
3   What operations follow the event?
4   Which people are involved with the events? (Security is again involved here because only certain people may be allowed to cause events, such as the request of a payroll analysis.)

Documentation also needs to be maintained for operations:

1   Which event(s) cause the operation to happen?
2   What does the operation actually achieve? (Data analysis.)
3   What data are involved? (An important tie with the data analysis.)
4   Are any other operations triggered off by the operation?
5   Can the operation be meaningfully broken down into sub-operations?
6   Which people are involved with the operation?

By taking the opening of an investment account as an example, here are some possible answers to the aforementioned questions.

Events

1 Customer wishes to invest some money.
2 Any time during opening hours.
3 Operation initiated is the opening of an account.
4 Customer and a cashier on a till (though many other possibilities exist and all should be listed, e.g. an agency, a letter and a cheque, etc.).

Operations

1 Customer asking for an account to be opened.
2 Placing of a new account on the investment file. The posting of a first transaction to that account.
3 Branch name, account number, opening data, initial receipt, customer name and address, account type, single or joint account, interest rate, and so on.
4 No, but see (5) following.
5 The operation might be split down into the following:
   (a) a receipt form is filled out,
   (b) a new account number is obtained/generated,
   (c) investment department of the new account is informed,
   (d) possibly a new customer record is generated if the customer is new to the bank,
   (e) a new passbook is issued.
6 People involved might be:
   (a) the cashier,
   (b) whoever issues the passbooks/account numbers,
   (c) investment department,
   (d) customer inasmuch as he/she will supply the necessary information.

Further examples of this process are given in Chapter 4.

3.11 Summary

Work of the data analyst has been likened in this chapter to that of the systems analyst, except that it is on a grander scale. Rather than a single area of the business being studied, all areas must be looked at: any omissions cause serious difficulties if they require insertion at a later stage.

From this global interpretation of the business, the data analyst will fill in a set of forms relating to the constituent entities, attributes and relationships of the organization, from which he or she will hope to derive a conceptual data model including a data model diagram. From these stages, in turn, they will pass on to the database design stages and the eventual implementation of the database. In theory, the data analysis has seemed a relatively straightforward if somewhat long-winded exercise, but the next chapter will show that this assumption is correct only on the second point and that the process of data analysis is far from straightforward and must ultimately be a 'patched together' analysis of all the business areas, rather than a true global overview.

4

Conceptual view: practice

4.1 Introduction

In the last chapter the theory of both data and functional analysis was looked at. In this chapter we see whether or not the theory can be put into practice.

4.2 Problems with data analysis

In Chapter 3 it was stated that data analysis should be performed at the global or organizational level, which implies a huge one-off exercise. Indeed, it should be a one-off exercise that does not have to be repeated even if a conventional file system is changed to become a database system, or there is any other major upheaval, and certainly not for minor changes such as updating the database level from, say, Oracle 6 to Oracle 7. The reasons for this are as stated previously: that the global conceptual model is implementation-free (a change to the computer environment should not change the way that the business is run).

Unfortunately, for a large business, it is difficult to see where such a global view of the organization might come from. In practice, all the data analyst can ever hope to do is visit all the user departments, extract all the information he or she needs and then consolidate the sum into a single global view. In other words, it is difficult to arrive at an implementation-free non-application-oriented view when it must itself be composed of a number of implemented application-oriented views.

Secondly, it was stated in the last chapter that the decision as to whether to implement manual files, conventional files or database files should be taken at the design stage. However, the decision to perform a data-analysis exercise is normally taken before a database system is implemented, and therefore there will exist a certain bias towards database systems, even if they are not wholly appropriate. In short, it is unlikely that a company will undertake n person-months of data-analysis study, unless it is committed at least partially to a database system to begin with.

4.3   A solution

It has been shown that the processes of data and functional analysis are closely related. We cannot define data items sensibly without noting in what processes they will be used. Similarly, we cannot define operations and processes without remarking on which items of data are involved.

Bearing this in mind, we can work on a compromise with respect to the data analysis by collecting the data as we perform the functional analysis (i.e. on a department-to-department basis), thus creating a set of conceptual submodels which we can piece together at the end of the exercise (see Section 4.17).

It must be borne in mind, however, that these submodels may not form simple subsets of the full conceptual model that we require. In short:

- entities in the full model may only be attributes in the submodel: for example, in the customer system, the entities of investment and mortgage may only be represented by their respective account numbers;
- relationships in the full model may be entities in a submodel; for example, a relationship in the full model, that a set of customers own an investment account (shown as a many-to-many relationship), might be shown in the investment department as an entity containing 'the set of owners';
- the degree and nature of any relationships in the full model might be different in a submodel; for example, in the global data model a mortgage might be shown as having a one-to-many relationship with insurances (e.g. a mortgage might have a buildings insurance, a contents insurance, an all-risks insurance, etc.), but to a buildings insurance department the relationship would be one-to-one because that department would not be interested in the other types;
- attributes of entities in the full model may be described as attributes of different entities in the submodels: for example, to the mortgage department, the customer name and address might well be included in the mortgage entity, but in the global model it would be more advantageous to have them in a separate customer entity accessible by all departments.

This process of performing data analysis at a functional level, though not theoretically correct, is helpful especially at the design stage because the resulting data submodels will, eventually, become our logical-database submodels.

4.4   Sources for analysis

Before looking at the practical side of performing data and functional analysis, we can define some general areas from which information can be gleaned in the general exercise:

- existing input documents, such as receipt slips and withdrawal slips;
- existing output documents, such as reports and balance sheets;
- existing computer files (if there are any);
- existing manual files;

- existing computer programs (very useful for process definitions);
- job descriptions (who does what, where and when);
- talking to all relevant members of staff in the functional areas and not just to the management.

4.5   Normalization

So far the process of data analysis might seem a fairly arduous but straightforward process of visiting user departments one by one and extracting all useful information from the sources listed in the previous section. Unfortunately, as it stands we have no way of knowing whether the entities arranged intuitively by natural grouping are good entities in that they will map nicely into compact, efficient data structures that display none of the problems outlined in Chapter 1 (e.g. data duplication, redundancy, etc.).

Once the database has been designed and is being implemented it will become progressively harder for any changes to be made at the root level. The data analyst needs some sort of tool for measuring the quality of their conceptual model before proceeding further. Such a tool is **normalization**, a process that owes much to the work of E. F. Codd on relational databases, but is suitable for most other database system types also.

The following definitions of the various normal forms may seem meaningless if stated simply; therefore a worked example has been included for clarity.

Suppose that we have a group of attributes grouped together intuitively to form a mortgage entity, these attributes being:

- Account number,
- Customer name (first named),
- Customer address,
- Amount borrowed,
- Amount outstanding,
- Supervising branch code,
- Supervising branch name,
- Account type (monthly repayment, weekly, etc.),
- Type of mortgage (repayment, endowment, etc.),
- Interest rate,
- Insurance type 1 (buildings, contents, all risks),
- Insurance company code 1,
- Insurance company details 1,
- Insurance details 1,
- Insurance type 2 (as above),
- Insurance company code 2,
- Insurance company details 2,
- Insurance details 2

and so on.

Note

For the moment the example will only deal with a single (first) named customer. The above may be a full list of all attributes the mortgage department wants with regard to a mortgage. It would seem natural enough to group it all in a single entity, but problems of data duplication may not be obvious until the database is implemented, and that may be too late. (Note that this simplified single-application view is reminiscent of many existing conventional file approaches.)

4.6 Unique identifiers

The first rule of normalization is that the entity should have an attribute or set of attributes that identifies an occurrence of the entity uniquely, such that no attribute can be removed from the key without the key losing its uniqueness. In other words, the key should be the minimum set of attributes that identifies an occurrence of the entity uniquely.

This is not such a strange idea because all non-computerized files and records will have such a key. In the mortgage example both the account number and a combination of customer's name and address would form unique identifiers for a mortgage record so we have two possibilities. What the unique identifier rule says is that there should be at least one identifier and that it is not worth having a composite key of all three because it would not contain the minimum number of attributes.

4.7 Functional dependence

An attribute of an entity is **functionally dependent** on a second attribute if and only if each occurrence of the first attribute has associated with it exactly one occurrence of the second.

4.8 First normal form

An entity is in **first normal form** if and only if the attributes that are not a part of the key are functionally dependent on the key. What this means is that there must be no repeating groups within the entity, because that would contradict functional dependence. Hence, in our example, insurance details should not belong in the mortgage entity because they repeat, and therefore they should be removed to form a separate entity. To do this we must bear in mind that the new entity must also have a unique identifying key (Figure 4.1).

Notes

1   Again there are various ways of representing both the normalized entities and the key attributes of each. Here we have designated the latter by asterisks and the former in a diagrammatic form that we believe shows the developed relationships more clearly.

2   It is an unwritten rule that when removing a repeating group the key of the originating entity goes with it whether or not it is required as a part key of the new entity. In practical terms it will be required for linkage if the database is implemented as relational (see Chapter 11). It will also prevent the formation of *m:n* relationships (see Section 4.13).

Here we must note that the insurance type, company code and account number are needed to identify uniquely the insurance entity because each insurance company will, no doubt, offer several types of insurance, but a mortgage will only have one type of each with one company (though buildings and contents policies may be with different companies). Also, it is apparent that the insurance company details are not functionally dependent on the whole of the insurance key, but only on the company code. In other words, given a company code we know the company without having to know the insurance type or the mortgage to which the details belong. This leads to a second set of definitions.

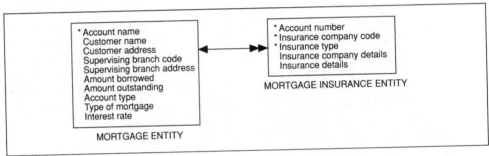

Figure 4.1 Mortgage data in first normal form

4.9   Full functional dependence

An attribute is **fully functionally dependent** on another attribute(s) if and only if it is functionally dependent on the second attribute(s) but not on any subset of the second attribute(s).

4.10   Second normal form

An entity is in **second normal form** if, and only if, it is in first normal form and every non-key attribute is fully functionally dependent on the identifying key. Clearly, this is not the case with the insurance entity which therefore needs to be separated further (Figure 4.2), by removing the data dependent on a subset of the key plus a copy of that subset which will become the key of the new entity.

The mortgage entity is already in second normal form simply because its key cannot be split into subsets and therefore the second normal form rule does not apply here.

Note that the possible key item of customer name and address has been removed from the diagram. This is because, for the sake of clarity, it is easier to represent only a single key at the moment and, in addition, the account number key is shorter and more meaningful to the business. However, other 'candidate' keys will not be forgotten but will be looked at later.

In the mortgage insurance details we clearly need to know the account number, the insurance type and the company code to uniquely identify the details. We have now removed some of the data duplication problems by having the insurance company details only held once. Inspection of the mortgage entity, however, reveals that the customer name and address may well be stored elsewhere (if the customer owns an investment account) and the supervising branch name certainly will be stored elsewhere. Such problems are removed by our third set of definitions.

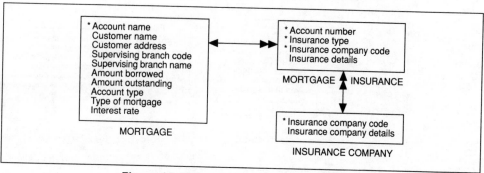

Figure 4.2 Mortgage data in second normal form

4.11   Transitive dependence

For three distinct attributes, if attribute 3 is functionally dependent on attribute 2 and attribute 2 is functionally dependent on attribute 1, then attribute 3 is **transitively dependent** on attribute 1 if, and only if, attribute 1 is neither functionally dependent on attribute 2 nor on attribute 3.

This may sound very confusing even after a couple of reads but relating it to the example it means that the branch name is functionally dependent on the branch code, the branch code is functionally dependent on the account number, but the account number is not functionally dependent on the branch code or the name. Similarly, the customer address is transitively dependent on the account number.

4.12   Third normal form

An entity is in **third normal form** if it is in second normal form and every attribute that is not a part of the key is not transitively dependent on the identifying key. Since an entity in third normal form must, by definition, also be in first and second normal forms, we can define a third normal form in terms of the conditions that the entity must have:

- a unique identifying key,
- no repeating attributes,

- no attributes that do not require the whole of the identifying key,
- attributes that are mutually independent.

A useful little catchphrase (origin unknown) is that for an entity to be in third normal form, every non-key attribute must be dependent on the key, the whole key, and nothing but the key.

Returning to our example, we now have the situation shown in Figure 4.3, in which the attribute dependent on the non-key attribute has been removed together with a copy of the attribute on which it was dependent which will become the key of the new entity. The relationship between customer and mortgage is one-to-one unless we assume that a customer can have more than one mortgage.

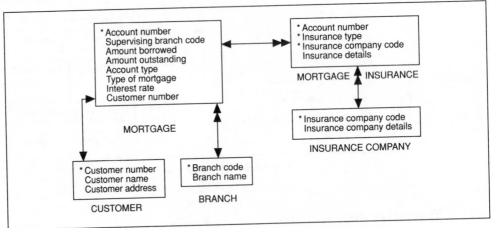

Figure 4.3 Mortgage data in third normal form

Notes

1   It is always useful to keep the entities named along the normalization path – if a name is not obvious then the entity should be named after a concatenation of the keys.

2   We now have data duplication with the supervising branch code, but it is a controlled redundancy because the item is never likely to change in value and cause problems. However, the 'bulkier' items such as the customer name and address, branch name, insurance details and insurance company details are now only in one place instead of on every account, so we have certainly reduced our storage capacity needs in comparison with the initial entity before normalization.

3   At this final stage we have had to invent a customer number because neither the customer name nor the customer address is a useful (or even possibly unique) key. Unless there is already in existence a customer number this will unfortunately be meaningless to the business and the customer, but short of concatenating the name and address it is the only way of identifying a customer uniquely (in fact even the name and address combined may not be unique if there is a father and son with the same forename living in the same house and both with accounts).

This problem of unique identifiers is common to every computer-based system. People's names are not guaranteed unique even in a small business. In general, any long alphanumeric items will not make good keys simply because, when they are entered, the keying-in must be exact. For example, if the address is the key and is stored as

> 5, London Road

then none of the following will find the record:

> 5 London Road
> 5, London Rd
> 5,London Road.

Frequently, the only solution is to create a unique identifying number even if it is purely internal to the computer system (i.e. is never used by the business as such). In the example, if the customer entity is only ever accessed from the mortgage entity then there will be no problems because the link would be provided by the DBMS and a customer number would not be needed. However, if the customer entity needs direct accessing then we will have to rethink.

4.13 An intersection entity

One result that did not actually occur in the example but, in general, frequently does, is that normalization removes all $m{:}n$ relationships by translating them into several $1{:}n$ relationships. For example, consider the investment system. Clearly, an investment account can have more than one customer, and a customer can have more than one investment account, so we have an $m{:}n$ relationship. If we normalized this in a similar fashion we would end up with the situation shown in Figure 4.4 (the reader can produce this as an exercise).

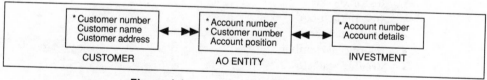

Figure 4.4 $m{:}n$ relationship after normalization

In this situation the central entity is known as an **intersection entity**. This is, in practice, a bridging entity placed between two existing entities to circumvent the $m{:}n$ relationship.

In the above example we have created an entity called Account Owners (AO) containing the account number plus a customer number plus a number to say whether that customer was the first named on that account (or second or third or fourth – such a numbering does have a meaning in the real world because, in general, only the first named is sent the statement). One account would have up to four associated AO entities but each AO would only relate to one account. Therefore we have a $1{:}n$ relationship. Similarly, a customer can be the first named on many accounts (i.e. have many associated AO occurrences), but each AO will relate only to one customer occurrence.

In the normalization example, described in Section 4.5, it was stated that we were only looking at a single customer per mortgage. Had we wanted more than one then the customer details would have been a repeating group and would have come out in first normal form. This would have produced a similar result to that above where an intersection entity would break down an $m{:}n$ relationship into two $1{:}n$ relationships.

4.14   A determinant

A determinant is an attribute or set of attributes on which some other attribute is fully functionally dependent. We can now study another third-normal-form definition which does not involve first and second normal forms. It is sometimes referred to as a **strong third normal form** (the prior definition being the weak third normal form) or as the Boyce–Codd normal form following an early definition by Boyce and Codd.

4.15   A strong third normal form

An entity is in strong third normal form if every determinant is a candidate key. An example should show this to be the case. Suppose we now look at the normalization of the branch entity. A branch might include:

- Branch code,
- Branch name,
- Branch address,
- Manager's name,
- Regional code,
- Area branch code,
- Sub-branch codes,
- Telephone number,
- Monthly statistics.

Here the region code is a numeric field denoting which region of the country the branch lies in. The area branch code is that of the area office (which is a branch in its own right), and the sub-branch codes are those of any branches controlled by the branch in question (i.e. if it is itself an area office).

This example is also useful because it shows that normalization should not be taken as the 'be all and end all' of data analysis. It sometimes produces unwanted results and, ultimately, there is plenty of scope for common sense when data structures are rationalized. The problem may be depicted as:

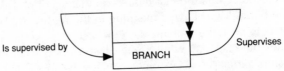

The entity branch has a relationship with itself because the area offices supervise other branches (a 1:n relationship), whereas sub-branches are supervised by an area office (an n:1 relationship). If we had regional offices that supervised area offices then the situation would be even more complex. Unfortunately, this linking of an occurrence of an entity to other occurrences of the same entity is quite common in the real world.

According to our definition of first normal form, the field shown as 'Sub-branch codes' is a repeating group which should not be a part of the branch entity. However, common sense tells us that from a business viewpoint it makes little sense to create a new sub-branch entity, containing only the branch code, and in turn linking back to the branch entity for the sub-branch details. (However, with certain DBMS formats, the above would be a useful structure to implement as it would provide an index file to the branches. This is not possible with all DBMS implementations so it will not be pursued here.) Here, we can gloss over the problem by declaring the sub-branch codes as sub-branch 1, sub-branch 2, and so on. Now they are disjoint attributes and no longer a repeating group.

Disregarding this problem we now try normalization techniques. First, with our definition of a strong third normal form in mind we look for possible keys. These would appear to be:

- branch code,
- branch name,
- manager's name,
- telephone number.

Are these the only determinants? To begin with we apply the definition of the first normal form (Figure 4.5).

There is no need to look to second normal forms because we have no split key. Consider the weak third normal form definition. Is the branch address transitively dependent on the branch code? The answer is 'no' because, although the address is functionally dependent on the name, the code is functionally dependent on both the name and the address (on the assumption that the branch name is unique), there being a 1:1 relationship between each pair.

There is a slightly harder task with the manager's name. Although managers can change branches, at any one instant the manager's name will be functionally dependent on the branch code and also the code will be functionally dependent on the manager's name. In other words, given a manager's name we can identify the correct branch. (Clearly, this assumes the manager's name to be unique. If this cannot be

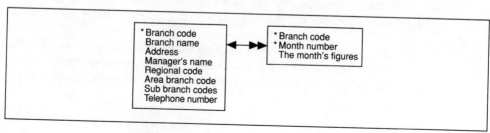

Figure 4.5 Branch data in first normal form

guaranteed then it can no longer be considered as a candidate key because it will not identify a single branch uniquely. Again common sense would rule this to be the case, coupled with the fact that over a period of time the manager is likely to change, and therefore his name would not make a suitable key.)

Looking at the branch entity, therefore, we have three determinants: code, name and phone number. A cursory glance will reveal there to be no further determinants and therefore the branch entity is in strong third normal form. (The case for a branch statistics entity being in strong third normal form is trivial.)

One lesson to be learned from this is that in the real world we would not dream of having either the manager's name or the telephone number as the keys to the branch, but if we are to undertake data analysis rigorously then we must recognize all possible candidate keys. The decision as to which actually will be used need not be made until design time.

4.16 Functional analysis in practice

All the normalization techniques mentioned so far have assumed that some intuitive processes already have occurred to develop natural groupings. Where can the data analyst find such groupings?

The answer can be found when existing reports and documents are looked at. In these the main nouns will usually be entities and the verbs will be the relationships between them. For example:

A customer owns accounts
A mortgage may be covered by an endowment policy.

As stated previously, functional analysis involves the study of each functional area of the organization and documentation of all the processes that it performs. The processes can be split into events and operations and, by defining the input needs and output needs for each operation, we can derive the data needs for the operation and, by extension over all operations, the data needs of the whole functional area.

An example of this process might be: a customer enters a branch to see the manager about a mortgage application. This is a process that can be split into an event (i.e. the customer coming into the branch) and an operation (i.e. the manager checking through the details with the customer). The application form is an input document that should provide the data analyst with a wealth of data items (Figure 4.6).

This shows a fine mass of information! The operation here would simply be to check that the customer has filled in the details correctly or to fill them in with the customer's guidance. Will any other operations and events be initiated by this process once the customer has gone? The following are some likely possibilities.

1   The manager checks his or her monthly quota to see if the branch has money to lend to the customer. This involves looking at some entity containing mortgage monthly quota statistics, presumably identified by the month number.

Month number
Monthly quota

Customer name
Customer address
Customer telephone number
Property address
Type of property (detatched, semi, terraced, flat, etc.)
Type of construction (brick, concrete, wood, etc.)
Loan required
Type of mortgage (repayment, endowment, etc.)
Repayment term
Investment account number
Solicitor's name and address
Estate agent
Vendor's solicitor's name and address
Husband's income
Husband's employers
Wife's income
Wife's employers
Valuation
Valuer's name

Figure 4.6 Mortgage-offer data

2 The manager must check the customer's investment record to see if they are regular savers and have enough for the deposit.

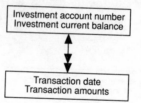

3 The manager must contact the husband's and/or wife's employers for references and check on their salaries.

Employer's name
Employer's address

4 If all is well the manager must contact the bank's surveyors and/or valuers to ask them to survey and value the property.

Valuer's name
Date of valuation
Valuation

5 The manager will presumably wish to check some details with the vendor's solicitor (and possibly the customer's also).

Solicitor's name
Solicitor's address
Solicitor's phone no.

6 Only if all is satisfactory can the manager make the customer a mortgage offer

that if accepted will, eventually, become a mortgage account with its own account number.

```
Customer's name
Customer's tel. no.
Mortgage offer no.
Mortgage acc. no.
```

This is a gross simplification but it does show how relatively simple events and operations can initiate others (each with their own data requirements) but, by following the chain of events through, the data analyst can build up a complete picture of the 'mortgage offer' function. By merely analysing the application form the analyst would only see half the picture. All the other detail could only come by a personal interview with a branch/mortgage manager as it is unlikely to be documented.

If the above six processes had been completed then we would have a full set of the data requirements for the mortgage-offer function. Normalizing this data we should obtain the results of Figure 4.7.

Notes

1   It is highly likely that the customer is already known to the business (through an investment account number) and hence the customer number (that unique identifier of the customer entity) can be assigned to the mortgage offer.

2   Although in practice the mortgage offer will not exist at the same time as the resulting mortgage, it is nevertheless correct and meaningful at the data-analysis stage to associate the mortgage account number with the offer in case the information is later stored for historical purposes.

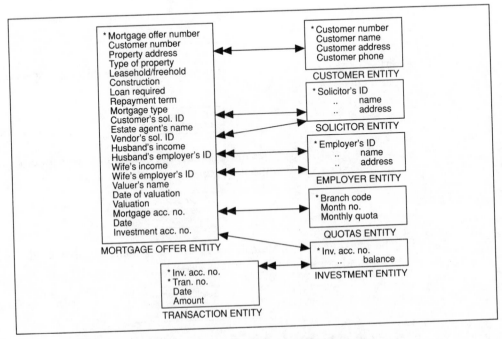

Figure 4.7 Mortgage-offer data in third normal form

3   Again, normalization has given us unwelcome results in terms of what we would expect in real life. Because we cannot assume the solicitor's name to be unique and because our third-normal-form definition insists that a solicitor's entity be split off because of transitive dependence, we have had to invent a solicitor's ID. The same applies to the husband's/wife's employers.

It may well be the practice of the business to keep a register of all qualified solicitors in the country in which case assigning them a special identifier may be a meaningful exercise. Alternatively, it may be more meaningful actually to implement the solicitor's name and address as a part of the mortgage offer entity. It would, certainly, be more sensible to store the employer's information on the mortgage-offer record; one of the advantages of normalization is that we end up with one fact in one place. However, unless most people living near a particular branch all work for the same employers, there is little to be gained by having the employer details as a separate entity with its corresponding increase in access times.

The moral of this is that these are implementation decisions that need not concern us here. The prime role of data analysis is to highlight potential entities and relationships, which may or may not be implemented as such.

A second problem of normalization is that it sometimes fails to show entities at all. If, in the above example, we had not included the process of checking the customer's investment balance, perhaps changing it to merely checking the existence of an investment record, then as we would only have the investment account number in the mortgage-offer entity and no repeating groups or transitive dependences, no degree of normalization will ever show investments to be an entity in its own right even though, intuitively, we know it should be.

Again this demonstrates that there is always room for common sense and intuition during data analysis and that any data models derived from it are not necessarily the data models that will be implemented.

4.17   Creation of a consolidated conceptual model

We shall now assume that the data analyst has visited all functional areas of the organization, has extracted all relevant information, and has created a set of submodels. How can he or she now consolidate these into a single global model? Bearing in mind the possible inconsistencies that were outlined in Section 4.3 the analyst may have problems.

4.18   The additive approach

Perhaps the most logical approach would be to take one of the submodels (arbitrarily) as the main model and then to add the other models to it one by one until the global picture is complete (Figure 4.8).

This is not a good approach. If submodel N is being added to the global model and contains an attribute A that conflicts with an attribute A already extant in the global model, then which takes precedence? It is very unlikely that the submodels are all

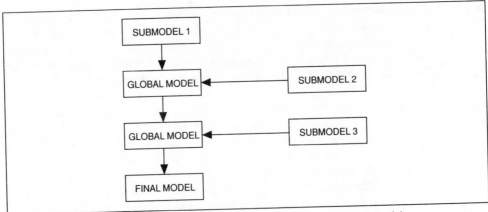

Figure 4.8 Additive approach to creation of a conceptual model

disjoint and so, whichever order they are processed in, there will almost certainly be problems of conflicting entity, attribute and relationship types.

4.19 The incremental approach

An alternative to the above approach might be for someone with a sound knowledge of the business to construct an intuitive first model based on a global view of the organization. Such a model may not be too complex, but it can be refined by the addition of the submodels one at a time. This is sometimes referred to as **stepwise refinement**. For example, a basic model for our bank might appear as in the diagram shown in Figure 4.9.

Such a model would probably, at best, show the functional areas of the organization plus a few ambiguities ($m{:}n$ relationships) though the latter should be removed by the stepwise refinement process.

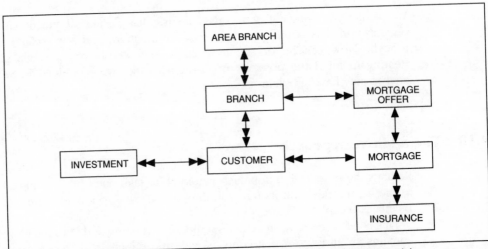

Figure 4.9 Incremental approach to creation of a conceptual model

4.20   **Problems with consolidation**

During the process of consolidation the data analyst must be aware of certain potential problems that must be eliminated before the design stage is started.

Synonyms

By bearing in mind that the pseudonyms described on the entity–attribute form are likely to refer only to synonyms within the particular area of study, in the global model the data analyst must determine whether or not two attributes with differing names are logically the same. For example, is the property address on the mortgage entity necessarily the same as the customer address on the customer entity? Is the date on the investment entity (for the opening of the account) necessarily the same as the date on the first transaction entity?

Homonyms

(These are words or phrases that look the same but actually refer to different things.) Does the account type in the mortgage entity (referring to whether the account is repayment, endowment or whatever) relate to the account type on the investment entity (here referring to whether the account is deposit, special shares, etc.)? Clearly not, in this case, but the data analyst must be aware that they should not be implemented, in general, with the same name.

It might be thought debatable whether or not to give the attributes longer and more meaningful names to begin with and check whether two attributes are the same, as opposed to their being given shorter names and checking to see if they are different, but in the long run it is far better to start off with meaningful (and different) names, particularly if consideration is given to data dictionary systems (Chapter 8).

Sub-entities

These consist of occurrences of subsets of the full entity. For example, if our business has a buildings insurance department and a separate contents insurance department, then the insurance entity generated from the building department will be a subset of the global entity insurance.

Recognition of sub-entities is important when we come to the implementation stage because they might show the need for different storage mechanisms for the differing subtypes (e.g. the buildings records may be required at different times/access speeds/frequency from the contents records).

It is also important when different conceptual views are highlighted. For example, overall we may have modelled a single investment transactions entity covering all transactions relating to an account. One particular department within the business, however, might only be interested in the transactions from the current financial year, whereas another might need all of them over the past five years. Normalization will not show the differing views, but there may yet be a need to split the transactions entity into a current and a historic, storing each in different ways on different devices.

4.21 Summary

In the last two chapters, we have looked at the process of data analysis; if it appears to be a long, arduous process then that is because it necessarily is so. Database design can be carried out after poor data analysis, but a poor database will result. In particular, any corrections or additions necessary at a later stage will generally be very difficult to implement. It is therefore far better to perform data analysis meticulously, paying many visits to the user departments and cross-checking all results, to ensure that the final model is as free from ambiguities as it can practicably be.

5
Logical database design

5.1 Introduction

We make no apologies for repetition when restating how important it is that database design is not initiated before the data analysis stage has been finished completely.

In practice, the processes of data and functional analysis are rarely performed except when a database is to be implemented. This is certainly to the detriment of many businesses that do not want a database solution and therefore do not gain this overall picture of the efficiency of their organization. For example, in large businesses it is not too rare to find two different departments spending n person-hours in producing independently exactly the same set of statistics, each for their own personal use. Data and functional analysis would highlight such wastage and eliminate the inefficiency in this autonomous environment.

With the database approach the theory shows that such inefficiency would be removed because all data would be shared and one fact will only be stored in one place. Such autonomy as is desired, particularly with respect to privacy, can be maintained adequately as shown in Chapter 7.

However, this is not to say that all data should be thrown into a single database as a cure for all evils. By considering the results of the data analysis exercise, the database administrator should have some ideas about how to implement each of his or her conceptual structures.

The design stage is therefore split into two distinct parts:

- mapping of the conceptual model into the logical data model,
- mapping of the logical data model into the physical data model.

5.2 Design objectives

In practice, the objectives of database design vary enormously from implementation to implementation. In general some of the following objectives are mutually exclusive, resulting in most implementations aiming for a suitable permutation of seven or eight from nine.

Efficiency

Efficiency is generally considered to be the most important. Given a piece of hardware on which the database will run and a piece of software (DBMS) to run it, the design should make full and efficient use of the facilities provided. Efficiency also means that the more important areas of the business are given more priority in the case of conflicting interests such that, for example, the database will not be tuned up around a program that only runs every third Tuesday. Any online work should also be taken into consideration such that interactive users have minimum response times.

Integrity

The database should be as accurate a reflection as possible of the business that it serves. Such considerations might seem obvious, but their importance can vary from business to business. For example, a financial institution maintaining a balance of £1058 for an account instead of the true £1059 is more likely to be 'found out' than a stock control system that shows the quantity of part A in stock as being 1058 when it is in reality 1059.

Privacy

The database should not allow unauthorized access to files, data items and relationships (at both the read-only and update levels) that would not be allowed in the 'real world'. Again, this requirement might vary from a business where the data held is public knowledge to one that maintains state-security data.

Security

The database, once loaded, should be safe from physical corruption, whether from hardware or software failure or from unauthorized access. This is a general requirement of most databases.

Implementability

The conceptual model should not be so complicated that it cannot be implemented as a logical database. Also it must not be implemented in such a way that it is very difficult for application programs to find their way through (navigate) complex structures and paths. This is another very desirable aim.

Flexibility

The database should not be implemented in a rigid way that assumes the business will remain constant for ever. Changes will occur and the database must be capable of responding readily to such change. Many traditional database types fall down on this point: they are very difficult to change.

Maintainability

The database must be implemented in such a way as to be comprehensible to any subsequent database administrators, as well as the present one.

Compatibility

Initially, the business data may be implemented as several disjoint databases. These should be compatible such that any future merging of data is possible. This is perhaps the least important of the objectives (unless we are considering distributed databases).

Portability

The database should be implementable on a variety of hardware and software. Most relational databases will run on a wide range of platforms because, in general, they have not been produced by computer manufacturers and therefore they need to appeal to as wide a market as possible. Traditional database types such as CODASYL, however, are notoriously non-portable because they are written specifically for one computer manufacturer, and are subsequently designed and tuned to run efficiently on one piece of hardware.

It must be borne in mind that, whatever the objectives, data analysis may have thrown out items that are not implementable on the chosen database. For example, $m:n$ relationships (if they have not been removed by normalization) and variable-length data items (it would always be desirable to implement names and addresses as variable-length fields but, unfortunately, not all database systems support them).

5.3 Efficiency vs privacy

Following the problems concerning privacy as outlined in Chapter 1, it would be highly desirable if privacy control could be implemented at all levels, that is, at database, structure, record and data-item levels, and, indeed, many systems allow this. However, processor overheads may be too high (i.e. if every time a record is accessed several checks have to be performed to verify the validity of the user with respect to that record and, possibly, also to some embedded data items) and the efficiency will suffer.

The alternative is to arrange the records so that the data items in each have the same level of privacy. Unfortunately, this is rather reminiscent of the conventional file approach where items had to be hived off into separate files, which itself was inefficient.

5.4 Efficiency vs logical data independence

As outlined in Chapter 3, one of the advantages of the database approach is that submodels (or views) can be defined allowing the user to see only what the user wants or is allowed to see in an application-oriented way, thus providing effective logical data independence. This mapping from logical model to submodel can be quite complex in general, and the more complex it is, the higher the processor cost will be. For that reason, it happens quite frequently that, whereas a given DBMS can support a more complex mapping, in practice the logical records are designed so the submodel is a simple subset of the logical model, resulting in a much simpler mapping and hence lower processor overheads. With this approach there is a danger of data duplication creeping in to 'save time'.

5.5 Problems with the operating system

As outlined in Chapter 2, most DBMSs leave the actual storing and retrieving of records to the operating system because, in general, this has been tailor-made for a particular machine and is therefore likely to be efficient. A problem here is that, to the operating system, the DBMS appears as a single user, as shown in Figure 5.1.

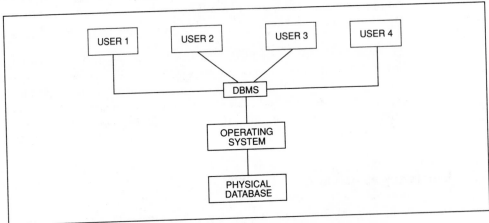

Figure 5.1 Influence of the operating system on data access

This means that the DBMS must route all data plus any error messages back to the correct user. This is a processor overhead in order to do something that is normally done very efficiently by the operating system.

A further problem is that the operating system might not allow the fine placement control required for maximum efficiency. For example, if data analysis has shown a need to store the investment record, its transaction records and the associated customer record close together because of frequent access, it would be ideal to store them on the same page. Such a convenience would be possible if we had separate storage and device data models. However, this is not the case and the operating system might not be equipped to follow such a request unless it had been written with the DBMS in mind. The end result is that the logical data model is often designed to combine logical records to ensure that all the related data are on the same page.

5.6 Database design methodology

Having looked at some of the pitfalls and limitations of current database-design techniques, we can now consider how the database administration (DBA) actually goes about its task.

First, we must assume that the relevant hardware has been decided on, and that its limitations have been taken into account, and, similarly, that a DBMS is available. Given this information the DBA must become fully conversant with the structure and usage of that DBMS and, in particular, with the structuring methods available with the associated data definition language (DDL). To achieve this they will probably be sent on a manufacturer-supplied course, but it is also important to stress the need for a good set of user documentation since this is what they will be using on a day-to-day basis.

Given, therefore, a conceptual model the DBA will probably at first try a simple mapping in which:

- entities become files,
- attributes become data items,
- relationships become primary and foreign keys (or sets in CODASYL).

Note: it is very difficult to generalize about database design without lapsing into the terminology of a particular database system.

Following this initial translation, the DBA must then decide whether the constraints described previously in this chapter are still present or are at least balanced correctly. For example:

- Will the privacy afforded by the DBMS facilitate items of differing privacy levels being stored in the same record?
- Will the DBMS allow related records to be stored physically on the same page?

Clearly, the second question should in theory be included in the physical database design, but following the assertions made in Section 5.5 all such considerations must be evaluated together.

If the result of the initial mapping is satisfactory in terms of constraints then the first model will become the final logical data model. However, if constraints are still extant then the initial model must be subjected to a process known as 'collapse and fragmentation'.

5.7   Collapse and fragmentation

This is the general process whereby entities are combined together (collapsed) or split (fragmented) to form new entities, for the purpose of removing unwanted constraints from the database design. A single example of each should be enough to outline their usage.

1   Suppose that as a part of our branch records we keep quarterly totals relating to data such as totals for receipts, withdrawals, new accounts, and moneys received through agencies. At the end of the year the four quarterly sets of statistics are totalled for the year and analysed to show the business progression of each branch. The data analysis revealed the need to store the individual quarterly statistics separately (i.e. normalization found them to be a repeating group) as shown in Figure 5.2. However, sometimes one of the managers in the finance department

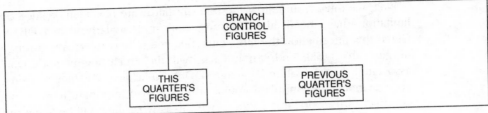

Figure 5.2 Fragmentation of the branch control file

wishes to run a statistical program that involves comparisons between statistics over the past four quarters. To prevent a high number of individual accesses it would be convenient if the four sets of data could be stored together on the same page, such that all the statistics for, say, branch 56 could be located with a single access; and so this is what is decided on at the data-analysis stage. However, at the design stage it is discovered that the DBMS will not afford such fine control. The decision must be made now as to whether to tolerate the high number of accesses or to collapse the two files into one, thus guaranteeing that for one branch we have one access.

There are no ground rules for such a decision, it is based purely on the importance of the 'offending' program.

It should be noted that if collapse is performed it will produce a result contrary to that necessitated by normalization. In other words, we have a repeating group as shown in Figure 5.3. Again this emphasizes that normalization is only a tool and does not always produce the final desired product.

```
BRANCH-FIGURES.
    BRANCH-CODE      NUMBER(3)
    Q-FIGURES     OCCURS 4
        etc.
```

Figure 5.3 Collapsed record as a file

2   Suppose now that the data-analysis stage produced a personnel entity composed of the attributes shown in Figure 5.4.

```
EMPLOYEE-RECORD
   WORKS-DETAILS
        EMPLOYEE-NUMBER      NUMBER(3)
        DEPT-NO              NUMBER(3)
        etc.
   PERSONAL-DETAILS
        ADDRESS              CHAR(30)
   MARITAL-STATUS            CHAR(1)
        etc.
   SALARY DETAILS
        TAX-CODE             CHAR(5)
        PAYMENT-METHOD       CHAR(1)
        etc.
```

Figure 5.4 Personnel data

As all the attributes were functionally dependent on the EMPLOYEE-NUMBER with no repeating groups or transitive dependences, then normalization produced the above as a collection of related data. Suppose that the privacy rights for this record are as follows:

The whole record	Only top management
MARITAL-STATUS	Only senior members of personnel department (bear in mind that this may include information such as divorced, living together, etc.)
CONDUCT-COMMENTS	Only top management
SALARY-DETAILS	Only top management plus wages department

If this entity were to be implemented as a single file, then every time a record is accessed the system would have to check whether the user is:

- top management,
- personnel department,
- wages department,
- any other valid user (such as the DBA?).

Such checking would be expensive in both processor time and disc access time, possibly too expensive, and the decision might be taken to fragment the personnel entity as shown in Figure 5.5.

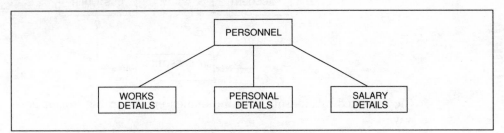

Figure 5.5 Fragmentation of personnel data

Clearly this decision must be taken in conjunction with the decision, as outlined in Section 5.4, as to how complex the model–submodel mapping is to be. If it is considered reasonable to have a more complex mapping then there is no reason to fragment, the entity can be kept as it is and can rely on the submodel design to provide any necessary privacy constraints (i.e. such that top management would have their own submodel, as would the personnel department and wages, resulting in only a single privacy lock being needed for each).

5.8 CODASYL relationships

As mentioned in Section 5.6, in the design of the CODASYL database, relationships in the conceptual model become *sets* in the logical model.

The rules concerning relationships as outlined in Section 3.7 can be mapped simply into CODASYL form:

Mandatory   AUTOMATIC

Contingent ⎤
                    ⎬   MANUAL
Optional   ⎦

(Note that this only applies to existence rules for members in $1:n$ relationships.)

Fixed   FIXED

Transferable   MANDATORY

Transient   OPTIONAL

(Note as above.)

Note that $m:n$ relationships cannot be mapped directly into the DDL. Instead an intersection link must be created such that each entity relates to the intersection link on a $1:n$ basis, for example:

becomes

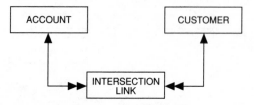

The involuted relationship with the branch entity can be broken down in the same way.

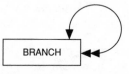

becomes

5.9 Program design

As shown in Figure 3.2, at the same time that the database design is being carried out, the database administration (probably in conjunction with a systems analyst) should also be designing the user interface. This will be as a result of functional analysis. Operations that involve the same data items and that take place at the same time will be grouped together intuitively to form conceptual programs. The problems of program design do not form any part of this book, but it is useful to state that the process can take place concurrently with database design, and that the connections between data submodels (views) and application programs should be clear at this point.

5.10 Efficiency

Having performed the mapping from conceptual model to logical model, and with any necessary collapsing or fragmenting having removed all hardware/software constraints, we now have a logical database. But how can we determine whether or not it will be efficient?

In practice, far too often a database is created, loaded and then monitored to see if it is efficient. If it is not, then the database has to be reorganized or restructured (see Chapter 8) to improve efficiency, but this is in general a time-consuming process. Instead, a little thought and effort at the design stage will save much work later (though this is not to say that the database should not be monitored continuously, as also outlined in Chapter 8).

At the design stage the DBA should look to the conceptual programs and determine how efficient they will all be with the database as it currently stands. (If there is no time to cover every process then at least the critical ones should be included, such as online programs or frequently used batch programs.)

The efficiency of such programs will depend on many facets of program design. Here we are interested only in those relating to database accesses. It is therefore useful to document these accesses at design time. An immediate benefit of having grouped like processes into the same program will be seen by the fact that a program performing both processes A and B on the same file (sequentially) should have half the access cost of two separate programs.

The task therefore is to list the major programs and the number of logical record accesses they will employ (the values used here will obviously have to be derived from an average run of the program in online terms, though in batch mode the number of records accessed is, usually, more fixed).

For example, it may be found that a critical program A at our bank is run daily and accesses:

750 000 investment accounts
3 000 000 investment transactions (average at half-year)
750 000 customer records

If this program is essential to the running of the business (e.g. it balances the accounts) then its importance may be enough to persuade the DBA to design the database around that one program. This situation is perhaps unlikely in a large organization, but many small businesses revolve around having a single very efficient online program to supply immediate information, and in such cases the database could be constructed around that program.

Such decisions cannot be quantified, nor can they be a part of collapsing and fragmenting. They are based intuitively on what is important to the business in question. An example of the documentation that could be used to show access costs is shown in Figure 5.6.

Notes

1   The program contains two separate processes that have been combined because both involve reading through the entire investment file (looking for today's transactions or new accounts) and that are both run at the same time (daily).

2   The estimate is the number of transactions daily and is available from business-supplied statistics.

3   The relevant files and relationships can be shown diagrammatically by:

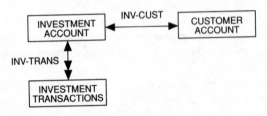

(Only first-named customers are accessed.)

4   All transactions need to be read, but only those bearing today's date are actually used.

Program description: to calculate moneys received on accounts today and to print out the names of any customers who have opened new accounts			
Record	Set	Number Accessed	Number Used
Investments	Direct sequential	750 000	750 000
Inv-trans	Inv-trans	3 000 000	30 000
Customers	Inv-cust	2 500	2 500

Figure 5.6 Access costs of a sample program

Conclusions

The program will be inefficient because of the point made in (4) (i.e. three million reads for 30 000 records is not a good hit rate). This problem assumes that the set INVTRANS has been implemented in the standard CODASYL manner:

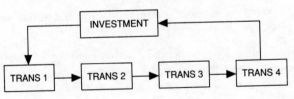

The investment record has a pointer to the first transaction which has a pointer to the second transaction and so on to the last transaction which has a pointer back to the investment account. Thus the only way to navigate through the transactions is to read them all until the required one is found. As today's transactions should always be the last ones there is much wasted I/O time when the first ones are read. It might therefore be decided that, if this program is important, the introduction of a second set of pointers is worthwhile:

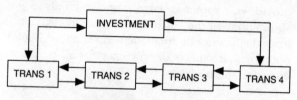

Now, by using these backward pointers, the program only has to access one or two transactions (until the date on them does not match today's date). This would have the effect of cutting down our transaction accesses to around 750 000 (since we must access at least one per account) – this is a saving of over two million logical reads! An even more drastic solution would be to have a flag on the account itself denoting whether there was a transaction today. This would cut the number of transaction accesses to 30 000 but would have the disadvantage of two extra updates to the investment record per day (one to add the flag, one to clear it).

Such decisions would become possible only at the design stage because only then is the information available. Data would almost certainly not show the possible need for a flag, as outlined above, on the investment record.

As a further example, consider the normalized accounts view in Figure 4.4. A normalized view from the customer perspective might be:

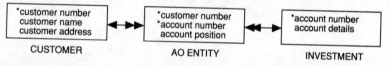

Are they the same? The only slight difference is that the customer and account numbers in the AO entity are transposed. Does that matter?

Consider how the data is stored based on Figure 4.4:

```
12345    17    1
12345    24    2
12346    84    1
12347    29    1
12347    17    2
```

Given an account number, all the information is contiguous, so access to the associated customer numbers will be fast. Now consider that, given a customer number, we do not have all the account numbers for that customer contiguous, so access will be slow (painfully slow if we are linear-searching). Similarly if the file is created as above it can be seen that information based on the customer number will be fast but access via the account number may be slow.

So they are not the same!

5.11 Summary

If a single piece of information is to be gleaned from this chapter, it is that there are no hard and fast rules for database design. It is the DBA's responsibility to ensure that the database:

- optimizes the usage of the available hardware and software;
- provides the required balance of constraints as outlined in Section 5.2;
- shows none of the hardware/software constraints outlined in this chapter (i.e. features that cannot be implemented on a given DBMS);
- optimizes all aspects of efficiency for all programs, particularly for those that are critical to the business.

6

Physical database design

6.1 Introduction

The processes of collapsing and fragmenting described in the previous chapter are concerned with how records should be stored, so already we have encroached on aspects of the physical database. This chapter looks at further aspects of physical database design. Since relational databases take many of the decisions about physical design away from the database designer, we will refer mostly to the CODASYL model in this chapter.

6.2 Data-item implementation

In the previous chapter we saw how a logical data model, free from constraints, can be derived and so now we can turn our attention to how the individual parts of that model can be implemented physically.

In the data-analysis process attributes were described largely by their functional relevance and there was little need to suggest how they might be implemented. For example, within the customer entity we might have had attributes described as:

```
TITLE - MR/MRS/MISS/MS/DR
MARITAL-STATUS - SINGLE/MARRIED/DIVORCED/WIDOW/WIDOWER
ADDRESS - NUMBER, STREET, TOWN, COUNTY, CODE
```

We now have to decide how these items can be represented in our DDL. It would seem sensible and is, indeed, usual to translate multivalue alphabetic items such as TITLE into multivalue numeric items such that we have

```
TITLE NUMBER(1)
```

and the application program can decipher its value as 1 for Mr, 2 for Mrs, and so on. Note that in all forms of data storage it is advisable not to have zero representing any definite value, unless there is need for a default value, because most database systems make all numerics either zero or null when creating records (although others might fill them with high values).

MARITAL-STATUS can be handled in a similar way, but there are many possible implementations of ADDRESS. It could be represented best as a free-format variable-length field or set of fields if the DBMS supports such types, or as a free-format fixed-length field of 70 characters or, indeed, one of the following:

```
ADDRESS.
    NUMBER              NUMBER(3).
    STREET              CHAR(20).
    TOWN                CHAR(20).
    COUNTY              CHAR(10).
    CODE                CHAR(8).

ADDRESS.
    ADD-LINE-1          CHAR(30).
    ADD-LINE-2          CHAR(30).
    CODE                CHAR(8).
```

Clearly, it will be stored in the way most suitable to the organization (e.g. if the address is used mostly for printing on letters then a letter-format representation would be the most suitable).

Having decided that an item is to be numeric, the DBA must now look to its usage. If it is only to be used for display purposes then they may wish to store it as a character field. If the item is required for extensive arithmetical operations, it might be wiser to store it as a binary field (again only if the DBMS allows the choice). As mentioned in the Preface, most database systems will store numeric data in packed decimal format by default, as this saves on storage space.

6.3   Checking functions

It is not only possible for the DBA to describe all data items in the DDL, but with most DBMSs it is possible within the DDL to describe formally any data checks that might be associated with a particular data item. Such methods allow data validation within the database code and lift the onus from application programs to perform such functions. Examples of this might be as follows.

- If a key item is described in DDL as being unique then the DBMS will not allow a new record to be stored with a duplicate key value.
- Range checking. In the example of the previous section, it could be stated that TITLE has to have a value v where $0 \leq v \leq 5$ (care must be taken to include all values: 0 might be acceptable if the customer is only known as J. Smith with title unknown).
- Value checking. If MARITAL-STATUS was implemented as a CHAR(8) field with possible values of married, single, and so on, then the DBMS could be required to check for a valid value.
- Existence checks. If an item has to be given a non-zero or non-null value before the record can be stored, then this can be described in the DDL.
- More complicated checks. The above are fairly simple and standard checking functions, but what if we wished to ensure that the interest due on an account was equal to the sum of all the interest dues stored on each transaction? For this, the DBA could specify a procedure name against the record. When that record is stored the given procedure is executed and the check performed.

It must be stated that the more complicated the checking required, the higher the processor and/or I/O cost at run time. Perhaps such a cost will be too high.

6.4 Direct access methods

The definitions of file storage and access methods given in the following sections are similar to those of non-database files. For those unfamiliar with such definitions, a brief outline is given in Appendix A. Where there are variations in terminology it is the CODASYL definitions that are used here.

The CODASYL definition for **direct access** is similar to the normal definition (i.e. that the user supplies an algorithm to translate the key (database or logical) into a physical address) but, in practice, most manufacturers of CODASYL products have implemented this so that the database key is the physical address (i.e. it contains the page number on which the record resides plus the position of that record on the page).

Direct access provides a very fast access mechanism with a maximum of one physical I/O (none if the record is in memory already). However, there is one big disadvantage in that the record is physically dependent on that address. If a restructuring takes place (see Chapter 8), and the record is moved physically during that process, then the Direct key must also be changed and hence programs will need changing; this is contrary to the desired features stated in Chapter 2.

So when might direct access methods be used? Clearly, when:

- very fast access is essential;
- the record structure is not likely to change (and cause the need for a restructuring);
- the file does not contain too many records (so that, if reorganizing or restructuring is necessary, the results will not be too traumatic).

6.5 Calc keys

This is also a direct access method but is more flexible than Direct and therefore in more common usage. An application program wishing to access a record provides a value for the key item (often more than one key is possible). Using this key value the DBMS can derive the physical address of the record in one of two ways: by hashing functions or by indexes.

Note that in CODASYL the two methods are described thus:

```
LOCATION MODE IS CALC
LOCATION MODE IS INDEX SEQUENTIAL
```

6.6 Hashing functions

Hashing functions are similar to those described for random files. Given the input key the DBMS can perform a transformation on it to derive the physical address. As with the random files, there are problems inasmuch as the range of actual keys will probably not be random so that clustering of records on certain pages may occur, with possible overflow problems.

The advantages are that a given record can be accessed, usually, with a single physical I/O (only more if overflow exists) and thus it is as fast as `Direct`. The disadvantage (and it may be very significant) is that there is no provision for sequential processing, that is, the file cannot be read in key sequence.

Note that in comparison with the `Direct` method the `Calc` key method may come out unfavourably if the hashing function is complicated and requires much processor time. However, as the physical addresses are not a part of the record, the application programs are physically independent of the storage position and will not require changing if the file is restructured or reorganized (though the hashing algorithm will need changing).

6.7 Indexing

Indexing is similar to the indexing techniques of non-database files as described in Appendix A. The most common type within database systems is **index sequential** whereby only the highest key for each page is stored in the index. Even so the disadvantage is that almost certainly two physical I/Os are needed to access a record (one for the index and one for the record) and, if the number of records is high, we may need indexes to the indexes to reduce table searching, with a corresponding increase in the number of I/Os. The advantage over hashing techniques is, of course, that records can be processed sequentially and, if several different indexes are possible, then I/O time for many varied application programs can be minimized.

Indexing is usually accomplished using a mechanism known as balanced trees or **B-trees**. B-trees act as a hierarchical index. The top level of the index may, for instance, indicate the location of keys 4, 23 and 57 and also contain pointers to sub-indexes for key values less than 4, between 5 and 22, and between 24 and 56. Each of these sub-indexes will itself contain some key locations and also some further sub-indexes. Each (sub)-index (known as a 'node') has a fixed size, indicating the maximum number of keys that it can hold. When another key is added to a node that is already full, the node is split into two nodes and a new key is added to the parent node. This may cause this parent node to overflow and itself split. In this way the index tree balances itself.

6.8 Other access methods

In general, there are no other direct access methods available with most database systems, but there is always use for a **serial or linear search** whereby the file is read in its physical ordering until the required record is found or until the end of the file if it is not found. This may seem to be an enormous overhead when `Direct` or `Calc` keys are available but in some cases where a file is accessed rarely, the overhead of maintaining an index may not seem worthwhile, in which case linear searching is the only solution. However, the process of searching can be improved if the DBMS offers some sort of placement control with records.

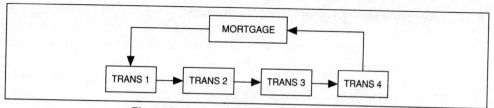

Figure 6.1 A set implementation as a linked list

Consider the scheme shown in Figure 6.1 and the desire to find all the insurance transactions resident in the mortgage transactions file.

It is unlikely that we would wish to implement a direct access method for every transaction with the key as the transaction code – the reasons being that the transaction file is too large and volatile for `Direct` entry, the hashing function method is likely to provide too high a processor overhead and the index sequential method too high an I/O overhead.

As CODASYL is very good at representing owner–member relationships (as sets), it would be wise to use those facilities, particularly as they also often allow related data to be stored in physical proximity. This would mean that the number of physical I/Os needed to search through all transactions would be minimized. Admittedly, the I/O time could be reduced yet further by grouping all transactions together, but this would rule out efficiency for the important and more frequently used relationship between a mortgage account record and its transactions (another example of important processes being given priority at design time).

6.9 Access-type decisions

Clearly, the decision as to the access type can only be made on a business-to-business basis, and in some cases the solution will be far from obvious. For example, the DBA will have to weigh up the different access patterns by each application program on each file and then prioritize them.

The most difficult decisions concern files in which insertions and deletions are commonplace, particularly if fast access is also required. Insertions will lead to eventual overflow situations occurring for `Direct` entry and `Calc` keys and overflow in tables occurring with index sequential methods. Similarly, deletions could lead to holes in files in each storage type unless the DBMS is good enough to maintain available space tables. Unfortunately, through lack of any alternative methods, one of the storage methods must be chosen, although problems can be relieved somewhat by the pre-allocation of storage space (i.e. creating blank records) if the DBMS allows it.

Thought must also be given as to how the file is likely to expand (if at all) in the future. It is fairly pointless having a database that is very efficient for its initial data population but degrades badly if the number of records increases. This is especially noticeable when overflow situations occur.

6.10 Relationship implementations

Possibly the greatest advantage of most database systems is their ability to show relationships between records and files in a manner that is generally unobtainable with conventional file approaches. The main ways in which this can be done are:

- linked lists,
- indexes,
- aggregates,
- foreign keys.

It is unlikely that all these would be available for one particular database system (for example, CODASYL is concerned predominantly with linked lists). The first three are described here, and foreign keys are described in Section 11.3.

6.11 Linked lists

These are constructed of an owner record (the 1 in a 1:n relationship) and a number of member records (the n), as shown in Figure 6.1.

The owner contains, as part of its record contents, a physical address pointer to the first member, and that member contains a pointer to the second member, and so on until the last member has a pointer back to the owner (in general), thus forming a closed chain. Such pointers are system-maintained and are, in general, invisible to the user.

Insertion of a new member in this structure is simple if the preceding member has been accessed already (ORDER IS NEXT in CODASYL). The forward pointer of the existing record is changed to that of the new record, and the old forward pointer is copied into the new record, as shown in Figure 6.2 where member N + 1 is being inserted.

However, this simple linked list is inefficient if the members are stored chronologically because to insert a new member (i.e. at the end) involves chaining through all existing members to reach the previous last member. This can be avoided by declaring a second set of pointers, this time backwards as shown in Figure 6.3 (ORDER IS PRIOR in CODASYL).

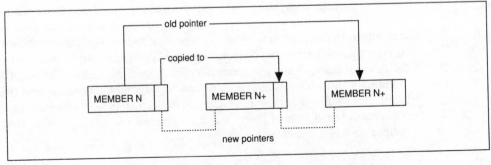

Figure 6.2 Insertion of a new record within a linked list

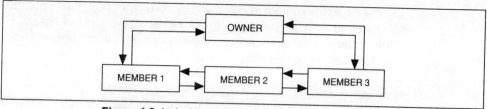

Figure 6.3 Linked list with forward and backward pointers

Thus, given an owner record we can find the last member record immediately.

Note that in all these examples, if a member record is inserted it does not mean that the other members are moved physically to accommodate it. In other words, the physical storage may be similar to that shown in Figure 6.4.

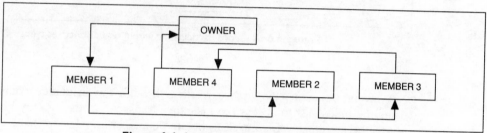

Figure 6.4 Actual physical ordering of a linked list

If the owner–members relationship involves much existence verification on the members then, clearly, all members would have to be read if the record does not exist and an average of $n/2$ if it does exist. To circumvent this problem it is possible to presort the members on a defined key (i.e. making them sequential rather than serial). Now $n/2$ reads are required on average to detect existence whether or not the record exists. The saving on this is dependent on the number of members per set, but to be set against that is the increase in overheads in having to sort the members in the first place. In CODASYL there is an ORDER IS SORTED clause which achieves this aim, but care must be taken if the physical ordering is likely to be similar to that shown in Figure 6.4 because with the existence of many members they are likely to be spread over many pages, and the number of I/Os needed to read through them could be high as shown in Figure 6.5.

	page 1	page 2	page 3
Members numbered	M1	M4	M2
in logical (i.e. sorted)	M5	M6	M3
sequence	M7	M9	M8

Figure 6.5 Possible I/O difficulties with linked lists with member records spread over several pages

To read through all members of this set could take eight physical I/Os.

Also, it must be borne in mind that if the members (as in the example of transactions) are created naturally in the required sequence (i.e. by date), then there would be a waste of processor time in having them sorted.

Consider what happens if our member records exist in two different relationships, with different owner types in each. For example, perhaps one of the mortgage transactions relates to an insurance payment. Thus one of the transactions has an owner record of both mortgages and insurances as shown in Figure 6.6.

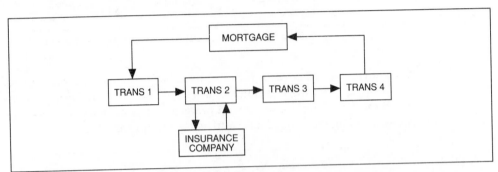

Figure 6.6 A record participating within two distinct set types

A certain process may involve reading through the insurance company records, using the linked list to access the insurance transaction. Also, it may be necessary to access the mortgage record itself to obtain details. From what we have defined so far, to reach the mortgage record from the insurance transaction involves chaining either forwards or backwards through the other transactions in order to arrive at the mortgage. Clearly, such a process is wasteful of processor and I/O time. If the process is an important one, then it might be deemed useful to be able to link each transaction to the owner record (LINKED TO OWNER in CODASYL), giving the situation shown in Figure 6.7.

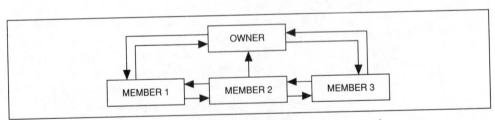

Figure 6.7 A set in which each member contains a pointer to the owner

Note that in this diagram each member contains three pointers (one forward, one backward and one to the owner). These pointers will probably take up a word of storage so that, if the member record is itself only a couple of words in length, we are adding a high percentage overhead in storage requirements in introducing all three pointers. In practice it is unlikely that all three will be needed in one relationship, but such considerations should be noted when it is decided whether or not to collapse small member records into their owners. Again it highlights the balance that must be found between high storage costs and efficiency.

6.12 Indexes

These date back mainly to early CODASYL systems. A `MODE IS POINTER ARRAY` clause was used to set up what was, basically, an index, in the form shown in Figure 6.8.

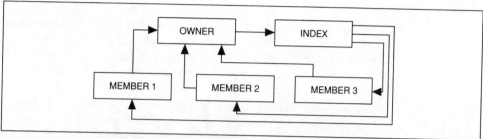

Figure 6.8 Early CODASYL index implementation

To access the members from the owner an index must be accessed (each owner–member set occurrence having its own index) and this contains a table of the addresses of each of the owners. The index can also maintain a set of key values against the addresses so that particular members can be chosen. This is a big advantage over linked lists but, because each member is only linked back to the owner, a disadvantage becomes apparent if we wish to chain through all member records. However, another advantage is that, because the storage addresses of the members are kept in one place (the index), if the members are physically moved (as they would be in a restructure or reorganize) then only the index needs changing and not all of the pointers on the individual member records. A third advantage lies in the fact that if we wished to access the members in some predefined sequence then that sequence can be maintained within the index.

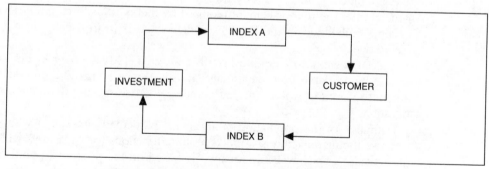

Figure 6.9 Indexes used to maintain an *m:n* relationship

Indexes can also be used to maintain *m:n* relationships such as that shown in Figure 6.9 between customer and investment records. From the customer we can go via index B to access all the accounts owned by that customer. From the investment we can go via index A to access all the customers who own that account.

Although it has been said how wonderful indexes are when used in this way, it must be noted that very few current CODASYL database systems actually use them!

6.13 Aggregates

This is the technical term for the situation in which normalization has insisted that all repeating groups be removed from an entity and then, for a possible variety of reasons, at the design stage we have decided to put them back.

This is of particular use when:

- the number of occurrences of the repeating group is fixed or at least variable within narrow confines, that is, the single consolidated record can be given a fixed acceptable length without having the great wastage described in Chapter 1;
- it is advantageous to access all the related data with a single physical I/O.

Thus if we were concerned only with a mortgage record and its (probable) two associated customers, then normalization would have split the customers away to form a separate entity, but the design stage would have shown (by common sense not theory) that the customers might as well be stored as part of the mortgage record. (Such a system might be used in practice were it not for customers' also owning investment accounts, and so to prevent data duplication we must store customers separately.)

The last point emphasizes the main problem with aggregates. If the members in question have relationships with any other owner types or are themselves owners in another relationship type, then aggregation is not appropriate because the other relationships would not be maintainable.

6.14 Device model

As has been mentioned previously, the theoretical database model gives independence to a device model which will place the database files on physical units of storage. In practice, this task is performed by the operating system which cannot in general offer the fine placement required by theory, thus forcing the device model to become embedded in the storage model which is in turn embedded in the logical data model.

The DBA should determine how big an area (file) is going to be (such statistics should be available from data analysis – see Figure 3.3), and then add on a suitable amount for future expansion, that percentage spare varying depending on the file in question.

Definition of the population of an area is particularly important with some DBMSs because the manufacturer-supplied hashing functions for Calc keys will often generate so many pages available for the file based on the proposed population: too high and disc storage is wasted, too low and overflow problems may follow. Similar considerations apply to table sizes with index sequential files.

Some systems allow for future expansion without the overheads of pre-allocation, for example:

```
AREA SIZE IS 1000 PAGES EXPANDABLE TO 2000 PAGES
```

(in CODASYL). Not many systems will allow the physical file attributes to be changed once a file has been created without the necessity to reorganize (Chapter 8): a high overhead as punishment for a lack of planning.

It should be noted that, with the above, most systems will have the extra available space at the end of the area, but it is often the case that physical grouping of records is desirable, and hence the need for spreading the available space across the area.

The DBA must specify also the required page size: too low a value and it might not be possible to store associated data on the same page with a resulting increase in I/O, too high a value and, for random access where only a single record is required, too much unwanted data is read into memory.

(The fine balance between I/Os and memory usage is described more fully in Chapter 8.)

6.15 Physical placement

It has been stated that often it would be very useful to be able to store associated records physically close to each other, but no mention has yet been made as to how this can be achieved.

If there exists a distinct storage-model implementation in a given database system (such as in CODASYL 78) then we might expect language clauses specifically for record placement. This is not to say that it cannot be done in existing database systems: for example, in CODASYL 73 there is a LOCATION MODE IS VIA SET clause which allows a certain degree of coarse placement. The DBMS will attempt to place the owner and members as physically close together as possible, and if there is no room on the same page an adjacent page will be used if possible, but the fine placement is out of the hands of the DBA.

6.16 Loading the database

Assuming that we have described the database fully using the DDL (examples of what such a definition might look like are given in later chapters), and have included the necessary storage and device mapping details, and have compiled the database with no errors, now we can look to how the data can be loaded physically on to the database.

First, the database areas must be created physically on disc. This is done as the last stage of compilation with some systems, though with others it is a separate process that has to be initiated by the DBA.

The loading of data is an extremely important exercise because the whole integrity of the database will disappear if the initial data are wrong. To that end some sort of load strategy should be developed which may well involve the need to:

1 write a program to load part of the data (perhaps mortgages and insurances);
2 load the data from their existing source (if currently on conventional computer files, it could be reorganized into a suitable format for loading);
3 check the data by using a file validation program;
4 if satisfactory, run the database system (with its own versions of application programs) in parallel with the older system for a reasonable period of time (usually weeks rather than hours) and compare outputs;

5   while the parallel running is taking place, the next functional area can be going through phases 1 to 3, and so on until all the data that should be on the database are loaded.

Note that many larger sites in practice have two central computers for backup purposes. This means that, in general, one can be used for testing.

The above approach works well in some cases, but in others problems arise where a lot of the functional areas and their data are interrelated. It becomes difficult to load part of the data and test the system comprehensively without loading all the data.

In our example, could mortgages and insurances be loaded without also loading customers? Or branches? Many of the mortgage programs will require customer or branch information, so any form of parallel running will be against only a part of the system. On the other hand, if we load the customer data, should we load all of it or just those customers who own mortgages? If we choose the latter, will there be difficulties in adding the investment customers later?

Probably, we could get away with splitting the conversion into two portions, investments and mortgages, but probably no more than two. Each part would involve many files and programs such that the testing and parallel running would take many months.

Conversion from non-database into database files can therefore be a long process even once the data analysis and design stages are complete. Conversion from manual into database files can take even longer. The following list highlights some of the problem areas.

- Many of the database users at this loading/testing stage will be using the software/hardware for the first time. Therefore errors of ignorance may occur.
- Any of the DBA's errors from the design stage (e.g. not allocating enough pages to an area) will come to light. Also the DBA may well actually be using the DBMS for the first time.
- The load programs are one-offs and as such may not be tested fully or as tuned up for efficiency as established programs would be. This is the opposite of what the load program should be: efficient and error free. Another factor is that record creation is generally the slowest database process because related pointers, table entries, and so on, have to be set up.
- An extremely arduous problem to solve during (or before) the load process is that caused by data duplication. In Chapter 1 it was stated that data duplication often occurs on conventional files with resulting inconsistencies. Now that data are being loaded to (hopefully) a single destination, in the case of inconsistency, which is the correct piece of data (e.g. there may be two different addresses for the same customer)? Load the wrong one and the integrity of the database disappears before we start. Often the solution is to load the two as separate customers and sort it out later. This, in turn, often means that:
  (a) the problem is put off indefinitely (there will always be more important things to do);
  (b) as mentioned, the integrity is lost;
  (c) if one occurrence is found later to be wrong and deleted, holes will be left in the files, impairing the efficiency.

There are several things that the DBA can do to alleviate the third problem above. The first is to make the load program restartable. This may involve the 'turning off' of rollback (Chapter 7) and the implementation of a simple record counter whose value can be determined in the case of failure as a restart point. Alternatively, it may be easier to keep rollback, but only load a certain percentage of the file in a single run (this way a run-time error is less disastrous).

A third solution is to write the load program to load the data in a specific and efficient way and not necessarily in the standard key ordering. Such a possibility is dealt with in the next section.

6.17   Load programs

It was mentioned in Section 6.15 that if the DBMS does not allow fine placement of records, then this puts the onus on the load program to achieve this aim. To aid this, often files are merged or sorted before the database load so that records that should be stored physically close are loaded consecutively. For example, in the existing conventional situation the mortgages and their transactions will probably exist on separate files. If these can be merged on to a tape file in the sequence

```
M1,T1,T2,T3,M2,T1,T2,T3,M3,T1,T2, ...
```

then, for example, if the LOCATION MODE IS VIA SET is used in the DDL, we can be reasonably certain that the transactions, when loaded, will end up on the same page as the mortgage (their owner) record.

Sometimes, there will be clear advantages in the file being sorted into key sequence, particularly if index sequential database files are to be created, because the pages/tables can be filled sequentially with a minimum of I/Os. Similarly, if the hashing functions for Calc keys are known and their results are predictable, then the input file can be presorted such that all database records being directed to the same page will be loaded consecutively.

6.18   Load versions of the database

The third method of optimization of load efficiency is for the DBA to create a special version of the database.

Checking functions as described in Section 6.3 are an extremely important part of ensuring database integrity. However, they do take up a large amount of processor time and so the load programs will be much slower if all input data have to be validated before the new records can be stored. Generally, it can be assumed that if the data already exist on computerized files then they will be valid. If this assumption cannot be made then the load program itself can do the validation (which will tend to be more efficient than the DBMS checking functions because the former will have the routines compiled into the machine code, whereas the latter will have the routines as separate code that will have to bound in at run time). Thus if we could turn the DBMS checking functions off, the load would be more efficient. Other functions of the DBMS may also be removable for the duration of the load. These might be:

- The UNIQUEness of a key can be determined by presorting the input file into key sequence.
- DUPLICATES NOT ALLOWED clause can be removed for similar reasons.
- Range, value and existence checks can be performed by the load program.
- The ORDER IS SORTED option can be removed from sets because the members can be loaded in the prescribed order.
- Any SET SELECTION clause can be removed because the selection can always be CURRENT OF SET (see Chapter 10).
- All recovery statements can be omitted if one of following has been decided on:
  (a) make the program restartable by conventional means,
  (b) have the program non-restartable.
  (This option will mean that there is no need to write to journal files with large subsequent savings in I/O and processor time.)
- All access controls can be removed in the assumption that the load program has the authority to create and access all data.
- With some database systems it is possible to create index sequential files without actually creating the indexes, which can be generated later; this process can save on index building, which is one of the slower of the DBMS functions, particularly if there is more than one level of table (such a strategy is not needed if the file is loaded in key sequence, but the desire to do that may conflict with the desire for fine placement control).

6.19 Summary

The possible storage/access methods for the physical database are extremely varied across current database management systems. The DBA must determine which methods are:

- available,
- most likely to produce an efficient database for their own application.

Many databases provide intricate storage mechanisms in terms of access mechanisms and/or placement control. Many of these will not be suitable for the database in hand. In other words, the DBA should not use every method merely because it is there.

The DBA should also be aware of the fine balance between a well-analysed and a well-designed database. You cannot have the second without the first, but this does not mean that a nice-looking conceptual model should be mapped piecemeal into a logical model. Some collapse and fragmentation may well be necessary to optimize the efficiency of the database.

Part Two
Database Administration

7
Integrity and recovery

7.1 Introduction

The three terms 'integrity', 'security' and 'privacy' are often confused in database terminology: integrity sometimes being synonymous with security and security often being synonymous with privacy. This book uses the following interpretations (with respect to databases).

Integrity

Once the database has been created and loaded, then each data item and relationship should be an accurate representation of their counterparts in the real world. Thus if Mr Smith has £10.25 in his account then the computer should maintain £10.25 and not accidentally round it to £10.26. Maintenance of integrity should therefore be a matter of prevention of invalid (as opposed to illegal) updates to the database.

As well as the obvious need for integrity on records and data items there are also relationships to be considered. The DBA should be responsible for setting up relevant relationships where there is a business need for them but thereafter those relationships should be maintained accurately. Thus if Mr Smith owns five investment accounts then he should be shown to have five accounts on the database, no more and no less.

Security

'Security' in the database sense involves ensuring that the database is corrupted by neither hardware nor software error, nor indeed by illegal updating, and it is here that security overlaps with privacy. If a database is corrupted then it loses integrity. Thus security revolves around recovery (see Section 7.12).

Privacy

Privacy is the prevention of unauthorized access of data. As mentioned previously, this usually revolves around letting the user see only what the user wants/is allowed to see, but there are different levels of privacy as discussed later.

7.2 Data redundancy and duplication

As a partial step towards guaranteeing integrity we should only allow one fact to be stored in one place on the database (since inconsistency automatically gives rise to a loss of integrity). To this end normalization is a useful tool because it guarantees one fact in one place barring key items which, clearly, can appear in several places (unless set structures and physical pointers are employed), but this would be a controlled redundancy and is unlikely to cause major headaches because any errors would be spotted quickly. However, as mentioned previously at the design stage, collapse and fragmentation may undo the normalization's guarantee (see Section 5.7) and an implemented database may no longer have one fact in one place. The problems here would have to be weighed up very carefully against the decision to collapse or fragment.

7.3 Integrity constraints

The integrity of the database is unlikely if errors are not trapped at the data analysis and design stages such that the database no longer accurately represents the business that it serves. This is one of the reasons why these initial stages are so important. If, for example, there is no reason why the mortgage interest rate cannot be in eighths of a percentage (i.e. three decimal places), but the database was only implemented as having two decimal places (since the DBA did not know better at the time), then as soon as the real-world interest rate becomes an odd eighth, the database can no longer maintain its integrity and will have to be restructured (see Chapter 8).

Once created, the database must be loaded and, as outlined in Section 6.3, the load program should bear the brunt of any integrity constraints to ensure that the initial database is free from inconsistencies (bear in mind that the conventional or manual files from which the database is to be loaded are even less likely to be integral).

Throughout its lifetime, the integrity of the database can be checked regularly by the applications software and/or the DBMS. The latter involves the application via the DDL as outlined in Chapter 5 of constraints such as range checking, uniqueness, and so on. If such bound-in procedures involve too high a processor overhead then sometimes it is easier to perform the checking through those application programs that actually create or modify the data.

7.4 Concurrency

As shown in Chapter 1, if two programs were allowed to update a conventional file, concurrently, then there would be no way that we could guarantee integrity. Database systems tackle this problem in one of two ways.

1   Two update programs are running against the file F, and program A accesses records 21, 17, 18, 3, 24, 5, while program B accesses records 4, 7, 9, 20, 18 as shown in Figure 7.1. While program A is running it locks each record before updating. The records updated by a program are only unlocked when that pro-

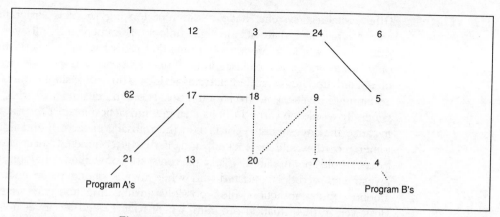

Figure 7.1 Access paths of two concurrent programs

gram terminates normally (i.e. does not terminate with an error condition). When program B reaches record 18 it finds it locked already and cannot therefore access it. Program B is therefore rolled back (see Section 7.17) to its beginning and all its records unlocked (rolling back will undo all of the updates that have been carried out by program B). If and when program A terminates successfully then program B will be allowed to run.

The reason why B cannot simply be suspended at its current point is that if, for example, program A later wants to access record 7, then it cannot do so because it has been locked by B. Thus A would be waiting for B and B would be waiting for A (this situation is called a **deadlock** or **deadly embrace** and is a serious problem of concurrency that must be avoided).

Note
A common variation on the above, and that employed by most CODASYL installations is for a whole page to be locked rather than each individual record. Thus if each row of the scheme shown in Figure 7.1 represents a group of records on a single page, program B could not have started at all because A would have locked all three rows in its first four reads.

Program locking of this nature does have its advantages in that a single program can be recovered without affecting other programs (other than having to wait for it), but it does have the disadvantage that it tends not to allow true concurrency. If A were an online update program performing page locks across a file randomly, it would more or less exclude all other update programs from running concurrently. If A updated investments and customers and B updated mortgages and customers (also online) then either of the following holds:

(a) A and B would have to be merged to form a single program,
(b) the customer file would have to be fragmented into two parts, one for investments and one for mortgages.

Either of these alternatives is likely to affect efficiency and/or privacy.

2 Other database systems have a different locking strategy. Program A locks a record while it updates it and then unlocks it immediately, allowing other programs to access it. If program B wants that record while A is updating it then it only has to wait a few milliseconds. However, deadlocks can still occur. A group of related updates is called a **transaction**. Thus, if a single event caused the updating of investment, investment transaction and customer records, this process generally would be carried out as a single transaction against the database. In this instance the investment record, then the transaction record, and finally the customer record would be locked, and, if that is completed successfully, then all three would be updated. (This prevents the unwanted situation wherein the investment record is updated and while that is taking place another program amends the transaction file, possibly invalidating the investment update.) However, in this situation program A may have locked the investment and transaction and be trying to lock the customer, while program B (an entirely different application) has locked the same customer record first and is trying to lock the investment and/or transaction. Hence deadlock!

Usually, this is resolved by a system of priorities used by the DBMS. If A has the higher priority then B's locking would be undone (and any updates performed in that transaction rolled back). Program A can now lock the customer, complete its transaction, and then unlock the records, allowing access to B. This method therefore allows true concurrency but the disadvantage lies in the fact that if a file has been updated by more than one program then all programs will have to be rolled back in the event of failure.

Note

The process of locking need not be exclusive to update programs. A statistical program may be processing the file sequentially to derive certain totals. If that file is also being updated then the totals may not be correct. To counteract this problem CODA-SYL has a USAGE IS EXCLUSIVE clause in its data manipulation language that prevents any other program from accessing the file while the current program is still active.

7.5 Error handling

In conventional systems errors are detected and reported by the operating system. The messages given are often written for general usage and cover a wide range of applications. For example, a program might terminate with an

```
END OF FILE
```

message without distinguishing between

```
END OF FILE - ALL RECORDS PROCESSED
```

and

```
END OF FILE - NO RECORDS FOUND.
```

Such a difference might be important to the application programmer who is trying to decide whether the task is completed or whether the wrong file was loaded in the first place. Thus the differences are important if each type requires a different response from the user. Too often the programmer/operator is left in the dark as to why the program failed and how to correct that failure.

As mentioned previously, most database systems pass requests for physical accesses through the operating system which treats the DBMS as a single user. For this reason any error messages passed from the operating system back to the DBMS have to be:

1   interpreted by the DBMS,
2   acted on by the DBMS if necessary (i.e. go into automatic recovery),
3   routed back to their originating program (if there is one).

Clearly, the DBMS must first decide what the error is and how it affects the integrity of the database. There are three levels of error, as follows.

1   If a disc has crashed or the DBMS itself has a software error, it is likely that all current programs will need to be suspended and an appropriate error message displayed. It is then often up to the DBA/operator as to how to proceed unless recovery is automatic.

2   If the error is serious, but has been caused by one particular program and no other programs are affected, the DBMS will terminate the program automatically and initiate a rollback (see Section 7.17), undoing all of its updates and preserving the integrity of the database, at the same time displaying an appropriate error message. Clearly, whether this option is possible depends on which of the two options, as outlined in the previous section, is available.

3   If the error is minor (such as end of file) the error is routed back to the originating program which, if designed correctly, will be able to handle that error and proceed accordingly. The error is usually returned as a 4-digit code which the program must have defined within itself as a variable. The first two digits might specify the error type as a broad category, such as OPEN ERROR, or FIND ERROR, and the last two digits define the subcategory of that error; for example, an error code 0321 might signify

```
FIND ERROR - NO MEMBER RECORD FOUND FOR
CURRENT OWNER
```

Knowing the exact error the program can detect that it is non-fatal and can proceed accordingly. Thus by testing the value of the DBSTATUS after each DBMS command the programmer can identify errors, and decide whether to:

(a) proceed normally because the error was expected,
(b) report the error and proceed,
(c) terminate the program.

Notes

1   Full lists of error codes and their meanings are normally given in the manufacturers' database manuals.

2   Some database systems will automatically zeroize the error-code field at the start of each database command but many insist on a 'manual' clearing by program before they will allow continuance (see Chapter 10).

7.6   Physical data checking

In the previous section it was stated that most database systems are good at error interpretation, allowing any problems to be corrected promptly. Most of these errors will have been detected initially by the operating system (for example, while trying to read a disc), but some database systems have their own physical data-checking functions.

In some cases this involves a checksum method by which all the on-bits within a block of data are counted and a checksum written at the end of that block (a similar idea to the parity bit on tapes, but on a wider scale). If the block is read then the checksum can be re-derived and tested quickly and any errors reported quickly. Processor overheads of such a system are high but, because every block is check-summed whenever the database is dumped, the DBA can be sure that:

- the dump is sound if no errors are detected,
- disc errors will not be extant on the disc for days/weeks without being detected.

7.7   Dumps and journal files

As with conventional files, the security of the database system is based on having a recent dump that can be reloaded in the case of hardware/software failure. Here the comparison ends because the database system can go one stage further in being able to recover right up to the time of the failure (or some conveniently close point) without having to rerun all programs subsequent to the dump. Such recovery is accomplished by use of journal files in a way described more fully in Section 7.14.

7.8   Database versions and time stamps

One of the easiest ways to corrupt a set of files is to accidentally run out-of-date programs (whose file format does not equal that of the current file) or reload the wrong version of files while trying to recover. Such errors are very difficult to either detect or avoid. Many database systems tackle this problem in the following way.

1   The database is compiled initially. The exact time of the successful compilation is stored by the DBMS as a database time stamp, each file (structure) in the database is given a format time stamp, and the update level of the database is set to 1.
2   Programs are compiled against the database by passing them through a pre-processor that appends the update level of the database and the format time stamp for each structure used by that program, to the object code
3   If at some time a database structure is reorganized or restructured (see Chapter 8), then the update level of the database would be set to 2 and the format time stamp of that structure would be changed to reflect the timing of that change.
4   If the DBA now recompiles all programs affected by that change, but accidentally misses one, the DBMS would prevent that program from running against the database because its format time stamp for the file in question would no longer equal

that of the actual file. Hence an old version of a program cannot corrupt the database. (Such a system works well, but its usage depends on the physical data independence of the program. If submodels were used extensively then the format time stamp could be affixed to only those submodels that are affected by the change.)

It must be noted that those programs not affected and not recompiled will still contain a database update level of 1. This is satisfactory; it is permissible for a program to run against a database with a higher update level as long as no time stamps are infringed, but not against one with a lower update level. Such a situation can arise in one of two ways:

- If an old database dump is reloaded accidentally, and the live one has been restructured since, then the loaded database will have an update level less than any programs recompiled since that dump and the DBMS will highlight the error quickly.
- It is often the case that a test database is derived from the live version (see Chapter 9). If this has been done to plan out and test a proposed future change to the production model (i.e. the live model has been restructured to create a test model), then the programs compiled against the test database will have an update level greater than that of the live model, and will not therefore be allowed to run against it without recompiling (which is precisely what we would want).

There are other possible time stamps. All changes to the database are recorded on the journal files, but with some database systems there is a utility to initialize a file (i.e. create a blank one), which clearly would have the effect of deleting all existing records on that file. Generally, this process is not audited (too time-consuming) which means that the file is no longer recoverable because of the discontinuity on the journal file. For this situation the structure would have a creation time stamp which would be the time when the file was last initialized (or originally created if it has not been initialized). Thus, if there was a need to roll back the database to a time before an initialization, the DBMS would report that this was not possible. Such a problem can be avoided by not using the initialize facility, but deleting the records from the file by program (such changes would be audited, but would take much longer than an initialize), or by dumping the database immediately after an initialize.

A final type of time stamp is that of the version time stamp which is the time at which a given structure was last updated; this is maintained by the DBMS as well as on the file itself: load a wrong version of a file and the DBMS will notice the discrepancy.

Thus by maintaining a variety of time stamps it is very difficult to corrupt the database accidentally and the security of the system can be maintained.

7.9   Traditional views of privacy

Almost before data began being stored on computers, people were worried about how much data was to be stored and how unauthorized access could be prevented. In the early days of computing the privacy aspect was a much simpler problem than it is today. All the work carried out on computers was performed within the confines of the computer room. Hence, if you prevented physical access to the computer room, your data were safe.

Unfortunately (from a privacy point of view), data lines were developed along with terminals and modems (and these days telecommunications, satellites and lasers), so that nowadays computerized data are passing under, around and over us. Buy a relevant receiver and those data are yours (hence Teletext, etc.). Therefore the only ways of securing privacy reasonably (though nothing is infallible) are to:

- introduce passwords into the system so that only authorized users can gain access,
- encode the data whenever they are transmitted in such a way that they could be intercepted.

Since we are interested predominantly in data-storage systems and not data communications, we shall study the first option.

Traditionally access to a computer is by user identifier and password. The former gives you your own area of disc to play with and the latter gives you access to that area. Alternatively, you might have a password to a more general area (not your own). Such passwords are usually maintained by the operating system: usually encrypted to prevent accidental disclosure in, say, a memory dump. And yet at most installations this set-up is not very secure: there are people who know other people's passwords (they have watched them type them in), either accidentally or deliberately. Passwords are, generally, fairly easy to change but there is apathy about changing them on a regular basis unless there is proof that they are known to other users. In addition, as outlined in Chapter 1, often there is only a single level of privacy. Thus, if the personnel department is a valid user, a single password will gain access to all of its programs and files and, as mentioned, sensitive data will have to be hived off into another system with a password known only to higher management with the problem that they will also want the non-sensitive data as a part of their system, and so the danger of duplication and inconsistency looms large.

7.10   Levels of privacy

Referring back to the documentation requirements of data analysis outlined in Sections 3.5 to 3.7, we notice the different levels with which access rights must be maintained (i.e. at attribute, entity and relationship levels). In general, we could define six distinct subsets of access constraints.

Read

This is whether or not a user can access a piece of data and read its value.

Change

There is a vast difference between simply being able to read a piece of data and being able to update it.

Delete

This is whether or not a user may delete a piece of data or record. An employee may be allowed to see their bad conduct record, but to be able to delete it would be another matter!

Create/extend

If the company has a special bonus record for staff eligible for a Christmas bonus then it is unlikely that you would wish just anyone to be able to create one.

Existence verification

This is often overlooked in the matter of privacy, but a user may not need actually to access data to be able to ascertain important knowledge. A finance company would only need to know the existence of a client's bad debts record to decline them a loan.

Execution

Execution is mentioned here because of the frequent occurrence of general-purpose query languages that can access the database, but also there is a requirement to restrict the usage of all programs that access data.

Of these, the traditional approach will, generally, only cater for the read/change constraints. Since all files and programs in a particular system are under a single password generally, having access to that password gives the user options to do all of the above. The read/change constraints are really only controlled by the valid user being able to describe a file as being read-only, though this can be changed easily by the unauthorized user if they know how.

7.11   Database approaches to privacy

Database systems that use submodels indirectly enforce privacy by only allowing the user to see that which he or she is allowed to see. This is very different from the all-or-nothing approach of the conventional system because by attaching a password to the submodel the user can ensure some form of privacy control.

In addition to this, most database systems allow the DBA to impose access constraints at the database/area/record/data item levels, giving all-round privacy control. Again a CODASYL model has been used to illustrate this as shown in Figure 7.2.

The reader is directed to Chapter 10 for a fuller description of a CODASYL schema, but it is sufficient here to note the usage of the ACCESS-CONTROL locks. In this example they have been defined at the schema, area and data-item levels. Since the areas GENERAL-AREA and WAGE-AREA each contain only a single file, an access-control lock at the area level is equivalent to one at the file level. Had the areas contained more than one file we would have had more options open. There are no sets defined here, but had there been we could have defined access-control locks on them (i.e.

```
SCHEMA
    ACCESS-CONTROL LOCK IS 'SESQUIPEDALIAN'
    AREA NAME IS GENERAL-AREA
    ACCESS-CONTROL LOCK IS 'GENDETS'
    AREA NAME IS WAGE-AREA
    ACCESS-CONTROL LOCK IS WAGE-LOCK
    RECORD NAME IS GENERAL-DETAILS
    LOCATION MODE IS CALC EMP-INDEX USING EMP-NO
    WITHIN GENERAL-AREA

    EMP-NO        NUMBER(5);
    EMP-NAME      CHAR(20);
    EMP-ADDRESS   CHAR(40);
    EMP-CONDUCT   CHAR(30)

    ACCESS-CONTROL LOCK IS PROCEDURE CONDUCT-LOCK;
    RECORD NAME IS WAGES
    LOCATION MODE IS CALC WAGE-INDEX USING WAGE-NO
    WITHIN WAGE-AREA

    WAGE-NO       NUMBER(5);
    BASIC-RATE    NUMBER(4,2);
    HOURS-WORKED  NUMBER(4,2);
```

Figure 7.2 Example of a database source showing access control options

access control on relationships). Of interest in the example are the three differing types of access-control lock available to the DBA. These are as follows.

1   Fixed constants. In line 2, access control to the database (schema) is via the password 'SESQUIPEDALIAN'. Obviously, this is easy to set up and maintain, but has two disadvantages. First, it is difficult to change without recompiling the schema and, secondly, it is available to anyone who gains access to the schema listing.

2   Variables. In line 6, access to the WAGE-AREA is via a variable called WAGE-LOCK. This means that at run time the user supplies a password which is checked against a value maintained by the DBMS in this variable. Such a variable can have its value changed easily by the DBA and is not visible in the schema listing.

3   Subroutines. In line 14, the access control to the data item EMP-CONDUCT is via a procedure CONDUCT-LOCK. Such a procedure will, in general, have been written by the DBA, and has the following advantages.

   (a) At run time a user could be checked against a table of valid users; such a table would be easy to maintain.

   (b) The procedure can be used to change dynamically the password on a day-to-day (or whatever) basis; for example, on a given day the password might be the day of the month plus the first three letters of the day of the week (an easy task for the computer and relatively easy for the authorized user). More complicated examples are certainly possible whereby an unauthorized user, seeing someone key in a password one day, could not possibly guess what the password will be the following day.

It is a pity that, in general, the tightest security is required at the lowest (i.e. data-item) level. Subroutines offer by far the best access-control mechanisms, but their processor overheads are high, particularly if that subroutine has to be performed at every record access.

7.12 Recovery

If a survey were to be carried out on all database users and the question asked, 'What is the most readily visible advantage of having a database system?', then most would mention the recovery facilities. Recovery of a non-database system is a nightmare, fraught with difficulties and prone to many errors.

There is, unfortunately, no computer yet built that does not occasionally crash on hardware/software errors. In addition, there are precious few programmers who will write programs that will never go wrong, even if they are tested fully.

In this book we shall define a **machine restart** as a time at which the computer halts itself (self-halt) or is halted by operations (forced halt), for whatever reason, and then is booted up again. At such times, if programs are restartable then they should restart automatically (though some operating systems would suspend them awaiting a manual restart), otherwise they are terminated by the operating system. Note that most systems know which programs are running at the time of a halt and can there-fore restart them automatically, though this does not mean that they can simply carry on from where they were; in most cases the program's environment is initialized and the program restarts from scratch.

The reasons for a machine restart (MR) are various, but a self-halt might, typically, be caused by a memory problem and a forced halt by the operations department being aware of a program looping. Whatever the reasons are, work is disrupted and clearly it is desirable to arrive back at a recovered state, ready for normal work to continue, as soon as possible.

It is unlikely that conventional programs will be restartable:

- Unless every update is written to a restart file, it is impossible to know exactly which updates have been affected. If restart files are used, then in a conventional system it is difficult to restart at the correct point because of the following.
- When is the update completed? Is it when the updated record has been passed back to the main memory buffer? Or when that buffer has been written back to disc? If the former, then some updates will be lost if an MR occurs while the update is being shuffled about in memory, and, with the latter, the process of writing the buffers to disc is out of the control of the program.

Thus, a program writing a restart record is not quite as simple as it seems.

Notes

1   There are cases where a single program can be written in such a way that it can redo updates if that program merely performs moves and not any arithmetic operations. Similarly, programs that create or delete records can be restartable if they contain some mechanism whereby records already created are not created again (i.e. a find is performed first). But in all these cases, the path is full of difficulties and it is often easiest to simply reload the last dump and rerun the programs.

2   These problems really only apply to update programs. It is normally fairly easy to restart read-only programs. If they are random reads then there is no problem. For sequential reads it is straightforward to maintain a restart file by writing

1   the latest key value,
2   any relevant totals to date every x records.

It is therefore one of the curses of conventional systems that so much time is wasted over (often relatively minor) errors as described in Chapter 1.

7.13   Transactions and checkpoints

Most database systems work on the basis that an application program is able to define when it is about to update the database (be that a single update or a collection of related updates), and similarly when the program has finished a particular update. These two times are generally referred to syntactically as a 'begin-transaction' and an 'end-transaction'.

During the time in between the two the program is said to be 'in transaction state'. As defined previously, all updates performed within a single transaction state (whether one or many) are called collectively a **database transaction**.

Now if an MR occurs whilst a program is in transaction state then the DBMS knows that an update was in the process of being performed and may or may not have been written to disc. It therefore knows that recovery is needed to maintain integrity (exactly how this is done is described in the following sections).

It would seem useful to define a point in time at which the DBMS knows that no updates are currently being performed and therefore no automatic recovery is needed (since the integrity is safe). Such a point is called a **quiet point**. Clearly, if no update programs are running then we have a quiet point, but what if update programs are running more-or-less continuously (such as during an online day)? In the event of failure we would want the database to be recovered back to the last quiet point. If we then have to rerun all programs, then we are not much better off than the conventional reload and rerun.

We therefore define a **checkpoint** to be a point in time when no programs are in transaction state. It is at this point when the DBMS flushes out all buffers to disc (in some systems half the buffers are flushed at alternate checkpoints – this will clearly affect the recovery procedures). The DBA can define a checkpoint as being so many transactions such that after that number of begin-transactions, the DBMS will not allow any more programs to enter transaction state until all current ones have reached their end-transactions, thus forcing a checkpoint. This may mean that programs sometimes have to wait, but the advantages of this system will become apparent after the next section.

7.14   Journal files

Databases, generally, provide recovery mechanisms by the use of journal (or audit) files. On these are kept a record of all updates that have been performed against the database.

The basic record will comprise:

- a **before image**, or exact copy of the database record before it was updated;
- an **after image**, or exact copy of the database record after the update.

To each of these records will be appended the:

- exact time of the update (from the machine clock);
- name of the program that performed the update;
- structure number/file name to which the update applies.

In addition there will be special records for:

- beginning of program runs;
- end of program runs;
- checkpoints;
- start of database dumps.

A journal file will therefore consist of many pairs of before and after images (though the after image corresponding to a particular before image may not appear juxtaposed if more than one update program is running), plus some checkpoint information. When the DBMS is able to signify a checkpoint, it can write a special record to the journal file, stating the time of the checkpoint. Thus an example journal file might contain records similar to those shown in Figure 7.3.

7.15   Restart recovery

Suppose that, for whatever reason, an MR occurs after the last record shown in Figure 7.3 has been written to the journal file. The DBMS can detect that program A is currently in transaction state, but will not know whether the actual record has been updated and written back to disc. Therefore, to be safe, it will rewrite the before image from the journal file back to disc, overwriting any possible update, and thus undoing the update. In practice, the DBMS will reapply all before images from all programs by reading the journal file backwards until it reaches a checkpoint. Here it stops, because it knows that the integrity is assured, for the following reasons.

1   When a checkpoint occurs, the DBMS suspends all programs until all system buffers have been written back to disc (which is why a checkpoint can take some time). Once this is completed the integrity is maintained.

TIMESTAMP	PROGRAM	STRUCTURE	IMAGE + DETAILS
09:53:2604	A	06	BEFORE ...
09:53:2643	A	06	AFTER ...
09:53:2721	CHECKPOINT		
09:53:8912	A	06	BEFORE ...
09:53:8931	B	07	BEFORE ...
09:53:8967	C	02	BEFORE ...
09:53:9002	B	07	AFTER ...
09:53:9048	B	07	BEFORE ...
09:53:9068	C	02	AFTER ...
etc.			

Figure 7.3 Example of the format of a journal file

2   If an MR occurs during a checkpoint then before images can be reapplied back to the previous checkpoint.

3   After this operation (which is done automatically), the DBMS knows the data to be consistent, but one of several things might now happen:

(a) If a particular program is restartable (and the ways of doing this within a database environment vary enormously) then it can be geared to restart from a checkpoint.

(b) If it is not restartable then at least it can be terminated in a controlled fashion. Following this the DBA will have several options open concerning the recovery of that particular program (see later sections).

7.16   Program rollback

In Section 7.4 we looked at the problems of concurrency with its possible deadlock situations, and stated that to avoid it one of the deadlocked programs would have to have its updates undone. By reviewing the journal file it is possible to see how this can be achieved.

When a program is initiated (or terminated), a special record is written to the journal file to signal the beginning or the end (BOJ or EOJ). Thus, given that the DBMS can determine a deadlock situation and has some method of choosing which program has priority, the other can be rolled back to its BOJ by scanning backwards through the journal file and reapplying all before images related to that program.

Exactly the same process applies if any program fails due to a run-time error: it will be rolled back to BOJ and, in general, this will be done automatically.

However, the two distinct approaches to journal file/locking management, as outlined in Section 7.4, must now be examined in more detail.

1   Page locking is performed such that if program A updates a record on a page then that page is locked and remains locked until A terminates successfully. Basically, this means that A has exclusive use of the file in question (and in gen-

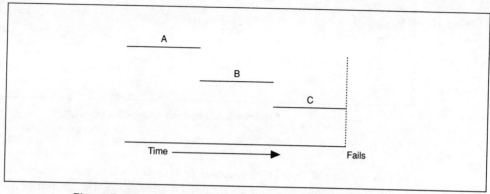

Figure 7.4 Program run chart where true concurrency is not permitted

eral this is forced by declaring USAGE IS EXCLUSIVE in the application program). Running against file F we have therefore the situation shown in Figure 7.4.

The advantages are clearly that if a program C fails, the most that needs recovering is that single program's updates.

The disadvantage is that only one update program can run against a file at any one time. This may not be a problem with batch work but it may be a huge problem with online updating.

2   Page locking is performed as before, but the page is unlocked when the transaction is complete. Clearly, this means that several different programs can update the same file, as shown in Figure 7.5.

This now has the disadvantage that if C fails then the file must be rolled back to the start of A. In general, this will mean that the whole database needs rolling back and not simply file F, because the chances are that each of the concurrent programs will update different combinations of files on the database and not simply F, as is shown in Figure 7.6.

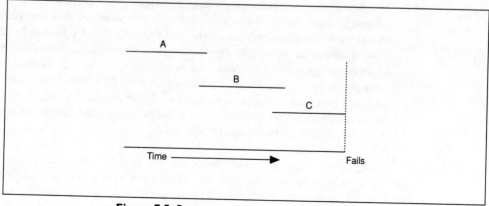

Figure 7.5 Program run chart with true concurrency

Program			Files updated				
A	1	2					
B		2		4	5		
C	1					6	Fails
D			3				

Figure 7.6 Complexity of program/file usage

In this diagram it would be impossible to roll back C without also A and hence B being rolled back. Program D should be unaffected, but in practice it too will be rolled back. Thus with this approach the most important aspect is to have frequent quiet points so that the database will not have to be rolled back too far.

Note

Since the scanning of the journal file for relevant entries could be a lengthy process, some systems employ a **transient before-image file**, if true concurrency is disallowed. Thus, while a program is active, its before images are written to its own journal file as well as to the master journal. If the program fails then its own journal file can be read and images reapplied quickly. If the program terminates successfully then the transient journal file is deleted.

7.17   Database rollback

Whichever journal-file method is adopted, situations will occur for which the entire database will need rolling back.

Briefly, these include the following:

1   A software failure occurs within the DBMS or operating system and it is possible that files may have been corrupted as a result. Of course, in general, it would not be known which data have been corrupted, if any, but the recovery mechanism will always assume the worst.

2   Program errors are discovered after the program has completed: perhaps that two programs were run in the wrong order. In this instance it is not sufficient merely to roll back the offending programs and rerun because subsequent programs may have updated the same file. For the second journal-file approach it does not matter because the entire database will need rolling back to a convenient quiet point anyway. Systems that employ transient journal files avoid any disparity by only allowing program rollback from this file. If the program finished and the transient file was deleted then the only course of action would be to roll back the entire database, which is the desired result.

In both these cases, the operators/DBA are usually given the choice of manually specifying when the database is to be rolled back to (i.e. it is not done automatically, unlike the program rollback mechanism mentioned in the last section). This can either be to a specific time (usually a 'not greater than' because the exact time stamp on the journal file will be unknown) or to a specific BOJ. The journal file is scanned backwards and all before images reapplied until the selection criterion is met. Usually, the journal file entries being used are destroyed as rollback proceeds, thus making a subsequent rollforward (see the next section) impossible and necessitating the accuracy of the supplied time/BOJ parameter.

Note that, whereas program rollback should not affect any current programs other than those waiting to use the affected files, database rollback is an exclusive function meaning that as soon as the error is determined all active programs (including read-only programs) must be terminated and cannot be rerun until the rollback has been completed successfully. In other words, if rollback fails for some reason and the DBMS is not sure of the integrity of the data, it will not allow any programs to proceed until it is sure.

7.18 Rollforward

The preceding sections have dealt with all forms of software error, but what of hardware errors? In the event of a disc crash or parity error it is not feasible to rollback because the disc would not be capable of having before images applied to it and, indeed, the DBMS may not be able even to apply the restart recovery. In the conventional-file situation the only possibility was to reload and rerun. With the database approach there exists a far more efficient solution.

Again, the last dump must be reloaded, but the journal file can now be brought into use by scanning forward, from the time of the dump (again noted on the journal file) and reapplying all of the after images, thus reprocessing all updates performed since the dump. Such an approach must be faster than rerunning the programs. In the latter case there are the program's processor and I/O times to be taken into consideration as well as those of the database, whereas with the former there is, basically, just a sequence of many simple read–write operations with very little processor time required.

How much time is saved clearly varies, but a typical saving of 90% in overall time is perhaps an underestimate.

Again, the operators/DBA are usually given a choice of where to roll forward to in terms of time or EOJ, but again it is essential that the completed task leaves the database in an integral state, that is, at a quiet point. Thus, if our DBMS only allows the option of rolling forward to the end of the journal file, then it may be necessary to rollback to the previous quiet point subsequently.

Note

Unlike rollback, the process of rolling forward does not destroy the journal file which means that if the operation is unsuccessful it can be tried again. This is useful particularly if we are trying to roll forward to, say, 10.47 and the DBMS encounters an error on the journal file at 10.42 and terminates. Since the integrity of the data is not guaranteed at 10.42 (not a quiet point) we might have to roll forward again to the quiet point before 10.42 (which will have been noted on the operator's log) and rerun subsequent programs.

As with database rollbacks, the rollforward process affects the whole database and is therefore an exclusive function.

7.19   Rebuilds

Some database management systems allow for the rolling forward of only parts of the database and this process is generally referred to as a 'rebuild'. This is useful especially if the database is spread across several discs and one fails or if perhaps just a single page is corrupted. It would seem a harsh overhead if all programs needed terminating to rebuild just a few records.

First, we would expect the DBMS to be able to inform us of exactly which pages are corrupt, which may occur when an application program is trying to read data or when a piece of checking software detects errors (such as checksums – see Section 7.6). A typical error message might be:

```
READ ERROR PAGE 17 OF FILE INVESTMENTS -
PAGE LOCKED OUT
```

The ROW LOCKED OUT message would mean that no programs could access that page until the error had been removed. Other programs using other files would be allowed to continue.

Armed with this information it would be useful to be able to reload page 17 from the last dump and reapply any updates that have been applied subsequently to page 17 from the journal file. If the related area of disc is corrupted then often the page in question could be rebuilt on a separate area of disc with associated pointers patched up automatically (though the ease with which this could be done clearly depends on the complexity of the physical model). If any program attempts to access that page while it is being rebuilt then the DBMS can return a suitable error message, otherwise all programs can continue. In a similar fashion options usually exist to rebuild several pages, files, areas or whole discs with the minimum of disruption to users.

Clearly, rebuilds of this type must be continued to the end of the journal file (and to this end the DBMS will eventually have to suspend all user programs at a checkpoint while the rebuild catches up and finishes), since rebuilds to a particular time would not guarantee the integrity of the whole database.

7.20   Other recovery facilities

From what has been stated so far, it might seem as if the DBMS can recover all situations. What can possibly go wrong? Examples are:

- the disc or tape on which the journal file resides may crash or have parity errors;
- recovery may fail because of errors on the journal file.

Both these cases can be catered for if the journal file is duplicated, and many database management systems will allow this. It may seem a high overhead in backing storage and I/O time to duplicate, but it does mean that if recovery fails with one journal file in error then the DBMS can automatically switch to the other and continue. This means that lightning would have to strike twice in the same place (which it probably will at some time) for recovery to fail and, if this happens, the DBA still has the option to reload and rerun.

In general, the maximum size of the journal file can be decreed by the DBA. Once this maximum is reached, some systems go into automatic restart recovery to the previous checkpoint and await instructions. The better management systems create a new journal file and, automatically, initiate an automatic backup copy of the old journal file.

In such cases continuity between the files is maintained by numbering the blocks on the file and continuing the sequence on the new file. With the older database management systems a new journal file is created after each database dump, but it is left to the DBA to ensure that the old one is backed up and that the new one is large enough to last until the next dump. Whichever method is available, it is always advisable to maintain a library of previous journal files (usually on the grandfather, father and son cycle), because there is little point in keeping old database dumps for recovery if there are no journal files to go with them.

7.21 Backup facilities

It has been stated already how backup plays an important part in rollforwards or rebuilds, but it was also stated in Chapter 1 that backups are taken infrequently because of the inability to be updating files at the same time. Most database management systems have various dump facilities to alleviate both these problems and others.

- It has been shown already in Section 7.6 how some systems recalculate checksums during the dump procedure and can therefore detect any disc errors (and hence allow them to be corrected) before application programs find them and crash.
- Another useful facility is the option of only dumping parts of the database instead of all of it. This facility generally only extends to whole files being dumped and not merely odd pages. Thus if we are currently pursuing mortgage processing, then at the same time we could be dumping the investment files, and vice versa.
- Perhaps the most useful backup function (unfortunately only offered by a few database management systems at present) is the ability to perform online dumps. The problems outlined in Chapter 1 meant that 24-hour online work/batch processing was impossible with conventional files, but if online dumping is available then all problems are removed. Whatever the recovery mechanisms available, it is still advantageous to dump as frequently as possible to reduce recovery times. Whereas with the conventional approach, online dumps are impossible because we would not know which updates are on backup medium and which are not, with database systems we do know because they are also on the journal file. Thus if the time of the commencement of the dump is noted then we can always reload the tape dump and roll forward the database to the end of the dump and thus reapply all after images that were created while the dump was taking place and hence maintain integrity.

With both online dumping and partial database dumping, mechanisms must exist whereby the integrity of the database can be assured. In Chapter 1 it was stated how easy it was to corrupt conventional files by reloading wrong versions at recovery time. In the next section it will be shown how the database approach counters this problem.

7.22 Time stamps revisited

This section uses the Burroughs DMS-II as an example. Other database management systems that allow online or partial dumping have their own mechanisms.

The whole database is controlled dynamically by a control file which contains data pertaining to the current state of the:

- audit (journal) files;
- usage of the database, whether it is in normal usage or whether a function such as recovery has exclusive usage;
- update level of the database;
- creation, format and version time stamps of all structures within the database.

The time stamps are also maintained on the files themselves and, at a database open, all such statistics are cross-checked. If any discrepancies are found, then no processing is permitted until the errors have been corrected.

Suppose that we have reloaded a partial dump of the mortgage files. The version time stamp (i.e. the time of the last update) on that reloaded file will not match that on the control file (assuming that the mortgages have been updated since the partial dump), and so we cannot continue with any processing until we have rebuilt the mortgage file. (While rebuilding takes place each after-image time stamp will be written as the version time stamp on the file. Thus when the last image is applied the version time stamp on the file will equal that on the control file.) In other words, yet again we cannot use the database unless it is consistent.

Note that if the file had been restructured since the dump (see Chapter 8), then the DBMS would not let us rebuild because the format time stamp on the file would not equal that on the control file.

As a more complex example, suppose that we have taken an online dump of the whole database as that shown in Figure 7.7. Note that at the end of the dump, the version time stamps on the disc control file and the disc file F are consistent but not those on backup because the control file was dumped before the file.

Suppose that for some reason we now have to reload the dump in its entirety. In doing so the disc control file and file F will be overwritten by the dumped versions. When we now come to open the database, the DBMS will flag that the control file's and file F's version time stamps do not match and will not let us continue until the

	END OF DUMP	
DUMPED CONTROL FILE VERSION TIMESTAMP FOR FILE F	17/08/86	14:27:3802
DUMPED VERSION TIMESTAMP ON FILE F	17/08/86	14:31:2639
ON DISK CONTROL FILE VERSION TIMESTAMP FOR FILE F	17/08/86	14:58:2914
ON DISK VERSION TIMESTAMP ON FILE F	17/08/86	14:58:2914

Figure 7.7 Example timings of an online dump

database has been rolled forward. Moreover, since the control file contains a pointer to the audit file and the control file is dumped first, by reloading the control file the DBMS will know where on the audit file to start the rollforward.

Clearly, this involves an overhead of having to use rollforward recovery every time we wish to reload a prior online dump, but against that is set the very great advantage of being able to dump files while they are in use and hence be able to have an uninterrupted flow to the data processing.

7.23 Summary

In general, the actual recovery procedures afforded by any one database management system vary in detail, but all provide similar basic features of rollback and rollforward, and, more importantly, ensure that following the recovery mechanism the user can be assured that the database's integrity is guaranteed; otherwise they would not be allowed to proceed. If all recovery procedures fail then there is always the original option of reload and rerun.

8
Other database facilities

8.1   Changing the database

To design a database system and hope that it will forever remain constant is a very blind outlook and, at most installations, flexibility is considered to be one of the main objectives of database design (see Section 5.2). Future changes can be varied in nature and most of them will be unpredicted at the time of the initial design. In particular, an organization may decide to:

- take on new areas of business (for example, our bank may launch a new type of account or a new type of mortgage insurance);
- change existing areas of business (for example, the way in which interest is calculated or the way in which insurances are handled);
- computerize existing manual systems, possibly through new innovations in technology (for example, there may be the possibility of computerizing management expenses if a scanner can read the varied documents on to the computer);
- change the volume of the business, either by external factors or by a conscious decision to market certain products more fully, increasing advertising, and so on (alternatively, a merger with another company may substantially alter the data storage requirements).

All of these are likely to affect the existing database, and the ease with which such changes can be incorporated might be critical. Suppose that government legislation means a radical change to the way in which tax is paid on investment interest – this involves changes to the investment file. The organization cannot say that it cannot be done or that it will take x amount of time; the change will have to be done as and when decreed.

There will also be times when the efficiency of the database is suffering because the way in which data are stored has changed. This may be because:

- there are varying volumes of data;
- deletions have left many holes in the file;
- insertions have led to overflow problems;
- patterns of access may have changed such that, for example, there is no longer a business requirement to access records from files A and B together and hence there is no longer a need to group related records on the same page.

The overall result of any of these would be, to a lesser or greater extent, that the neat efficient database that was set up carefully by the load programs, has degraded in performance with an overall loss in efficiency. (As to how such a degradation might be noted, see Section 8.12.)

The general desire in such a situation might be to 'shuffle the data around a bit' such that spare space is consolidated, overflows are eliminated and natural groupings are restored. Any approach to shuffling the data around has to be considered carefully.

Again, the terminology varies from database system to system, but the definitions used in this book will be as follows.

- If changes are required to the logical structure of the database, by adding or deleting areas, structures, records, sets or data items, or by changing the size/type of data items, then these will be performed via a **restructure**.
- If changes are needed to the physical storage of the database, then these will be performed by a **reorganize**.

8.2 Restructure

Changes to the logical structure of the database could involve the addition, deletion or amendment of:

1 record types (tables),
2 data items (attributes),
3 set types (changes to key status).

It must be stressed that these changes initially will be made known to the business as changes to

1 entities,
2 attributes,
3 relationships,

respectively, and it is the DBA's task to decide how such changes will affect the existing database.

For example, it may be decided to include the address code as a separate item on all stored address data, perhaps because the post office has decided on a postal rebate if all mail is sent with the address code included. The DBA must find all occurrences of an address field and make decisions as to how the extra field will be implemented. For example:

- Is the address code already in existence, perhaps stored on the end of an attribute called county?

  COUNTY CHAR(20) (e.g. 'Lancashire LA1 4YR')

- Is it to be implemented as a separate item or can COUNTY be broken down into two separate items?

- Would it be useful to have the address code as a key item such that all customers living in a particular area can be identified quickly?
- What are the consequences of there not being an address code available immediately (such as on new housing developments)?

It is important that the DBA looks to the conceptual model and its associated documentation to map out any proposed changes, because it is here that the changes' effect on the organization will show. To this end he or she should be aided by the data dictionary if one exists.

It is likely that the systems analysts will have been informed (and they may even be the originators) of the proposed change, such that it will be left to them to decide which existing application programs require amendment or whether new ones will need to be written (and again the data dictionary will be able to help them with the former) but it is very important that they liaise with the DBA about the new submodel requirements and the time scales involved in pursuing the change.

8.3   Unload and load

The actual processes involved with restructuring vary from system to system. With many, the data must be unloaded logically from the database. This entails a special dump program being written to copy the data from disc to disc or a tape streamer, in some predefined sequence that will make the reloading as efficient as possible. Once the data are dumped, the old file can be destroyed and then recreated in its new format. Generally, this process is supervised by the DBMS which will create and store a new-format time stamp for the structure and also increment its update level by 1. The dump tape can then be used by a specially written load program to load the data back on to the new file. Such a load program will be written with similar considerations to those outlined in Section 6.17.

A database dump is unsuitable for this process for two reasons:

1   the update level is changed by the restructure which means that the DBMS will not allow a prior dump to be loaded at the wrong update level;
2   even if the first problem could be overcome, a database dump will neither be in a logical ordering of records, and will hence make the load inefficient, nor will it be in a form easily readable by an application program since it will contain checksum data, page control data, pointers, and so on, which are normally invisible to the user program.

Clearly, such a process can be very time-consuming and for a large file the time scales could be of the order of days rather than hours. Moreover, a restructure is an exclusive function which means that all application programs will have to be excluded while it is being performed. Thus we are considering weekend schedules at the best and for some restructures we may have to be planning for the next 3- or 4-day public holiday.

Owing to the possible size of the task, the onus is clearly on the dump and load programs to be as efficient as possible. To that end they will have to be written very carefully and tested thoroughly before they are actually employed, preferably with testing against a database of similar data volume to be able to gauge an approximation for the time scales.

Some database management systems broach part of this problem by using fourth-generation software. The DBA feeds the proposed changes to the DBMS (usually in interactive mode) and the latter generates code that will dump and reload the required file. Usually, it is source code that is generated which means that the DBA has the opportunity to modify it before compilation. For example, normally the DBMS will generate code to dump and load a file in the order of its prime key. There may be reasons why the DBA wishes to reload in a secondary key order and this can be achieved easily. Generally, the dump will be directed to another disc area, but there is often the option of the restructure being performed *in situ*. Thus a new structure is generated by the DBMS and the old data is physically mapped on to it without needing a secondary medium. At the end of the process (if successful) the original file is removed and the new one becomes a part of the database. In the event of failure the original is still there and can be used.

From the data dictionary, the DBA should have been able to compile a list of application programs that will require amending and/or recompiling as a result of the restructure. Those of the former category will be passed to the programming teams, but there may be difficulties in recompiling and testing such programs before the actual restructure is done. This is simply because the testing is, as usual, essential before usage but there is no suitable database to test against. A possible solution to this problem, using test databases, is outlined in Chapter 9.

At the end of the restructure, the DBA can at least rest assured that, if the DBMS uses time stamps or some equivalent, then any programs that slip through the net and are not recompiled will not be allowed to run against the database and will therefore not be capable of corrupting the database.

It should be noted that some restructuring exercises will not require the unloading and loading of data nor the recompilation of programs. For example, the addition of a new file or record type will probably only entail the recompilation of the DBMS code to flag that it exists and provide the new accessing code, followed by the structure's initialization and readiness for use by (usually) new programs.

8.4   Change of record layouts

Perhaps the most common form of restructuring exercise revolves around one of the following:

- change of the format of an existing data item, such as addition of an extra digit to a numeric field;
- addition of new data items to an existing record.

Deletion of data items is a process seldom contemplated.

If items are no longer used then, because of the large amount of time required to restructure and remove them, often they are left unused on the record. Similarly, the change of data-item names (which would make unused items reusable) is generally avoided because usually it means deletion of the old item and addition of the new via a restructure, even if the two are of the same length and type (though, of course, there is no reason why the unused item cannot be renamed in subschemas).

Suppose that a record for a customer is as shown in Figure 8.1. Note how the two odd-number-of-digit items have been grouped together to minimize storage requirements if numeric data can be packed. The total number of bytes required for storage is 73 (with packing). Suppose that the computer is a word machine with four bytes to a word. This means that the customer record will actually be allocated 19 words of physical storage. In other words, three bytes are wasted (this assumes that there are no pointers on the record which, generally, add one word to the length for each pointer). Some database management systems allow us to use those three bytes by declaring them as a filler item (similar to the COBOL filler, except that they must appear at the end of the record). If now we wish to restructure the record by adding a two-digit code then we can simply redefine the existing filler into a two-digit identifier plus two bytes of filler. In this way the physical size of the record has not changed and hence no dump and reload is necessary. Also the only programs that will need changing are those that will want to use the new item whether or not subschemas are used.

```
CUSTOMER-NUMBER    NUMBER(7).
SEX                CHAR(1).
NAME               CHAR(20).
ADDRESS-1          CHAR(20).
ADDRESS-2          CHAR(20).
POST-CODE          CHAR(8).
AGE                NUMBER(2).
```

Figure 8.1 Example customer record

If such a provision as fillers is allowed for by a DBMS it is generally sensible to make the record size into a whole number of words and, if the structure of the record is likely to be particularly volatile, then there is no reason why we should not add on a filler of any number of bytes and, as long as it does not increase storage overheads, this will be worth the saving in future work.

8.5 Reorganization

This is the process whereby, for a variety of possible reasons, we wish physically to move data around on disc. The usual reason is either to consolidate space or to resituate data that has become less ordered or grouped than we would like and is therefore impairing the efficiency of the database. Other reasons might be as follows:

- As a direct consequence of a restructure. By adding new records/data items or by deleting or amending them we may have more/less data on each page than we require.
- Patterns of storage and access may have changed. For example, there may now be a business requirement to produce an important report daily. Such a report might involve files Fl and F2 that were previously unrelated. It might be decided

that there is just cause to implement the new relationship by storing associated records of Fl and F2 on the same page physically.

- Volumes of data have changed and the efficiency of the database has degraded. For example, a file originally may have been created with CALC access in the belief that it would not contain more than 1000 records. With that value in mind, table and/or page sizes were set accordingly. Over a period of time the number of records may gave gone up to 5000 and the result is many overflow pages being used. (When designing a database the DBA should predict what will happen to the business over the subsequent five years or more. In practice this is extremely difficult.)

The actual reorganization (sometimes called 'physical placement reorganization' or 'garbage collection') often requires a logical unload/reload of the data in similar manner to the restructure (although again some database management systems allow this to be done *in situ*). The difference between a restructure and a reorganize is that, with the latter, no user programs will need recompiling (in general).

8.6 Tuning the database

The efficiency of the database we have constructed would soon degrade if we simply loaded it up and let it run, and every time it crashes, for whatever reason, find out what the trouble is and fix it. It is a part of the DBA's job to try to foresee problems (particularly with regard to future restructures and reorganizations) and to try to cure or circumvent them before they have had time to develop. To this end, most database management systems supply (usually at extra cost!) a set of software designed specifically for monitoring the performance of the database.

This software can take any of the following three forms:

1   software that is run occasionally to scan the physical database and produce a report of disc usage, wasted space, overflow situations, and so on;
2   software that runs concurrently with the database (and usually is a part of the DBMS code) and produces statistics on the dynamic workings of the database such as the memory management, read times and physical I/O times for each program that runs against the database;
3   a combination of the above two.

Given a piece of software of this nature, clearly it is up to the DBA to run it as and when required, in the case of (1), and to interpret the results produced and decide:

(a) what has caused the results (if unusually good or bad). Was it a special year-end or one-off program the efficiency of which we may not be too bothered with? Were there known hardware problems at the time to account for the results? Was the program itself inefficiently written? Could the database design be at fault?
(b) based on the deductions from (a), what can be done to improve the situation (be those improvements to the program or to the database).

Much of this and the following sections concern parameters that on some database management systems are easy to change dynamically, whereas others require a re-organize and possibly a database recompilation. It is essential that the DBA be aware of exactly what they can or cannot do at a dynamic level, when the database is designed initially as, clearly, this may affect the design. For example, if they cannot add extra space to an area without having to recompile the database, then that spare space will have to be designed into the original model.

8.7 Program statistics

Many DBMSs produce program statistics that can, if taken independently of any other information, produce results that are very misleading. Database processor and I/O times can vary enormously from one run of a program to another, depending very largely on what else the computer is doing at the time (this is contrary to most theory). The DBA must collect together several sets of statistics for a single program, determine (usually from the statistics) whether the same volume of work was carried out by each run of the program, and weight the results accordingly to produce an average.

For example, if an online inquiry program performs a single enquiry, the database statistics might produce an I/O time of 1.07 s, which might make it appear that the DBMS took 1.07 s to locate a single record. Running the same program with two inquiries might show a time of 1.09 s. From this the DBA could reasonably deduce that a database I/O takes 0.02 s and the rest of the time is taken in the database being initialized, buffers initialized and all the necessary DBMS code read into memory. Of course, in practice, the number of enquiries in a true sample would be very much greater than one or two. A typical set of statistics produced by a program run might appear similar to that shown in Figure 8.2.

PROGRAM MTG04
Total DB processor   time   00:02:23
I/O   time   00:31:21
elapsed   time   00:47:53

STRUCTURE	RECS READ	PHYS READS	TOTAL I/O	AVE (ms)	RECS WRTN	PHYS WRITES	TOTAL I/O	AVE (ms)
MORTGAGE	7283	4283	00:03:29	49	7283	4283	00:04:12	59
MTG-TRANS	21426	48	00:00:03	62	7291	52	00:00:03	58
MTG-INDEX	7283	3741	00:02:11	35	0	0	0	0
MTG-CNTRLS	7283	6108	00:00:54	58	7283	6108	00:04:10	41
CUSTOMERS	7249	7041	00:05:11	44	0	0	0	0
CUST-INDEX	7249	6914	00:04:09	36	0	0	0	0

Figure 8.2 An example set of program statistics

Given that there is one MTG-CNTRLS record for each of the 200 branches, that MTG-CNTRLS is a CALC file whereas MORTGAGE and CUSTOMERS are both index sequential, and that a physical read (from disc) does not take place if the record is already extant in memory, we can infer that:

- There were no mortgage records created, otherwise there would be writes to the MTG-INDEX, but the mortgages are being updated.
- The number of mortgage records being written is very similar to the number of MTG-TRANS records being written.
- Customer information is only being read.

The most likely scenario is therefore that the program is adding mortgage transactions to the file (amending existing transactions is far less likely given the nature of the business and the quantities being written), updating the mortgage record, updating the MTG-CNTRLS record and reading related customer information (for a printout?).

There is evidence in the results to show that mortgages are being read in random order:

- were the mortgages being read in sequential order, we would expect far fewer reads on MTG-INDEX;
- if the input file were in branch order, we would expect a maximum of 200 physical reads for MTG-CNTRLS even if they are blocked.

All of this the DBA should know from the program documentation, but their conclusions should be the same, as follows.

1. It would appear that, in all but 48 cases, the existing mortgage transactions are on the same page as their owners (since no further physical reads were required to access the transactions). This is good news as it shows that our physical-placement strategy is still reasonably efficient, but from the number of logical transaction reads it is clear that the program is having to serially search through the existing transactions before the new one is inserted. This problem will worsen as the number of transactions grows throughout the year. It implies that either no mechanism exists to FIND LAST (see Section 6.11), or else one exists but the programmer is not using it (i.e. the program is inefficient and not the database). It is hoped that it is the latter because to correct the former will involve a restructure and should have been foreseen when the database was designed.

2. A general conclusion might be to presort the transactions before running the program (into account-number order). If the account-number ranges are linked to particular branches, then this will not only cut down on the number of mortgage and MTG-INDEX physical reads, but also those for MTG-CNTRLS. We would not expect the customer statistics to be improved because they will always be random, the number of physical reads being slightly less than the number of logical reads purely because of the occasional chance siting of two consecutive (as processed) records being on the same page (which was therefore still in memory).

The result of this might be to save several minutes of I/O time, but consideration must be taken of how long the presort will take. It is likely to take several minutes, so would we be saving really? An alternative might be as shown in the next section.

8.8 Buffer management

Supposing that our database has had two buffers allocated for each structure (the extra one being to allow for READAHEAD if the accessing is sequential). If we could change this apportioning of memory at run time dynamically, then certainly we could improve the efficiency of the database. For example, the MTG-CNTRLS record is 50 bytes long and is blocked in tens, and there is a total of 200 records.

In the normal running of the above program, with two buffers, there would be 20 MTG-CNTRLS records in memory at any one time. If the next required record is not one of those 20 then one of the buffers will have to be flushed (discarded or written back to disc if it has been updated) and the new page read in. Thus for a random read we have a 0.9 probability that a physical read will be required for each record. Suppose that we could now alter the number of buffers to 20 dynamically. The memory overheads are small but only 20 physical reads are necessary to read all the pages into memory such that, thereafter, no more physical reads are needed (although the buffers will still need flushing at checkpoints). The time difference between records being read from disc and being read from memory is very significant (less than 2 microseconds from memory compared to 10 milliseconds from disc). So the result of the number of buffers being increased will save nearly all of the original I/O time (approx. 6 min) without the need to presort transactions.

Other programs might only require a single MTG-CNTRLS record and so it would be inappropriate to read all 200 into memory. Therefore it is highly advantageous for the buffering to be controllable dynamically (and perhaps to be included in the operating instructions for the program).

A further example of memory management might be seen with the investment index. If we allow 20 investments per page (with their transactions), then we would need 50 000 table entries in the index. By dividing these into 50 entries per table (see Appendix A), we need 1000 tables. For these we would need 20 subtables and one sub-subtable (in other words three levels of table). Thus to access an investment record via the index takes four reads. If we only have two buffers available then we would need to:

1 read in the sub-subtable,
2 read in the relevant subtable,
3 flush out (1) and read in the relevant table.

Clearly, it would be advantageous to allocate at least three buffers to the index such that the sub-subtable can be kept in memory permanently (since the sub-subtable is needed for every find it will never be flushed out except at checkpoints).

8.9 Readaheads

If a program is reading a file sequentially, then it will read in a page of data, process it, and then read the next page. However, there will be a certain delay while the next page is being read in – a delay that could be avoided if the computer could pre-empt the call for the next page and read it in while the previous page is being processed.

Such a device is said to be **readahead** and, clearly, requires a minimum of two I/O buffers in memory. The question now is, how does the DBMS know that the file is being read sequentially? On some systems there is a special DDL syntax for sequential reading that flags the program's intentions to the system. On others, a record is kept of the I/O requests. If three or four consecutive pages are read into memory, one after the other, then the DBMS assumes that accessing is sequential, switches to a readahead mode and reads in the fourth or fifth page before it is requested. (It should be noted that this is not exclusive to database management systems and that many operating systems perform readaheads on non-database files.)

If the records on a file are blocked (block = page) correctly, then most sequential programs will be processor-bound, that is, having read a block into memory it will take longer to process every record on that block than it will to read in the next block. However, if the program involved is doing very little processing (for example, perhaps just dumping the records to backup), then it is more likely to be I/O-bound and time can be wasted waiting for the next block to be read in, even taking read-ahead into consideration.

A useful weapon in the DBA's armoury might therefore be the ability to alter the unit of physical access from a block into a superblock dynamically when performing sequential reads. Thus, instead of reading in 10 records at a time (or whatever the blocking factor is), the DBA can specify a superblock to be equal to 10 blocks, and thus 100 records are read in at one time. Again the memory overheads are increased, but this feature is of great use on a dedicated task where time is of the essence.

8.10 Memory management

Those database management systems that produce program statistics usually also produce a summary listing of the database usage every time the database is opened (if various programs overlap in their running then the database will only be opened once by the first and closed once by the last to finish). As well as a summary of I/Os against each structure used, as shown in Figure 8.2, there might also appear a summary of the memory usage.

Examples of these, and their significance, follow.

```
1   MAXIMUM ALLOCATED MEMORY = 100000 WORDS
    MAXIMUM MEMORY USED = 96329 WORDS
    NUMBER OF OVERLAYS = 2386
    NUMBER OF FORCED OVERLAYS = 487
```

When creating the database, the DBA often has to specify a maximum amount of memory that the database will use. If there is too much then other programs, utilities and/or system software may not have enough memory to function. If there is too little the following problems may occur. If more than the maximum is used, the system should not fall down but the number of forced overlays will increase. A forced overlay occurs when the system has to write a buffer back to disc at a time when it would not normally do so to make room for another page to be read in. This means an increase in I/O time and a decrease in efficiency.

The DBA should therefore be aware of times at which memory usage peaks: at certain times of the day or with certain programs. To aid them, many manufacturers provide software that will produce memory maps of usage over a given period. Using this information the DBA may decide that the memory allocation should be increased dynamically at certain times. (The actual database memory usage, clearly, depends on the buffer sizes and any use of superblocks may affect it radically.)

```
2   TOTAL NUMBER OF PHYSICAL READS = 4206
    TOTAL NUMBER OF PHYSICAL WRITES = 683
    AVERAGE WAIT TIME PER I/O = 14.3 MS
    CHANNEL 1 - NUMBER OF READS = 1032
    NUMBER OF WRITES = 293
    AVERAGE WAIT TIME PER I/0- 79 Ms
    CHANNEL 2
```

and so on. The DBA can use these statistics to determine whether certain I/O channels are being overloaded. In general, it is wise not to have databases on the same disc as the operating system or any often-used system files if it can be at all avoided, because that channel will be in constant use and the DBMS will have to wait for its I/Os. The DBA must therefore be careful as to which files are stored where.

In the same way care must be taken that disc-head movements are kept to a minimum. Normally, this is achievable by spreading the database across several discs so that structures likely to be in use at the same time are on different discs. For example, we might have:

```
DISK 1   INVESTMENTS
         CUST-INDEX
DISK 2   MORTGAGES
         INV-INDEX
DISK 3   CUSTOMERS
         MTG-INDEX
```

Clearly, the restriction on efficiency is the number of discs available.

```
3   CURRENT JOURNAL FILE NUMBER = 97 (28% FULL)
    CURRENT JOURNAL FILE PAGE NUMBER 3842
    CHECKPOINT = 10 TRANSACTIONS
    AVERAGE TIME FOR CHECKPOINT = 0.9 S
```

General journal file information can be very useful to the DBA. The journal file is a file that is written to just like any other file and so its I/O times are equally as important, particularly with regard to checkpoints. A checkpoint can take the DBMS a considerable length of time (comparatively speaking), largely because *all* updated buffers are written back to disc. If the current work being carried out is mostly online with perhaps 10 to 15 transactions per minute, then we could afford to take one or two checkpoints during that time, since a delay of a second in a minute would not be noticeable. However, if the work is batch and we are processing, say, 5 transactions per second, then 30% of the time is taken up checkpointing and this will drastically increase the program's run time. Certainly it would be beneficial if the DBA could dynamically alter that value of 10 transactions per checkpoint to, say, 100. Now only 3% of the time is taken performing checkpoints.

8.11   Summary of run-time statistics

What must be stressed at this point is that features mentioned so far in this chapter are certainly not features available with every database management system. Moreover, other systems have their own, equally useful, features. Those given here are merely representative of the kind of options that can be open to the DBA and that, if used correctly, can increase the efficiency of the database greatly. In particular, the database can be altered dynamically to improve the throughput of every program if desired, by changing its own environment.

Clearly, if it is necessary to restructure or reorganize the database merely to change the memory allocation or buffer sizes, then tuning of this nature is severely restricted.

If it is possible, then the database statistics, as shown, provide the DBA with the best indication of how the database is performing, structure by structure, on a day-to-day basis. By maintaining these statistics over a period of time, the DBA can ascertain whether the efficiency of the system is degrading. For example, if the average I/O time to read a record of a particular file shows a marked increase over a period of weeks, then problems with the file's structure are likely and the DBA may have to resort to another piece of software to determine what the problems are: namely, the database analyser.

8.12   Database analyser

Such a piece of software will, generally, be database-manufacturer-supplied and will read through the whole, or selected parts, of the database to analyse the content of each structure. The report produced will show the DBA where inefficiencies lie and can point out where possible restructure or reorganize requirements are likely.

The reports generated vary from system to system but given here are two examples that display some of the information produced and the action required.

```
1   FILE - INVESTMENTS
    ACCESSED BY INDEX - INV-INDEX
    TOTAL RECORDS = 978326
    RECORDS PER PAGE = 50
    TOTAL PAGES = 37286
    % SPACE PER PAGE = 16.4 (AVERAGE)
    INV-INDEX TABLESIZE = 100 ENTRIES
    NUMBER OF TABLES - LEVEL 1   9
                       LEVEL 2   420
                       LEVEL 3   20983
    NUMBER OF OVERFLOW TABLES = 904
```

In this example, for simplicity, investment transactions are not stored on the same page as their owner investments. The DBA could glean some important information from these results. First, each page is only 83% full, presumably the space coming from deleted records (unless some spare space was pre-allocated at the design stage). The DBMS may maintain available space tables, in which case the space will be re-used eventually, but if this is so then the ordering will suffer, with a corresponding increase in I/O time when the file is read sequentially. If this is the case then the DBA may consider a reorganization to recreate the investments file in index order, which will also have the benefit of consolidating any spare space on the file.

A second observation would be the number of overflow tables in the index, which is far too high. The DBA may therefore consider it worthwhile reorganizing the index, such that each contains 150 entries but that each is only 75% full initially, thus allowing room for future expansion without the need for overflow.

```
2   AREA - MORTGAGES
    AVERAGE MORTGAGES RECORDS PER PAGE = 9
    AVERAGE TRANSACTIONS PER PAGE= 67.81
    UNUSED SPACE PER PAGE = 58.19 TRANSACTIONS
```

In this database system we have allocated space for 9 mortgages plus 126 transactions (14 per account) on each page (the DBMS allows for physical placement). This means that each page should be full at the end of the year (although the mortgages with 54 transactions will clearly cause overflow problems) but, at the beginning of the year, most of each page will be empty. The DBA might decide initially to define a page as holding 15 mortgages, but each with only 6 or 7 transactions, and then, partway through the year, reorganize the data into the above framework.

Thus, by using the analyser program, the DBA should be able to monitor the physical state of the database and be able to predict any future problem areas and inefficiencies, so that they can be amended before the performance degrades too seriously.

Note

It is here, in particular, that we see the advantages of having disjoint logical and physical models. If this is so then we can afford to change blocking factors, page sizes, page contents and the like without affecting user programs.

8.13 Data dictionaries

In Chapter 3 it was stated that the user's view was defined to be the conceptual model whereas the implemented database was defined as the logical model. It may appear that there is no direct link between the two except through the reams of paper generated by the data analysis exercise, but in reality most database suppliers now provide a computerized data dictionary system which has the benefits of being:

- complete,
- up-to-date,
- easy to use,
- able to provide quick cross-referencing.

That is, it is the complete opposite of what a manually based system may be.

Data dictionaries are created and maintained by the DBMS by extracting information about files/data items when they are created. In the case of relational databases the information is actually stored as data in tables, and can be accessed by the user (given the correct level of access rights). Thus, for example:

```
SELECT * FROM TAB;
```

would display all the tables to which a user has access. There are further options to access other tables with columns containing sizes, date created, last access dates, and so on, which can be very useful to the user.

```
DESC tablename
```

would list all the data items that constitute a table, together with their data sizes and types.

For the DBA (with added privileges) there is the possibility of getting a system overview of:

- who has access to tables (by password);
- the ability to change user rights and privileges;
- the size of each table, creation dates, and so on;
- overall database information such as total database size, free space, buffer sizes, clustering information.

For the old CODASYL systems there is an added requirement to keep track of all the application programs that access the database. Because the general methodology for 3GL programs is to pass the source code through a compiler (usually a special database-related compiler), then that process can extract information from the source code concerning that program's usage of subschemas, areas, records, sets and data items, and often whether the program is update or read-only.

With this information from all programs bound into a centralized dictionary it is relatively easy for the database administrator to interrogate this dictionary (usually in a 4GL manner) whenever the need is there. For example, if a restructure of the investment file is about to take place, which will affect data items d and e then the DBA can be given a list of all programs that access investments and, indeed, which programs use subschemas containing items d and e. This prevents most of the problems dealing with out-of-date documentation outlined in Chapter 1.

8.14 Summary

This chapter has briefly looked at some more standard database features and utilities available with most database systems. It is true to say that some are more important on some systems than on others. For example, it is relatively easy to restructure a relational database (see Chapter 12) without affecting users, so relatively little planning needs to go into the actual process of restructuring, although there is still a requirement to review what effect the change will have on the efficiency of the system.

9
Database administration

9.1 Introduction

Throughout this book so far we have referred to the database administration as the DBA without defining who, exactly, they are or if, indeed, there is a team rather than a single person. In this chapter we try to remedy that deficiency by looking at the actual role played by the DBA within an organization.

By listing the tasks performed by the DBA, it might be possible to understand the sort of person(s) required for the job. They must have sound knowledge of:

- data analysis,
- database design methodologies,
- how to implement the database on the particular machine in question,
- imposition of privacy rights as access controls,
- the definition of backup and recovery strategies,
- control of changes to the database,
- how to monitor the database on a day-to-day basis,
- prediction of future changes needed to maintain efficiency and minimize storage requirements,
- applications support,
- operations support,
- how to tune the database,
- the creation of test databases.

Clearly, from this list, it can be seen that if a database exists already then the first three items will have been performed (though the DBA will still need the documentation that was produced at the time); presumably, the applications department will be familiar with database accessing techniques, documentation for operations will have been written, and recovery strategies will have been thought out. This may sound as if there is nothing left for the DBA to do, but that is not the case. As with all other system software, the DBMS will be updated by the manufacturers every so often, some features will be phased out, some added, and these enhancements will need passing on to the programmers and the operations department. More areas of the business may be computerized and this may, in turn, involve the design of further databases. (Although, as mentioned, the original data analysis should not need repeating, because it should have covered the entire organization, there are still also the important areas of monitoring, tuning and changing the database.)

It may be possible for all of this to be carried out by a single individual, but in a large business a team is more likely, and if there is no database in existence then one would expect the task of data analysis and design to be too much for one person.

9.2   The database team

Having opted for a team approach, we must enrol some members and look at the special skills that they will need.

First, in charge of the team we would need a database administrator to coordinate the development of the database in much the same way that the systems analyst co-ordinates the development of a project. This implies that the database administrator should possess the usual management qualities of:

- planning,
- coordinating,
- motivating,
- communicating (with many other people).

He or she should also have a specialist knowledge of the systems software and hardware available and, in particular, an intimate knowledge of the database management system and its utilities. They may or may not have a detailed knowledge of the workings of the organization (certainly it would be useful, but it is not essential). If they haven't then there is, clearly, the need for someone close at hand who has. In general, this will be a systems analyst, though it must be borne in mind that many systems analysts tend to specialize in one particular area of a business (especially in a large organization) and thus all of the analysts are likely to be called on individually at some time. As they will each have their own work to do as well, they will not be permanent members of database administration. A diagrammatic representation of a database team might therefore be similar to that shown in Figure 9.1.

The database analyst(s) will be responsible for the collection of data in the analysis stages, for interviewing users about their requirements, for searching out existing documentation and/or programs, files, and so on, and, by the process of normalization or by any other methods, eventually creating a conceptual data model.

Concurrently with this process, the same or, more likely, a different database analyst will be looking at the functional areas of the business and will be drawing up lists of the events and operations involved. Eventually, this should lead to a conceptual

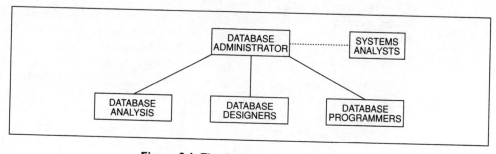

Figure 9.1 The database administration team

process model. (It may have been decided to extract the data requirements for the business from this study of the functional analysis, as outlined in Section 4.3, in which case probably only a single database analyst will be required.)

These two processes should generate reams of paperwork (unless the data can be fed directly into a data dictionary), which should be properly maintained and kept in a readable form for future reference.

From what has been said, it is likely that the database analysts will extract their information by working in small teams, the members of which will vary depending on the various systems analysts available and also the user department currently being looked at, at any one time, because that user department will usually supply a member of the team.

Following the successful conclusion of the data-analysis stage, the database analysts should no longer be needed. This is not to imply instant redundancy; it is more likely that they were recruited from existing programming staff on a temporary basis and can now return to their former duties.

It is now the turn of the database designers who must pick up the conceptual model and somehow turn it into an implementable logical model. This task is mutually exclusive of the analysis stage in theory but, in practice, as soon as the particular database management system has been decided on, the design team must learn about the languages to be used, the design options available and the general constraints imposed by the specified hardware and software. To this end they will tend to be a different set of people from the database analysts, though by no means does this have to be the case. Having designed an appropriate database, then probably they will liaise with operations over a relevant load and testing strategy.

Since future changes to the database, and even the day-to-day monitoring, affect the aims and objectives of their database design, it is likely that at least one database designer will be a permanent member of the DBA.

In conjunction with the designers, there may exist database programmers who will be asked to write various pieces of software to support the database. These might include data-validation or access-control procedures that eventually will be bound into the DBMS. Once the database is designed it will be the database programmers' task to write and test the load programs (as outlined in Section 6.17) and, indeed, any other one-off programs needed to create and initialize the database. For this they will obviously need to be good experienced programmers who have been taught the workings of the DBMS and who will be able to interface with it, generally by using a high-level programming language.

As mentioned, the database team may only be temporary in nature (with the exception of the database administrator) and may be drawn from existing data processing (DP) staff. For example, the database analysts may be existing systems analysts or senior programmers who should already know much of the workings of the organization (though their own concepts should not cloud the important data-analysis task of interviewing user departments). The design team might consist of programmers and maybe even operators (who better would know the shortcomings of an existing machine?). The database programmers could also be existing programmers. However, it may be necessary for them to be versed in more than a single high-level language. The load programs will almost certainly be written in the host language, but the various DBMS subroutines may well be written in the operating system language, such as ALGOL or FORTRAN, or PL/SQL for relational databases (see Chapter 13).

Having finished their allotted tasks, the various team members may be allowed to return to their original jobs, hopefully having gained from their experience. This would leave the database administrator plus, possibly, a single designer/programmer, to perform the remaining tasks and generally monitor the database.

In this section the stages of analysis, design and implementation (bar the tasks mentioned in subsequent sections) have been covered. Most of this work will be the direct responsibility of the database administrator.

9.3 Privacy

Privacy, as an important consideration in both the analysis and design stages, was dealt with in Chapter 7, but there are still a few points that need clarifying.

First, it is not the database administrator's task to decide who can see which data, or what they can do with them. These are organizational decisions that must be taken at a higher level than the DBA. Given those constraints, the administrator must then find ways in which to guarantee that the access controls that he or she imposes on the data will uphold those constraints.

The real problem here is that the constraints are rarely written down in practice. Given a manual system, it is, usually, a matter of 'who has the key to the filing cabinet'. So, access controls are generally on an all-or-nothing basis with no regard for individual data items. A member of staff either has access to all of the contents of the filing cabinet or none of them. Thus the DBA can gain something by knowing who has the keys, but they may not know whether all such data are at the same level of privacy. Indeed, there may well be members of staff whose own jobs would be simpler and more efficient if they had immediate access to some of the other data in that filing cabinet, but who are denied access because of the confidentiality of some of the data. This is identical with the problems of the conventional computerized filing system as outlined in Section 1.9. To avoid these problems, and also the related ones of data duplication (see Section 1.10), the DBA must clarify all access-control decisions at the analysis stage, for example, by correctly filling in the privacy parts of the forms shown in Figures 3.3 to 3.6.

9.4 Backup and recovery

Before the database becomes a 'live' concern, the DBA must have drawn up some form of recovery procedures. Preferably, they will have tried and tested as many of the error conditions as they can manufacture, and will have documented the outcomes. The operations department may well have been through some initial training courses relating to the usage of the particular DBMS (and, indeed, these courses may have been given by the DBA themselves), but courses are second best to experience, and experience in recovery techniques will be essential. This is perhaps the strangest area to operations, whose natural instincts may well be to reload and rerun.

At some sites, the recovery of a database is only ever carried out by the DBA no matter what time of day or night, but we can see no reasons why, after an initial period of a few months, operations cannot perform this (usually) relatively simple task, especially if they have a good set of documentation. There are, after all, few options open. Either the database will recover itself (as in restart recovery – see Section 7.15) or it will not. If not, then it is a case of one of the following:

- rollback and retry (if rollback is not automatic),
- rollforward and retry,
- rebuild a disc/page (or whatever is necessary),
- reload and rerun if none of the above work.

Given the actual syntax for the three types of database recovery, there is no reason why the nearest operator should not perform them. Moreover, operations are far more likely to know exactly what work has been done and when the last dump was, than the DBA.

Some decisions will only come from experience. For example, given the following timetable,

5 p.m. Database dump ends
6–7 p.m. A single update program is running
7–11 p.m. Various concurrent programs,

if a program crashes at 11 p.m., clearly it will be necessary to recover to the last quiet point (7 p.m.). Will it be quicker to rollback, or reload and roll forward?

Occasionally, events will occur that cannot easily be solved by recovery. Possibly the worst thing is an unknowing operator performing a non-DBMS-controlled disc-to-disc copy of a database file while it is in use, and then starting to use the new disc. This would be non-recoverable because the DBMS has no knowledge of the copy and cannot therefore mark the journal file (compare with online dumping, described in Section 7.20). The only solution is to reload and rerun. This emphasizes a general point that has not been discussed yet. Given a database, it is essential that general housekeeping duties such as copying be performed only by DBMS routines and not by normal operating system commands, otherwise all integrity checking and guarantees are bypassed. The DBA should have impressed on operations the need to dump the database as frequently as possible. Clearly, exactly when they do so is up to them, and a lot will depend on whether online dumping facilities are available, and whether their workload is on a day-to-day basis.

The DBMS will dictate whether manual recovery is required to the last quiet point (in which case there should be frequently scheduled quiet points), or whether the DBMS will rollback the faulty program automatically. Whichever is the case, operations should be aware of all forms of automatic recovery and what they achieve, and what the options are once they have finished.

It is very likely that, as well as the database(s), there will also be some conventional files in use that will not be recoverable in the database fashion. Operations should therefore be clear as to which files these are, when they will need dumping, and which to reload in the event of failure.

9.5 Changes

When restructures or reorganizes are forced on the database through changes to the business or by degradation of database efficiency, the DBA needs to control these changes and coordinate all other people involved. With relational databases the actual process of restructuring the database is often trivial (although pre-written SQL or PL/SQL statements may still need to be altered). The following paragraphs may still, therefore, be appropriate.

Restructures

These changes will have been passed to the DBA from elsewhere, usually from a user department via a systems analyst. It is the DBA's task to evaluate these changes and plot the effect that they will have on the database and existing programs.

Normally, this will be done in conjunction with the data dictionary (if one is available), which should be able to project proposed changes across the breadth of the conceptual and logical models and supply listings of all structures/programs/queries affected. The DBA can decide therefore on how long the work will take (by experience or guesswork), and arrange a proposed timetable. The list of affected programs can now be passed to programming with time scales of writing and testing (the latter will clearly revolve around when a test database will be available – see Section 9.9).

Come the day of the restructure, a detailed schedule must be drawn up for operations (if the DBA is not present). Probably, this will show a critical time after which the exercise must be abandoned and the old database and its software reloaded (to be able to carry on with the day-to-day work).

Reorganizes

Essentially, the programming department will not in theory be involved with this exercise, but if the logical and physical models are merged, a change of (for example) blocking factors may well involve the recompilation of programs. A similar schedule is needed for operations.

9.6 Monitoring

The process of monitoring the database has been dealt with extensively in Chapter 8 and so little will be said here other than the fact that it is the DBA's most important role on a day-to-day basis. Statistics must be collected and collated such that future problems can be detected and, ideally, corrected before they have time to develop. The DBA should also provide the run-time parameters for each program relating to allowed memory, blocksizes, checkpoints, and so on, to operations, to ensure the maximum efficiency of the database.

9.7 Applications support

While the database is being designed and implemented, the DBA is likely to spend some time instructing the applications programmers on what the database will mean to them, and how they should use it. (This option will generally be cheaper than sending them all on a manufacturer-supplied course and the results hopefully will be comparable.)

The interface to the database is likely to be through an **application program interface** or API (i.e. the program calls the relevant DBMS routines to access the database). It is vital that the programmers be taught how to trap DBMS errors within their programs and how to deal with them. It is not uncommon to have a set of standard error routines that can be compiled into a program by the use of a library call. In particular, each update program must be able to handle a deadlock situation (the DBMS itself will resolve the deadlock, but the program must decide whether to terminate and await rolling back or simply to wait a few milliseconds, depending on the mechanisms available – see Section 7.16).

If it were merely a case of syntax learning, the DBA's instruction task would be simple, but there is also the more important job of teaching the programmers how to make the most effective and efficient use of the database; this may be more difficult because the DBA may not, at this stage, be aware of the full workings of the DBMS.

The programming department also will need to be informed of:

- any proposed changes to the database in terms of restructures (if they are not the originators of them);
- any reorganizations if they are likely to affect the running of programs;
- any changes to the DBMS software (i.e. new releases), which may affect programs or else provide new techniques of interest to the programmer;
- how to use any existing query languages (subject to any access constraints).

Note

It may also be appropriate for the DBA to teach the usage of query languages to any other user groups that are allowed to view certain areas of data and may wish to extract information quickly without having to make a new program request.

9.8   Operations support

Recovery and backup strategies have been mentioned already, but operations will also want information about the day-to-day running of the database, for example, as follows:

- How and when to change and dump the journal file (if it is not automatic).
- How and when to change the database dynamically (if that is possible). It may only be feasible to restrict these changes to the differences between online and batch work, but if it is possible on a program-to-program basis then details should be incorporated in the program's operating instructions.
- How the DBMS interacts with the online control program (if there is one), particularly with regard to recovery. (Many online systems revolve around sophisticated message control systems that pass data from the communications network directly to the application programs and, as a result, often have their own mechanisms for recovering messages in the event of failure.)

9.9 Test databases

At most sites there is a distinct need for a test database on which the programmers can develop and test application programs before 'putting them live'.

While they are becoming accustomed to using databases it is probable that any database vaguely similar to the live version will suffice, but, as their confidence grows and the various systems develop, there will become an ever-increasing need for the test model to be as near as possible to the live version. This would allow full testing of all possible data and error variations. Clearly, the main problem is resources. If the site can afford the processor power and disc-storage capacity to be duplicated entirely, then the programmers will benefit. It is more likely that the database administrator will be asked to create a submodel containing enough data for reasonable testing to be performed (though the actual loading of data to this test database may be left to the programmers who will know exactly what they require).

Most database management systems provide the facility for the DBA to update the live database to form the test model. Since the new schema and its software are moved elsewhere (usually to another machine) the live model is not actually affected. Clearly the advantages of this are that the programmers are working on the most up-to-date version. Other considerations are outlined in Section 7.8. If the live database is restructured (though not if it is reorganized), a new test database will need to be created as soon as possible.

Other database systems allow the live DBMS software to be used for the test versions directly without having to regenerate it. This is made possible by the fact that the variable data concerning the database, such as resident disc names, journal-file information and memory allocation, are not compiled into the DBMS code but are maintained elsewhere (for example, in the control file). The DBMS is thus a combination of the logical and storage models, but not the device model. If we generate a new control file with the test-database disc names and run-time parameters then the DBMS itself will not need recompiling.

The actual loading of the test database is a complex task. It is usually not sufficient merely to dump and reload every tenth record (or whatever) from the live version. The test model will have to be consistent, all member records in a particular set occurrence will have to exist, and all control totals will have to balance. In a complicated network model, and indeed in the object-oriented model, it is often very difficult to separate out records that are not linked to others that are themselves linked to others, and so on.

In such cases, it is often wisest to allow the programmers to populate the test database with their own contrived data, rather than try to extract any from the live version. This may be achievable through a query language, if one exists and allows the creation of data.

Whatever the method, this will be a very slow process if the amount of data loaded is to be significant, because there is little sensible testing that can be carried out on half a dozen accounts if the live database contains half a million. Moreover, it will not be just the programmers who will use the test database. The DBA will also want to experiment with future restructures, monitoring and tuning exercises, and the results may not be meaningful unless the volume of data throughput is a significant proportion of that in the live situation.

Part Three
Existing Database Systems

10

CODASYL: a network approach

10.1 Background

Throughout the first two parts of this book, many of the theories, definitions and examples have used the original concepts of the CODASYL database. This is not to say that all CODASYL approaches are identical – indeed they are not – but they are all bound together under a common architecture and a common philosophy and, as such, are widely used throughout the world of commercial databases. For that reason, the brief history of the CODASYL database, as outlined in Section 2.2, is expanded here to show its full relevance.

Following its success with the rationalization of COBOL, the CODASYL group decided to extend its activities to related areas, and in 1965 formed a List Processing Task Force to look at the list-processing capabilities of COBOL. Two years later this was renamed the Data Base Task Group (DBTG). In October 1969, the DBTG submitted a report to the Programming Language Committee (PLC) proposing a data description language (DDL) to describe a set of linked structures, and a data manipulation language as an extension to a host language (COBOL), to be used for the access and manipulation of the data.

This report was revised in 1971 to incorporate two DDLs: one for the global model or schema, and one for the submodels or subschemas, and it was accepted by the PLC. In the same year the Data Description Language Committee (DDLC) was formed and within two years it had produced a journal of development outlining its proposals.

In 1973 two task groups were set up by the DDLC: the Subschema Task Group (SSTG) in the USA and the Data Base Administration Working Group (DBAWG) (for the development of tools for use by the DBA) in the UK. The latter's preliminary report in 1975 included work on a data strategy description language (DSDL) for reorganizing the database, and for the provision of concurrency and data protection. This was included as an appendix in the CODASYL journal of development in 1978. In 1976 a CODASYL FORTRAN database facility was published and incorporated into the journal of development in 1977. The 1978 report was important in that it included, for the first time, a data storage definition language which would provide the physical data independence lacking in the earlier models. From this brief history it will be observed that CODASYL is run by a selection of committees and task groups. It is not a manufacturer of databases, but rather a group of users, manufacturers and software houses that was established to try to rationalize and standardize the concepts of database design and current technologies, by producing a set of system specifications.

Since it was brought into existence, CODASYL has influenced the thinking of all the major manufacturers (though some, notably IBM, have since deviated from the CODASYL architecture).

10.2   CODASYL architecture

The CODASYL network model has structures grouped as in a Bachman diagram (see Figure 3.7) of which a simple example is shown in Figure 10.1, with some records (owners) related to others (members) in a 1:n relationship. Member records can themselves be owners in other relationships (e.g. mortgages and investments in Figure 10.1).

The **schema** defines the logical data model, and is itself written in a special language, the **data definition language** (DDL), which describes the various records, their constituent data items and the relationships between them (implemented as sets). The schemas of CODASYL 73 models also describe the storage data model, but the CODASYL 78 proposals put forward an independent data storage definition language.

The logical data submodels are defined as being subschemas that are derivable from the schema. A subschema is essentially an application-oriented view of the database. It is not possible to restructure the data within the subschemas: for example, to define new sets that do not exist in the schema.

The CODASYL approach to data manipulation is one of a host language (usually COBOL or FORTRAN), with extensions to allow for communication with the database, and the manipulation of the data in the subschemas. The programmer invokes the relevant subschema at program compilation time and the user work area (UWA) is copied into the object code for that program.

Thus, overall, we have the architecture shown in Figure 10.2.

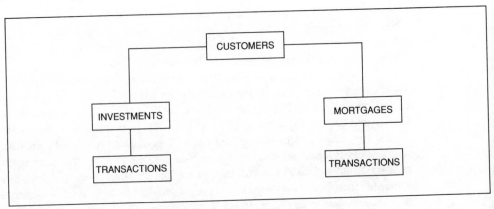

Figure 10.1 A simple CODASYL network

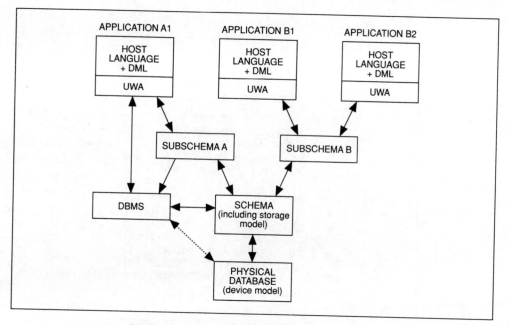

Figure 10.2 A generalized CODASYL architecture

10.3 Schemas

The schema is written by using the DDL which describes records and sets. Records can be readily equated to COBOL records, whereas sets describe relationships between records, generally on a $1{:}n$ basis ($m{:}n$ are not directly maintainable on most CODASYL implementations, as mentioned in Section 4.13).

The schema itself should always be representable by means of a Bachman diagram (see Section 3.8), though the processes of normalization, collapse and fragmentation are still highly relevant.

To describe the data definition language itself really requires an example (Figure 10.3); the one used here is a basic study of the customer–investment–transaction set of relationships as shown in the left-hand half of Figure 10.1.

SCHEMA entry

The schema name must be a unique identifier within the system (i.e. there cannot be two databases with the same name). An access-control lock is optional, the various possibilities having been discussed in Section 7.11.

AREA entry

The total storage requirement for the database is divided into areas. For each record defined in the schema, an area name must be specified using the WITHIN clause, in which the record will be placed when created. In fact, more than one area can be defined for each record, in which case the decision as to where to store the record could be made by:

```
SCHEMA NAME IS ACCOUNTS
  ACCESS-CONTROL LOCK IS DB-KEY

  AREA NAME IS CUST-AREA
    ACCESS-CONTROL LOCK IS CUST-KEY
  AREA NAME IS INV-AREA
    ACCESS-CONTROL LOCK IS INV-KEY

  RECORD NAME IS CUSTOMER
    LOCATION MODE IS CALC CUST-INDEX USING CUST-NO
IN  CUSTOMER
    DUPLICATES ARE NOT ALLOWED
    WITHIN CUST-AREA
    CUST-NO          NUMBER(7);
    CUST-SEX         NUMBER(1) CHECK IS VALUE 0 THRU 4;
    CUST-NAME        CHAR(20);
    CUST-ADD-1       CHAR(20);
    CUST-ADD-2       CHAR(20);
    CUST-ADD-CODE    CHAR(8);
    MARITAL-STATUS   NUMBER(1)
      ACCESS-CONTROL LOCK IS MARITAL-KEY;

  RECORD NAME INVESTMENTS
    LOCATION MODE IS CALC INV-INDEX USING
      INV-ACC-NO IN INVESTMENT
    DUPLICATES ARE NOT ALLOWED
    WITHIN INV-AREA
    INV-ACC-NO        NUMBER(10);
    INV-OPEN-BALANCE  NUMBER(8,2);
    INV-CURR-BALANCE  NUMBER (8,2);
  NO- OF-OWNERS       NUMBER(1) CHECK IS VALUE 1 THRU 4
  ACCOUNT-TYPE        NUMBER(2) CHECK IS TRAN-TYPES

  RECORD NAME IS INV-TRAN
    LOCATION MODE IS VIA I-T SET
    WITHIN INV-AREA
    ON STORE CALL IT-CHECK
    IT-NO            NUMBER(3);
    IT-DATE          NUMBER(6);
    IT-TYPE          NUMBER(2);
    IT-SOURCE        NUMBER(1);
    IT-AMOUNT        NUMBER(7,2);

  SET NAME IS CUST-INV
    OWNER IS CUSTOMER
    ORDER IS PERMANENT
    INSERTION IS FIRST
  MEMBER IS INVESTMENT FIXED AUTOMATIC
  SET SELECTION IS THRU CUST-INV OWNER IDENTIFIED BY
  CALC-KEY;

  SET NAME IS I-T
    OWNER IS INVESTMENT
    ORDER IS PERMANENT
    SORTED BY DEFINED KEYS
  MEMBER IS INV-TRAN FIXED AUTOMATIC
  SET SELECTION IS THRU I-T OWNER IDENTIFIED BY
  CALC-KEY;
```

Figure 10.3 An example of schema listing

- the DBMS,
- a DBA-written procedure,
- the application program storing the record.

This could be an important concept for larger files. For example, the investment file could quite easily be spread across several areas, and in which particular one a record is stored might depend on the account type which itself could be determined by either the second or the third of the above options.

As to what an area is in physical terms, this varies greatly from machine to machine. It is perhaps with the concept of an area that we see how much physical database design has encroached into the logical model, since it is related both to how and to where the record is to be stored.

As mentioned previously in Section 7.11, the AREA clause can also contain access-control locks.

RECORD entry

The main difference between the schema record definition and that of a COBOL record definition is the specification of a location mode to state how and/or where the record is to be stored (again a direct relationship with the physical data model).

An important concept in CODASYL is that of the database key. In theory this is defined as being the uniquely identifying key that distinguishes one record from any other. However, in CODASYL it is often synonymous with the physical address. At run time, a program can supply this key and hence gain fast and efficient access to the requested record.

The problem with the physical-address approach is that if the programmer obtained such a value and stored it as a data item for an application's usage, a subsequent restructure would change the physical address of the record but not that in the data item. Current DBTG proposals would mean that the database key is available to the programmer solely on a read-only basis and it cannot be moved or manipulated.

By bearing this in mind, there are four possible location modes.

1   DIRECT. Each record has a unique database key equating to the physical address that the program supplies when it wishes to access that record. The advantage is that a very quick access is afforded. The disadvantage is that a restructure necessitates program amendments.

2   CALC. A data item or group of data items within the record form the key, and this is passed through a hashing algorithm (Appendix A) to produce a physical address. This algorithm is either provided by the manufacturer or written by the DBA. This is probably the most common form of access method in CODASYL databases since it combines a relatively fast access method with physical data independence (the program does not need to know the physical location).

3   VIA. A record can be stored depending on its relationship with another record type (i.e. through a set). This is very useful for storing member records physically close to their owners and thus reducing I/O overheads.

4   SYSTEM. This access/storage method is by means of DBMS-supplied software. It is the default value if the DBA is not bothered how the record is to be stored or accessed, and leaves the decision to the DBMS.

Notes

1 There is no method of sequential access defined in LOCATION MODE.
2 It is important to realize that location modes are not the only access methods. A serial read can always be performed by a

FIND NEXT WITHIN Areaname

clause.

Duplicates

In most CODASYL databases it is possible to have two keys with the same value: for example, if a mortgage is covered by two endowment policies (as is often the case), the key for each occurrence of the endowment record would be the mortgage account number. If duplicate keys are not required then the DBA must specify

DUPLICATES ARE NOT ALLOWED

and the system will guarantee that no two records will be stored with the same key value.

On store

The ON STORE CALL procedure name can be used to invoke a pre-written procedure when the record is stored, and this is particularly useful for data validation. As with other CALLed procedures this one will be written by the DBA.

For example, if the possible values of an item are fixed then each can be assigned check values such as those for CUST-SEX and NO-OF-OWNERS, but if the values are likely to change (as are tax rates or hourly payments), then it is wiser to incorporate them into a procedure that can be readily changed without having to update the schema. In the schema example given, such a procedure might check that the:

* transaction number (IT-NO) is one higher than that of the last stored transaction,
* date is valid,
* account type has a correct value,
* source is valid,
* amount is within predefined limits.

Sets

The distinguishing feature of CODASYL databases is the set concept by which relationships between differing record types can be expressed. In general, only $1:n$ relationships can be represented directly using owners (1) and members (n), and the following rules apply.

1 A record type may be an owner in one or more set types (e.g. a customer can be an owner in both customer-mortgage and customer-investment sets).

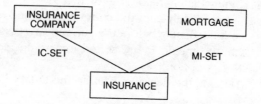

2   A record may be a member in one or more set types (e.g. an insurance record can belong to both an insurance company and a mortgage record).

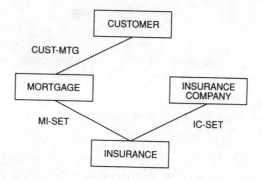

3   A record can be an owner in one or more set types and a member in one or more set types. This provision allows for true networking facilities.

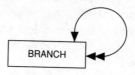

4   A set occurrence contains an owner and any number of member records (including none).

5   A record cannot be both an owner and a member in the same set type. This condition means that we cannot directly have

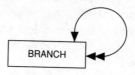

6   A record cannot appear in more than one occurrence of the same set type. This prevents, for example, a transaction belonging to more than one account at any one time.

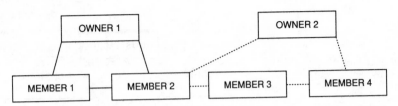

For every set defined, an ORDER IS clause must be specified to define where the DBMS is to insert a new member record when it is created (if the AUTOMATIC option is used; see later). The options are:

- FIRST, immediately after the owner;
- LAST, immediately before the owner;
- NEXT, immediately after the currently accessed record;
- PRIOR, immediately before the currently accessed record;
- SORTED, the members are sorted into some redefined ordering (via the KEY IS ASCENDING option);
- IMMATERIAL, the decision is left to the DBMS.

Some of these are shown on the following diagram:

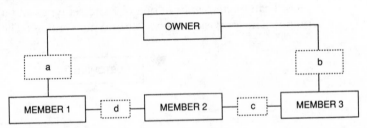

Again, DUPLICATES ARE NOT ALLOWED can be specified, usually with sorted sets, to prevent the duplication of sort keys.

Existence

The FIXED entry states that the particular occurrence of a member record can exist only in that particular set occurrence (i.e. it cannot be moved to another owner) and must be deleted from the entire database to remove it.

The second alternative is MANDATORY which means that the member can be removed from a set occurrence, but only to another occurrence of the same set type. For example, a member of staff could be moved to another branch, if desired, but they must belong to a branch somewhere.

The third option is OPTIONAL which means that the member can be moved to another set type, or not be associated with any set type. This would be useful at year-end when a transaction could be removed from the I-T set and be placed in a historic transaction set.

Insertion

The AUTOMATIC entry refers to how the record will be stored: in this case a new member will be inserted automatically into the set by using the guidelines of the

ORDER IS clause without need of a specific INSERT within the application program.

The alternative is MANUAL which implies that the insertion point within the set is determined by the application program (which must read through the members until it finds the required point).

Set selection

This clause states how a particular occurrence of a set is to be identified. There are many possibilities, of which only one is used in the example, namely OWNER IDENTI-FIED BY CALC KEY. This means that the application program will provide a key value for the CALC KEY routine. This format is often used when the member record does not itself contain the key of the owner record.

Another useful alternative is the OWNER IDENTIFIED BY CURRENT OF SET. If we have the example

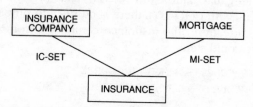

then having accessed the insurance record through the MI-SET, and then wishing to access the insurance company record, the rules defined dictate that each insurance record can belong to only a single insurance company record, and thus the required insurance company record will automatically be the owner of the insurance record. By using the pointers the insurance company record can be located.

Singular sets

The advantages of sets lie in the fact that the application program can navigate through all associated records in some predefined way by using pointers. It might also be considered advantageous to navigate through all customer records in some predefined manner, also by using pointers. From what has gone before, the only way to do this would be to define a new record type, called (for example) CUST-OWNER, that owns all customer records in a new set type. Unfortunately there exists no natural 'owner' of the customers. The way in which this is achieved in practice is usually to define a **singular set** which has the system as an owner. The system is a dummy owner that cannot be accessed as a normal record type. The set is called 'singular' because there is only one occurrence of the relationship.

Thus we could add to our schema definition

```
SET NAME IS CUSTS OWNER IS SYSTEM
  ORDER IS PERMANENT INSERTION LAST
MEMBER IS CUSTOMER FIXED AUTOMATIC
SET SELECTION IS THRU CUSTS SYSTEM;
```

Identifier

As a further step away from the equation

database key = physical address

CODASYL 78 has introduced the concept of identifiers. This equates to the candidate key concept of Section 4.15, the syntax being

```
IDENTIFIER IS INV-ACC-NO IN INVESTMENT
```

A record could have many, one or no such identifiers.

Source and results items

Although not mentioned in the example, CODASYL includes several other useful ideas. By referring back to the normalization process of Chapter 4, it was determined that the insurance record should be disjoint from the insurance company record, with the former containing a company code which was the key to the latter. It was also stated that, although this was data redundancy, it was at least a controlled redundancy. In CODASYL there is no need to physically store the same item twice. If it exists already in the insurance company record then within the insurance record itself we could state

```
01 CO-CODE IS VIRTUAL SOURCE IS
    COMPANY-CODE OF OWNER OF IC-SET
```

To an application program the CO-CODE appears actually to be stored in the insurance record and is made available as if it were. However, to physically obtain the value for CO-CODE, the DBMS must access the current owner of set IC-SET and find the value there. Again, there has to be a trade-off between storage space and possible duplication with inconsistencies, against an increase in I/O and processor times.

A second example of virtual items is as follows. Suppose that the insurance record contains a field called PREMIUM which is the yearly premium amount due. We could now define an item TOTAL-PREMIUM in the insurance company record as:

```
01 TOTAL-PREMIUM NUMBER(8,2) IS VIRTUAL
    RESULT OF ADD-PREMIUMS ON MEMBERS OF IC-SET;
```

ADD-PREMIUMS would be some pre-written procedure. No item TOTAL-PREMIUM is stored physically, but when a particular set occurrence is accessed, an item is created. The procedure ADD-PREMIUMS is then called and this reads through all the insurance (member) records, accumulating the PREMIUM amounts and finally storing the result in TOTAL-PREMIUM (in memory, not on disc) which can then be accessed by the application program (on a read-only basis, of course).

Note

If in this example it was necessary to store the field TOTAL-PREMIUM on disc, then it could be defined as above but using the term ACTUAL instead of VIRTUAL.

10.4   Subschemas

The application's view of the schema can be defined as a subschema such that a database will contain one or more subschemas (all implementations insist on at least one subschema even if that one defines the whole of the schema for a single application), with the possibility that a particular subschema could be shared by more than one application program. The various subschemas will not, in general, be disjoint. In particular, a subschema can omit (from the schema definition):

- one or more areas,
- one or more record types,
- one or more set types,
- one or more data items.

In addition, certain amendments to the schema definition are allowed:

- areas, sets, records and data items can be renamed in the subschema,
- access-control locks can be changed (affording different passwords for different users),
- the ordering of data items within a record can be changed,
- data items can be omitted,
- data items can be given different data types (for example, a NUMBER(8,2) can be redefined as a CHAR(8) in the subschema),
- different SET SELECTION clauses may be defined.

In general terms, the subschemas of a CODASYL database provide the logical data independence, as defined in Chapter 2, that is missing in non-database approaches.

At present, CODASYL subschemas are usually written in either COBOL- or FORTRAN-oriented languages.

COBOL subschema

Supposing that we have a schema as defined in Figure 10.3 and also that we have an application that reads through the investment file and checks the current balance (INV-CURR-BALANCE) against the sum of all of the transaction amounts added to the opening balance (INV-OPEN-BALANCE); whether the amount is actually added to or subtracted from the total depends on the value of the transaction type (IT-TYPE). For this application we could define a subschema similar to that shown in Figure 10.4.

We have thus defined everything that the particular application requires (in fact if we had defined a virtual item TRANS-AMOUNT-TOT within investments and had written a subroutine as described previously, then there would be no need to have the program other than to print out discrepancies). If any other database items change via a restructure, then this program would not be affected (i.e. it is as logically data independent as it can be).

TITLE DIVISION

This is used to give the subschema a name (which must be unique) and to state to which database it belongs.

MAPPING DIVISION

This is used to give any alternative names that might be used. Thus long self-explanatory names within the schema definition can be shortened for the programmer's convenience.

```
        TITLE DIVISION
        SS BALANCE-CHECK WITHIN ACCOUNTS


        MAPPING DIVISION
        ALIAS SECTION
        AD INVESTMENTS BECOMES INVS
        AD INV-TRAN BECOMES TRANS


        STRUCTURE DIVISION
        REALM SECTION
        RD INV-AREA
        SET SECTION
        SD I-T
        RECORD SECTION
        01 INVS
           03 INV-ACC-NO        PIC 9(10)
           03 INV-OPEN-BALANCE  PIC 9(6)V99
           03  INV-CURR-BALANCE PIC 9(6)V99
        01 TRANS
           03 IT-TYPE           PIC 99
           03 IT-AMOUNT         PIC 9(5)V99
```

Figure 10.4 An example of COBOL subschema listing

STRUCTURE DIVISION

Within this division, which is used to define the logical structure of the subschema, are the:

1 REALM SECTION; because 'area' is a reserved word in COBOL, the word realm has to be used as a synonym in the subschema definition; a realm does not have exactly the same connotations as the schema's area because it can contain subsets of the records in one or more areas;
2 SET SECTION which names the required acts;
3 RECORD SECTION which describes the records and data items to be used within the subschema.

Note

The FORTRAN subschema (not described here) affords very similar features but for one major difference. In COBOL, access-control locks can be specified in the schema definition, and these will take priority over any conflicting locks specified in the schema definition. In the FORTRAN subschema, the reverse is true.

10.5 Data manipulation language

As mentioned previously, the CODASYL approach to data manipulation language (DML) is one of a host language (i.e. extensions to an existing language, in this case usually COBOL or FORTRAN). Before defining the various extension verbs, it is important to grasp the concept of currency, which forms a central part of the CODA-SYL DML philosophy.

Currency

Since a database is likely to be composed of many record occurrences and many set occurrences, it is important that the DBMS can keep track of where an application program is with respect to the database at any one moment. The basic concept of currency therefore is that the database key of the current record is stored.

This concept extends to other portions of the database. In particular, currency status indicators are maintained for the following:

1 **realm**, for each realm accessed by a program, the most recently accessed record within that realm is termed the **current of realm**;
2 **record type**, for each record type accessed, the most recently accessed is termed **current of record**;
3 **set type**, for each set type accessed, the most recently accessed owner or member is termed **current of set**; this is because a set itself does not have a database key but, by bearing in mind the rules for sets (the Sets subsection in Section 10.3), either an owner or a member will identify uniquely a particular set occurrence;
4 **any record**, the most recently accessed record of any description is termed **current of program**. (In CODASYL terminology, a program is often alternatively termed a 'run unit'.)

The other important concept is one of a DBERROR or DBSTATUS by which an error code can be passed back to the application program so that appropriate action can be taken. A typical implementation would be a four-digit code, of which the first two digits would specify the DML verb being used at the time of the error and the last two digits would be a subcategory of that error.

10.6 DML verbs

ACCEPT

This is similar in principle to the normal COBOL ACCEPT statement. In DML it allows a program to read into its user work area any of the currency-status indicators (clearly on a read-only basis). For example, if a record R has just been stored and the program wishes to note exactly what database key has been assigned to that record, then it can use

```
STORE R.
ACCEPT WS-RKEY FROM (CHOICE) CURRENCY.
```

where (CHOICE) is the realm name, record name or set name of the required currency indicator. The data item WS-RKEY (or whatever) must have been declared with a USAGE IS DB-KEY clause.

BEGIN-TRANSACTION (START-TRANSACTION)

This verb is usually used to specify that a transaction (update) to the database is about to take place. This is a very useful function for reasons stated in Chapter 7.

CLEAR

As mentioned previously, not all database management systems zeroize the error-status field after the next successful database instruction. To avoid possible confusion, therefore, the task must be performed by the application program. For example:

```
IF DBERROR > 0 PERFORM CHECK-ERROR-TYPE
            CLEAR DBERROR.
```

Note that the actual data item DBERROR can have different names on different systems.

CONNECT (INSERT)

Suppose that we have just created an investment record and wish to relate it to an existing customer record (i.e. place it in the set CUST-INV). To be able to do this we need three operations:

```
1   FIND CUSTOMER
2   FIND INVESTMENT
3   CONNECT INVESTMENT TO CUST-INV
```

Note that the set CUST-INV will normally have been specified as MANUAL. If it was specified as AUTOMATIC the DBMS itself would have inserted the new record in accordance with the ORDER IS option.

DISCONNECT (REMOVE)

This statement (not surprisingly) does the opposite to the connect verb. If we wished to remove an investment record from an occurrence of the CUST-INV set we could use:

```
1   FIND CUSTOMER
2   FIND INVESTMENT
3   DISCONNECT INVESTMENT FROM CUST-INV
```

With this done, then the investment record can still exist within the database if CUST-INV is specified as OPTIONAL.

END-TRANSACTION

Used to signal that the update to the database has been completed by the application.

ERASE (DELETE)

This option is used basically for deleting records. There are three possible sub-options:

```
FIND INVESTMENT
ERASE INVESTMENT      {PERMANENT}
                      {SELECTIVE}
                      {ALL}
```

- If no qualification is specified, then the investment record will be deleted only if it is the owner of no member records in any set occurrence, otherwise an error is returned.
- If PERMANENT is used then the investment record is deleted along with any MANDATORY and FIXED members for which the investment is an owner in all set occurrences. Note that OPTIONAL members will only be removed from the set occurrence and not deleted from the database.
- If SELECTIVE is employed, then the effect is the same as that when PERMANENT is used except that OPTIONAL members are also deleted, but then only if they are not members of other set types.
- If ALL is specified then the investment record and all of its members are deleted, no matter what their standing.

It is important to note that if any deleted members are themselves owners, then the same ERASE statement applies to their members and so on. Thus great care must be taken! With a complex network database it is possible to delete half of the database (or more) with a single ERASE statement. If ERASE is used then the current of program is set to null. No other currency indicators are affected.

FETCH (OBTAIN)

This combines a FIND and GET (see subsections following) into a single statement. Thus

```
MOVE 1234567890 TO INV-ACC-NO.
FETCH ANY INVESTMENT.
```

FIND

This is the most complicated DML statement because there are several distinct possibilities. For all options the FIND locates a particular record in the database and makes it the current of program, current of realm, current of record type and current of all set types in which the record participates. The options are as follows.

Direct access

```
FIND INVESTMENT DB-KEY IS INV-KEY
```

In this statement INV-KEY is a program data item (i.e. in the Data Division of the COBOL program and not in the database) which has been declared as USAGE IS DB-KEY. At the time the above statement is executed the program must have placed a valid database key into that item.

CALC key access

```
MOVE 1382941603 TO INV-ACC-NO.
FIND ANY INVESTMENT.
```

Here the key field INV-ACC-NO must appear within the relevant subschema. The DBMS applies its hashing function to the key value to provide a physical address where the record is located.

Linear searching

Suppose that there existed a need to scan through all transactions for a particular account, adding the individual amounts together in passing. We could use

```
MOVE 1384216803 TO INV-ACC-NO.
FIND ANY INVESTMENT.
FIND NEXT INV-TRAN WITHIN I-T.
IF    I-T EMPTY PERFORM NO-TRANSACTIONS
        ELSE PERFORM LOOP UNTIL END-OF-SET.
LOOP.
... processing ...
FIND NEXT INV-TRAN WITHIN I-T.
```

Before the first FIND NEXT statement, the current of set I-T will be the investment. Thus a FIND NEXT will locate the first transaction. The word NEXT can be replaced by PRIOR, FIRST, LAST, an integer or the name of a data item having an integer value. In the last two cases, a positive number indicates the number of occurrences of the transactions to be read in a NEXT context, and a negative number would be the equivalent for the PRIOR. Thus if we knew that the transaction we required was the third from the end, then we could specify

```
FIND -3 INV-TRAN WITHIN I-T
```

(This of course assumes that backward pointers are available.)

Current record

This is used to make the current of a set the current of program (which may not necessarily already be the case).

By assuming the current of I-T to be a transaction and not the investment:

```
FIND CURRENT INV-TRAN WITHIN I-T
```

This situation would be possible if, for example, we had found an investment, found the relevant transaction, and then gone off to read the customer record. This would make the transaction the current of set but the customer would be current of program. The latter could revert to the transaction by using the above. In a sense, this is not a true FIND because the record had been found already: it is merely a means of updating currency indicators.

Find owner

If the current of program was an investment record and we wished to find its owner customer record (in the CUST-INV set), then we could use

```
FIND OWNER WITHIN CUST-INV.
```

Another linear search

To illustrate this mechanism, the example must be changed to that of the insurance company and mortgage records that both own insurance records via the IC-SET and the MI-SET respectively.

Suppose that we wished to find the premium on the contents record for company 014 for mortgage number 9876543211. Clearly, we could either find the mortgage record and scan the MI-SET until we found the contents record with insurance company code 014, or we could find the insurance company record and scan the insurance records through the IC-SET. In this instance, the former would be far more efficient in general, because the mortgage will own fewer insurance records than the company.

Thus we could use:

```
MOVE 9876543211 TO MTG-ACC-NO.
FIND ANY MORTGAGE.
IF MI-SET EMPTY GO NO-INSURANCES.
MOVE 014 TO IC-CODE IN INSURANCE.
FIND INSURANCE WITHIN MI-SET CURRENT
USING
   IC-CODE IN INSURANCE.
```

If CURRENT is omitted from this example then the SET SELECTION statement would be performed. There are other possible variations on the FIND statement but they will not be discussed here.

FINISH (CLOSE)

When a program has finished work on a particular realm, it is most efficient if it releases that realm for use by other programs. Thus:

```
FINISH INV-AREA.
```

FREE

This statement nullifies a KEEP statement (see the subsection following).

GET

We have already looked at the FIND verb which locates a required record, but does not return it to the user work area (UWA), although the outcome of the FIND can be checked (i.e. a NOTFOUND condition would be returned to the program). To obtain the record, the program must contain a GET verb. Thus

```
MOVE 1234567890 TO INV-ACC-NO.
FIND ANY INVESTMENT.
IF NOTFOUND GO NO-FOUND.
GET INVESTMENT.
```

In this example, the final noun INVESTMENT is superfluous, because GET acts on the current of program (i.e. just GET would have sufficed).

KEEP

Some CODASYL systems allow concurrency by placing the onus on the application program to maintain integrity. In this situation, the current of program is said to exist in a 'monitored mode'. If a second program wishes to update a record after it has become current of the first program, then the first program will terminate with an error. In other words, MONITOR is as it sounds and not a locking device. The monitored mode ends when a record ceases to be current of program. However, a program may extend monitored mode by KEEPing the record until it is explicitly FREEd.

If a program requires a set of records for a set of consistent updates, then it could FIND all records and KEEP them until it has finished. However, if while doing this one of them is updated by another program, an error will occur. To prevent this happening a REMONITOR command can be used which effectively KEEPs all the desired records, but only after the last has been accessed.

The general idea behind this old-fashioned method of allowing concurrency (generally used before page locking became common practice), is that a program using KEEP and/or REMONITOR can detect whether a record, that it has obtained as current of program, has been updated by another program since that time and can act accordingly, that is, it can decide whether to terminate or simply to reread the record. This prevents the possible loss of integrity problem outlined in Section 1.7, although the onus is on the application program. Normally the DBMS will lock all required records at the time of the execution of the BEGIN-TRANSACTION.

MODIFY

This verb is used to alter existing records within the database. For example:

```
FETCH INVESTMENT.
ADD TRANS-AMT TO INV-CURR-BALANCE.
MODIFY INVESTMENT.
```

Thus the record must have been found previously, moved into the UWA and updated, and then MODIFY stores the record back on to the database. If MODIFY specifies a record name then the entire record is written. Alternatively, if MODIFY specifies certain data items then only those items are replaced. Thus, in the example, the same effect could have been achieved by using

```
MODIFY INV-CURR-BALANCE.
```

ORDER

The ORDER statement can be used to impose a new ordering on the member records of the current occurrence of a particular set. This can only be done if the program has exclusive retrieval or protected retrieval declared against the relevant realm (see 10.9). For example, if ORDER IS SORTED is specified in the schema definition, then an application program could use

```
ORDER I-T LOCALLY ON ASCENDING KEY IT-TYPE IN INV-TRAN.
```

Note
The change is only temporary and the ordering reverts to its original state whenever the realm is FINISHed.

READY (OPEN)

Before a program can use a realm it must READY it and declare its required usage type. This can be one of the following:

```
UPDATE
RETRIEVAL
UPDATE EXCLUSIVE
UPDATE PROTECTED
RETRIEVAL EXCLUSIVE
RETRIEVAL PROTECTED
```

The differences between these are highlighted in Section 10.9 following. An example would be

```
READY INV-AREA USAGE-MODE IS RETRIEVAL.
```

STORE

This command is used to create a record occurrence (as opposed to MODIFY which is used to change an existing record). Thus to create a transaction record we would use

```
MOVE 15 TO IT-NO.
MOVE 010786 TO IT-DATE.
MOVE 37 TO IT-TYPE.
MOVE 2 TO IT-SOURCE.
MOVE 26.38 TO IT-AMOUNT.
MOVE 1234567890 TO INV-ACC-NO.
FETCH ANY INVESTMENT.
STORE INV-TRAN.
```

The seventh line is necessary because the set I-T was declared as AUTOMATIC which means that when an INV-TRAN is stored the DBMS will store it automatically within the I-T set, and therefore the correct investment must be identified and fetched.

USE

This DML statement implies usage of named procedures, perhaps to action database error reporting or to control privacy locks or validation routines. For example:

```
IF I-T EMPTY USE NO-TRANS-ERROR.
```

An example

It is perhaps difficult to visualize the construction of a DML program without a full example to reference. For that reason an example is given in Figure 10.5, the program in question being one that checks through all investment transactions, checking the balance against that stored on the investment record itself.

Please note that the program is not structured in a program-design sense, and also that the syntax is not standard across all computers employing CODASYL products. The subschema does not appear in the listing but would be invoked in the subschema section by a precompiler or during the compilation itself. It is, however, the same format as that described in the COBOL subschema subsection in Section 10.4.

```
                    IDENTIFICATION DIVISION.
                    PROGRAM-ID.  INV/01.
                    ENVIRONMENT DIVISION.
                    INPUT-OUTPUT SECTION.
                    FILE-CONTROL.
                      SELECT PRINTOUT ASSIGN PRINTER.
                    DATA DIVISION.
                    SUBSCHEMA SECTION.
                    DB BALANCE-CHECK WITHIN ACCOUNTS.
                    FILE SECTION.
                    FD PRINTOUT.
                    01 P-LINE          PIC X(132).
                    01 PR-LINE.
                       03 ACC-NO       PIC 9(10).
                       03 FILLER       PIC X(5).
                       03 ACTUAL-AMT   PIC Z(5)9.99.
                       03 FILLER       PIC X(5).
                       03 CALC-AMT     PIC Z(5)9.99.
                       03 FILLER       PIC X(96).
                    WORKING-STORAGE SECTION.
                    01 CALC-TOTAL      PIC 9(6)V99.
                    PROCEDURE DIVISION.
                    OPEN-UP.
                      OPEN OUTPUT PRINTOUT.
                      READY INV-AREA USAGE-MODE IS PROTECTED
                    RETRIEVAL.
                      FIND FIRST INVESTMENT WITHIN INV-AREA.
                      GO GET-INV.
                    INV-LOOP.
                      FIND NEXT INVESTMENT WITHIN INV-AREA.
                      IF END-OF-FILE GO CLOSE-DOWN.
                    GET-INV.
                      GET INV-ACC-NO INV-OPEN-BALANCE INV-CURR-BALANCE.
                      MOVE INV-OPEN-BALANCE TO CALC-TOTAL.
                    TRAN-LOOP.
                      FIND NEXT INV-TRAN WITHIN I-T.
                      IF END-OF-SET GO CHECK-BAL.
                      GET IT-TYPE IT-AMOUNT.
                      IF IT-TYPE < 20 ADD IT-AMOUNT TO CALC-TOTAL
                        ELSE SUBTRACT IT-AMOUNT FROM CALC-TOTAL.
                      GO TRAN-LOOP.
                    CHECK-BAL.
                      CLEAR DBSTATUS.
                      IF CALC-TOTAL = INV-CURR-BALANCE GO INV-LOOP.
                      MOVE SPACES TO P-LINE.
                      MOVE INV-ACC-NO TO ACC-NO.
                      MOVE INV-CURR-BALANCE TO ACTUAL-AMT.
                      MOVE CALC-TOTAL TO CALC-AMT.
                      WRITE P-LINE BEFORE 1.
                      GO INV-LOOP.
                    CLOSE-DOWN.
                      FINISH INV-AREA.
                      CLOSE PRINTOUT.
                      STOP RUN.
```

Figure 10.5 An example of a COBOL host language program

Note:

The actual numerical values of DBSTATUS implying end-of-file or end-of-set vary enormously from machine to machine.

10.7   Data storage description language

As mentioned previously, the CODASYL 78 report introduced a separate language for the storage model which was to become independent of the logical model.

By referring back to the schema definition in Section 10.3, it is of particular note that:

- a database key relates to how and where a record is to be stored, literally if it is a physical address itself;
- location mode clauses are concerned with how a record is to be stored and accessed;
- virtual or actual clauses state how a record is to be derived and from where (thus giving them physical data dependence).

Not surprisingly, CODASYL 78 has sought to remove these from the DDL. Instead, within the DSDL, it has implemented the following three constructs.

- A storage record. This is 'a variable length addressable container for data and pointers associated with a single schema record'. Basically, what this entails is a $1:n$ mapping with each storage record relating to a single schema record, but one schema record possibly producing many storage records.
- A mapping that is defined by a MAPPING DESCRIPTION entry and is the mapping between schema and storage records. If the mapping is $1:n$ then the storage records for a particular schema record may overlap with duplication of data items. The DBMS will be able to control such duplication (e.g. a mortgage record could be stored in two parts, one current data and one historic data, but each might contain the account number, customer number, etc.).
- An index that is defined as 'a set structure which supports access paths to storage records'.

There is no mention of set storage constructs in the CODASYL 78 report. Any set associations are defined via pointers and indexes in the storage record definition. In particular, location mode has been replaced by a PLACEMENT clause for which there are three possible values:

- RANDOM used for quick accessing,
- SEQUENTIAL used for accessing by key sequence and randomly,
- CLUSTERED used for storage of associated records on the same or adjacent pages.

10.8   Privacy

In a CODASYL database all access to the data must be done through subschemas (except for query languages – see Chapter 8), which themselves afford a considerable amount of access control. The DBA can allocate a subschema to an application program which contains exactly what the application wants (or is allowed to see). In addition, the DBA can also specify access-control locks at the schema, realm, set, record and data-item levels, and it is possible for different locks to be applied for different users (through the use of subroutines). It is also possible to set different locks for different operations (e.g. insert, remove, delete, etc.).

At the schema level the functions that can be controlled are ALTER (updating facilities), DISPLAY (read-only), LOCKS (displaying the access-control locks in the schema) and COPY (to define a subschema).

At the other levels, the possibilities are:

```
SUBSCHEMA    ALTER DISPLAY LOCKS
             COMPILE
AREA         RETRIEVAL (PROTECTED OR EXCLUSIVE)
             UPDATE    (PROTECTED OR EXCLUSIVE)
RECORD       DELETE FIND GET INSERT MODIFY
             REMOVE STORE
SET          FIND INSERT ORDER REMOVE
DATA ITEM    GET MODIFY STORE
```

For all these possibilities, the relevant access-control key must be supplied by the application program before the function can be performed.

Note

The COMPILE subschema option simply implies the ability to invoke the subschema at compilation time.

10.9   Integrity

The last section dealt with how access-control locks can be used to maintain privacy (and hence maintain that aspect of integrity). The DBA can also define various validation procedures that can be invoked (usually at the time of a STORE or MODIFY) to check that the content of the current record obeys predefined rules. These procedures can be CALLed either by the application or by the DBMS (if they are defined in the schema).

Loss of integrity by concurrent updating can be avoided by the USAGE-MODE clause as outlined in the previous section. The meanings of EXCLUSIVE and PROTECTED are as follows:

- EXCLUSIVE means that once a program has used READY on a realm in exclusive mode, no other program can READY that realm (and thereby use it), be it for update or retrieval.
- PROTECTED means the same except that other programs may READY the same realm for retrieval only.

A program that has readied a realm for UPDATE or RETRIEVAL only (i.e. without the EXCLUSIVE or PROTECTED clauses) must cater for the fact that another program may be updating the same realm at the same time. In this instance, the DBMS uses the notify protocol to inform the program if, after it has made a record current of program, another program updates that record (see the KEEP subsection in Section 10.6).

Such a system has come under severe criticism because there is no locking mechanism and no guarantee that integrity cannot be lost if the programs have been written badly. For this reason, most CODASYL implementations have taken to realm/page/record locking as an alternative and, since this is a far neater and safer methodology (the onus for maintaining integrity is placed on the DBMS), this trend is likely to continue.

10.10   Restructure/reorganization

It is perhaps in this area that the CODASYL implementations have been traditionally weak. Because of the complex relationships afforded by a network model, in particular the reliance on database keys as physical addresses and physical-address pointers, it is often very difficult to restructure a file without having to 'fix up' the pointers of all related record types.

The result of this is that too often large parts of the database have to be dumped to backup medium by program, the database restructured and then the data reloaded (i.e. recreated) in its new format by another user-written program.

For example, in our customers–investments–transactions network, if we wished to restructure investments we would have to bear in mind that pointers exist on both customer and transaction records that are dependent on the physical location of an investment record. If the latter are moved physically, as they would be in either a restructure or a reorganize, then the related pointers would need to be changed. To do this we would need to:

1   dump the investment records logically;
2   delete all investments, leaving all occurrences of CUST-INV empty, and leaving all transactions without owners (only possible if I-T is OPTIONAL which is not what we would normally want);
3   restructure investments;
4   reload the investments and hope to patch them into the relevant CUST-INV occurrences along with all their related transactions – a process that is not easy when each transaction does not have a unique identifying key (the reason it does not is that it is not needed in a network model).

By bearing these factors in mind it would be condonable to:

1   dump customers, investments and transactions logically;
2   restructure;
3   reload and recreate all three (assuming that they were dumped in such a way as would facilitate this).

Those of you who are observant will have realized that the customers also are connected physically to the mortgages which are connected to their own transactions, insurances, endowments, and so on. Therefore we cannot dump and delete customers without mortgages and, by extension, nearly every other file on the database.

These problems stated, it must also be said that CODASYL is currently working on a common restructuring language which hopefully will alleviate these problems when it is implemented.

11

Relational databases

11.1 Basic concepts

Relational databases involve data being stored in tables, subject to the following rules and definitions.

Rules

1　Each position in the table contains a single value.
2　All positions in the same column are of the same kind.
3　Each column is distinct (i.e. has a distinct name).
4　Every row in the table is unique (i.e. there are no two rows that contain identical values).
5　The ordering of the rows and columns is not significant.

Definitions

1　The set of all tables is the **data model** (equivalent to the database in CODASYL).
2　A single table is called a **relation**.
3　A single row in the table is called a **tuple** (equivalent to a record).
4　The number of tuples in a relation is termed the **cardinality** of the relation.
5　The columns of the relation are termed **attributes**.
6　An individual item of data is called a **component**.
7　The number of components in a tuple (and hence attributes in a relation) is termed the **degree of the relation**.
8　The set of all possible attribute values compose a **domain**.

An example (Figure 11.1) is used to illustrate these definitions, and the same example will be used throughout Chapters 11–13. For brevity, only a few attributes for each real-world entity have been used (except for CUSTINV) and the account number has been reduced to five digits. In this example we have a single data model comprising three relations: investment, customer and CUSTINV, the intersection entity between the many-to-many relationship. Studying the investment relation in particular, we have:

1　a cardinality of six tuples,
2　five attributes,
3　the degree of investment is thus five,

ACCNO	ACCTYPE	DATE OPENED	BALANCE	BRANCH
14682	1	12-MAY-92	60.85	101
15214	6	23-JAN-97	482.20	104
13852	4	02-NOV-94	4.25	103
19651	6	14-SEP-95	1625.00	107
13173	1	16-JUN-96	184.00	101
12745	5	30-MAY-94	742.58	104

INVESTMENT relation

CUSTNO	SURNAME	STREET	TOWN
46	WILLIAMS	15 BULL LANE	PRESTON
17	KING	17 CEDAR DRIVE	WIGAN
23	STEVENS	48 STANLEY RD	STOKE
82	DAVIES	14 FIELDING ST	BRADFORD
12	BARNARD	18 FYLDE RD	BLACKPOOL
29	JENKINS	12 PLOUGH LANE	PRESTON

CUSTOMER relation

CUSTNUM	ACCNO	POSITION
12	15214	1
17	19651	1
17	12745	2
23	19651	2
46	12745	1
46	13173	1
46	14682	2
82	14682	1
82	13852	1

CUSTINV relation

Figure 11.1 Example relations

4   the domain of DATE_OPENED is all the possible values (presumably excluding
    Sundays).

It must be noted that there is a distinct element of data redundancy here: the investment account number appears in two separate places, as does the customer number.
The reason for this is that relational databases have no physical pointers acting as
links such as those that appear in network models. Associations between different
relations are shown by there being common attributes, and all tuple accessing and
data manipulation are based on this commonality, as will be seen. It is of interest to
note that an involuted relationship (an entity related to itself) can be expressed within
the relational model. For example, branches are controlled by area offices which are
themselves branches, as shown in Figure 11.2.

```
        AREA          BRANCH
        BRANCH

        101           101
        101           102
        101           103
        104           104
        104           105
        106           106
        106           107
```

Figure 11.2 An involuted relationship (the area-branch/branch relation) as a single relation

11.2   Normalization

At this stage we must return to normalization (though perhaps 'return' is the wrong word, as the process of normalization was developed by E. F. Codd for work on relations and only later adapted for other database systems).

The only rule for relations is that: every attribute value in each tuple is atomic (i.e. cannot be broken down further).

What this means basically is that each attribute within a tuple must consist of a single item and not a group of items. Thus our CUSTINV relation in unnormalized form would be as shown in Figure 11.3.

```
        ACCNO     CUST NO & POSITION

        14682     82   1    46   2
        15214     12   1
        13852     82   1
        19651     17   1    23   2
        13173     46   1
        12745     46   1    17   2
```

Figure 11.3 An unnormalized relation

11.3   Keys

A **candidate key** is defined as being an attribute or set of attributes which uniquely identify tuples in a relation. Thus ACCNO is a candidate key for the investment relation as is (ACCNO, ACCTYPE) or (ACCNO, DATE_OPENED). Clearly, in this example, ACCNO is common to all candidate keys and itself identifies uniquely a tuple. This is therefore termed the *prime key*.

The attribute ACCNO would not uniquely identify a CUSTINV tuple. For this we would need (ACCNO, CUSTNUM). That there must be at least one key is shown by rule (4) in Section 11.1 which states that each tuple must be unique. Therefore we are guaranteed a primary key even if it consists of every attribute in the tuple.

When there are two candidate keys, each containing no superfluous attributes (for example, CUSTNO and SURNAME/STREET/TOWN), we would arbitrarily choose one to be the primary key; in this case we might choose CUSTNO because it is shorter although the other has the advantage of being more meaningful and 'easier to remember in the outside world'.

An attribute, or group of attributes, of a relation A is termed a **foreign key** if it is not the primary key of A but its values are the values of the primary key of some other relation B. An example exists in the CUSTINV relation. The attribute CUSTNUM is a foreign key because its values correspond with those of the primary key of the relation CUSTOMER. For similar reasons, ACCNO is a foreign key.

Foreign keys are an important part of relational databases as they help to maintain integrity (see Section 12.3). We would not wish to be able to create a CUSTINV record if either the customer or the account did not already exist.

11.4   Data definition language

Suppose that we wished to implement the data model shown in Figure 11.1 as a relational database. An example of the data definition language might be as shown in Figure 11.4. It is noteworthy that by declaring domains we can include check value

```
DOMAIN    ACCNO          NUMBER(5)
DOMAIN    ACCTYPE        NUMBER(1)
DOMAIN    DATE_OPENED    DATE
DOMAIN    BALANCE        NUMBER(6,2)
DOMAIN    BRANCH         NUMBER(3)
DOMAIN    CUSTNO         NUMBER(5)
DOMAIN    SURNAME        CHAR(15)
DOMAIN    STREET         CHAR(20)
DOMAIN    TOWN           CHAR(15)
DOMAIN    POSITION       NUMBER(1)

RELATION INVESTMENT(
    ACCNO,
    ACCTYPE,
    DATE_OPENED,
    BALANCE,
    BRANCH)
RELATION CUSTOMER(
    CUSTNO,
    SURNAME,
    STREET,
    TOWN)
RELATION CUSTINV(
    CUSTNUM  DOMAIN CUSTNO,
    ACCNO,
    POSITION)
```

Figure 11.4 An example relational database definition language

controls. This is similar to CODASYL, except that the declarations are not specific to any record type but are specific to certain attributes that may be common across several relations.

Also of note is the fact that within the relation declaration, attribute names can be changed. This is a consequence of being able to have many different attributes belonging to the same domain. For example, if we were to have a domain called simply DATE and it was subject to the restriction that the day and the month were valid, then we could have within it various relations (for a fuller data model):

```
DATE_OF_BIRTH      DOMAIN DATE
DATE_OPENED        DOMAIN DATE
TRANSACTION_DATE   DOMAIN DATE.
```

The syntax of the above example is not standard simply because there is no standard syntax for relational databases. There is no mention of key items in this example (although some relational languages do allow for their definition). This is not of great consequence because keys represent neither physical database keys nor necessarily separate structures (such as indexes) and, as will be seen in the next two sections, the user can navigate the relations without using keys at all.

11.5 Relational algebra as a data sublanguage

The relational algebra approach to data manipulation is based on two parts. The first is traditional set theory involving unions, intersections, differences and Cartesian products, and the second is special relational operators such as select, project and join. Both components are described below.

1 Traditional set theory can be extended to cover relations if the relations are **union compatible** for at least the first three definitions below. This means that the relations must be of the same degree and that the corresponding attributes must be from the same domain (i.e. one relation cannot have a year whose domain is 83, 84 and another have a year whose domain is 85, 86).

   (a) The **union** of two relations X and Y, written as $X \cup Y$ or X union Y in relational algebra, is the set of tuples belonging to either X or Y or both. This set of tuples itself forms a relation.

   (b) The **intersection** of two relations X and Y, written $X \cap Y$ or X intersection Y, is the set of tuples belonging to both X and Y.

   (c) The **difference** between two relations X and Y, written $X - Y$ or X minus Y, is the set of tuples belonging to X that do not belong to Y.

   (d) The **Cartesian product** (or simply **product**) of two relations X and Y, written as $X \times Y$ or X times Y, is the set of tuples such that each tuple is the concatenation of a tuple belonging to X with a tuple belonging to Y, and such that the set contains all such tuples. For example, if X = [Xl, X2] and Y = [Yl, Y2] then the Cartesian product would be:

   $$X \times Y = ([X1,Y1], [X1,Y2], [X2,Y1], [X2,Y2])$$

2 To illustrate the special operators needed, the relations customer and custinv as shown in Figure 11.1 will be used.

(a) SELECT is an operator used for constructing a subset of tuples for which a given condition is true. For example,
- SELECT CUSTOMER WHERE TOWN = 'PRESTON' would give full customer details for Williams and Jenkins.
- SELECT CUSTINV WHERE POSITION = 2 would give

```
17  12745  2
23  19651  2
46  14682  2
```

(b) The PROJECT operator is used for construction of a subset of attributes. Any duplicates are not shown. For example,

PROJECT CUSTOMER OVER SURNAME would give a list of all the surnames (and no other customer details)

(c) The JOIN operation can be used to combine two relations as, for example,

JOIN CUSTOMER AND CUSTINV OVER CUSTNO to give

```
46  WILLIAMS   15  BULL LANE     PRESTON   46   12745   1
46  WILLIAMS   15  BULL LANE     PRESTON   46   13173   1
46  WILLIAMS   15  BULL LANE     PRESTON   46   14682   2
17  KING       17  CEDAR DRIVE   WIGAN     17   19651   1
17  KING       17  CEDAR DRIVE   WIGAN     17   12745   2
```

and so on.

Note

Customer 29 would not appear on this list as they do not appear on any CUSTINV tuples. Note also that there is a degree of redundancy here, the customer number appearing twice. In most implementations of relational databases redundant items would not appear in the result.

The OVER CUSTNO refers to the attribute common to both relations on which the system can make a comparison (although the attribute names are different, CUSTNO and CUSTNUM, they belong to the same domain). Alternatively, we could have used:

JOIN CUSTOMER AND CUSTINV WHERE CUSTNO = CUSTNUM

(d) The only way to illustrate the divide operation is to give an example and then explain what has taken place.

PROJECT CUSTINV OVER CUSTNUM ACCNO GIVING SS
DIVIDE SS BY 17 OVER CUSTNUM

The result would be

```
19651
12745
```

Note the use of naming the intermediate result (SS here), which is itself a relation (though only temporary), so that it can be used in subsequent operations.

Explanation

In its simplest form we are dividing a relation of degree 2 by a relation of degree 1 to give a result of degree 1. Both dividend and divisor must have an attribute belonging to a common domain. If we were to generalize and define the dividend as (X, Y) and the divisor (Z) where Y and Z are of a common domain, then the result would be those X values whose corresponding Y values include every component of the divisor (Z).

What would be the result, then, if we were to:

```
DIVIDE CUSTINV BY (17,23) OVER CUSTNUM
```

Here, the result would be all occurrences of ACCNO where the CUSTNUM is 17 and 23, namely 19651.

11.6   Retrieval by using relational algebra

From the definitions of the previous section and the relational database as described in Figure 11.1, the next stage is to look at some examples of data retrieval.

1   Obtain the account numbers of all customers who are second named

```
SELECT CUSTINV WHERE POSITION = 2 GIVING R1
PROJECT R1 OVER ACCNO GIVING RESULT
```

Note that it is possible to combine the above two statements. Thus:

```
PROJECT (SELECT CUSTINV WHERE POSITION = 2) OVER ACCNO GIVING
RESULT.
```

2   What are the names of the customers who have an account type of 6?

```
SELECT INVESTMENT WHERE ACCTYPE = 6 GIVING R1
PROJECT R1 OVER ACCNO GIVING R2
JOIN R2 AND CUSTINV OVER ACCNO GIVING R3
JOIN CUSTOMER AND R3 OVER CUSTNO GIVING R4
PROJECT R4 OVER SURNAME GIVING RESULT
```

As with example (1), these five statements could be combined into one by the use of parentheses, but the result would be less understandable to the human eye despite producing a faster turn-round of results.

In general, the more complicated the required process, the more ways there are of actually achieving the goal by combining different statements in different orders. Clearly, some will be less efficient than others.

11.7   Storage by using relational algebra

Insertion and deletion as operations on a relation are performed relatively easily by use of the union and minus operations. For example:

1   Add a new CUSTOMER tuple where CUSTNO = 32, NAME = 'EVANS', STREET = '41 TOWN WALK', TOWN = 'DUNSTABLE':

```
CUSTOMER U (32, 'EVANS', '41 TOWN WALK', 'DUNSTABLE') GIVING CUS-
TOMER
```

2   Delete a CUSTOMER tuple where CUSTNO = 82:

CUSTOMER - (82, 'DAVIES', '14 FIELDING ST', 'BRADFORD') GIVING
CUSTOMER

3   Delete all CUSTINV tuples for student 46:

CUSTINV - (46, '*', '*') GIVING CUSTINV

In the last example, the '*' acts as a 'wild card' and implies that the second and third attributes of the specified relation can contain any values. In theory, updates could be performed by removing the old version of the tuple and then adding the new, but in practice a special update operator would be supplied.

11.8   Relational calculus as a data sublanguage

The basic differences between relational algebra and relational calculus are that:

- calculus combines the SELECT and PROJECT commands into a single statement, GET or RETRIEVE or similar, by using a selection-criteria WHERE statement;
- whereas the JOIN command of relational algebra can only apply to two tables, in relational calculus the GET can JOIN many tables.

The attribute names within each relation must be qualified by a relational name prefix if they are the same in two or more relations. In general, they are always prefixed in this way. Thus, in the examples given we have used prefixes on each attribute name even though the actual names as described in Figure 11.4 are all different. Again, there is no standard for syntax and so the following are in a fairly generalized form relating to no particular system.

Simple retrieval

What are the account types?

```
GET (INVESTMENT.ACCTYPE) INTO RESULT
```

The result here would only show 1, 4, 5, 6 (i.e. there would be no duplication).

Qualified retrieval

What are the account numbers where the balance is greater than 400?

```
GET (INVESTMENT.ACCNO) INTO RESULT WHERE INVESTMENT.BALANCE >
400
```

Retrieval with ordering

What are the account numbers of all accounts in branch 101 in numerical order?

```
GET(INVESTMENT.ACCNO) INTO RESULT WHERE BRANCH = 101 ORDER BY
INVESTMENT.ACCNO
```

Limited retrieval

Give the account numbers of any two accounts owned by customer 46.

```
GET (2) (INVACC.ACCNO) INTO RESULT WHERE CUSTNUM = 46
```

Note that this would not necessarily produce 12745 and 13173; there is no guarantee to the order of processing.

Complex retrieval

The selection criteria specified after the WHERE can be quite complex. For example: what are the names of the customers who have accounts for branch 104 and whose balance is greater than 500?

```
GET (CUSTOMER.SURNAME) INTO RESULT WHERE
        CUSTOMER.CUSTNO = CUSTINV.CUSTNUM AND
          CUSTINV.ACCNO = INVESTMENT.ACCNO
AND BRANCH = 104 AND BALANCE > 500
```

As can be imagined, what started out as meaningful attribute and relational names now involve an onerous chore in keying in all the prefixes and identifiers. For this reason, many implementations allow abbreviations to be declared. This is often by means of the RANGE command, for example:

```
RANGE CUSTINV CI
GET (CI.CUSTNUM) INTO RESULT WHERE CI.POSITION = 2
```

Other common features of relational calculus implementations not used in the examples here include:

- OR and NOT operators as well as the AND;
- key words such as COUNT, MAX, SUM, AVE can be used within the GET clause instead of an attribute name, for example:

```
GET (COUNT) INTO RESULT WHERE INVESTMENT.BRANCH = 104
```

This would produce the number of accounts for branch 104.

11.9 Storage by using relational calculus

Updating

Some implemented relational calculus database systems allow for a tuple locking system in which the user can HOLD a tuple or tuples (the update equivalent of GET), modify his or her user work area and then use the UPDATE command to write the modified tuple(s). For example, change the balance for account 19651 to 1125:

```
RANGE INVESTMENT I
HOLD (I.ACCNO, I.BALANCE) INTO RESULT WHERE I.ACCNO = 19651
RESULT.BALANCE = 2
UPDATE RESULT
```

The last line would write the user's temporary relation RESULT back to the relation INVESTMENT.

Note
The primary key of the required relation (in this case I.ACCNO) must also be held, but it cannot be updated. If updating were needed, the tuple would have to be DELETEd and then INSERTed.

Following a HOLD, the system will not allow any other user to access that tuple until the update is completed. Whereas GET can be used to access many relations, HOLD is restricted to only one, and if more are required then more HOLDs will also be needed.

Insertion

The general function name for this is INSERT, though on some systems it is PUT. For this we must assume that an implementation allows for the setting up of a blank user work area of a specified tuple format (R). An example should explain its usage. Add a new customer tuple:

```
R.CUSTNO = 52
R.SURNAME ='ADAMS'
R.STREET = '15 ABBEY RD'
R.TOWN = 'PLYMOUTH'
INSERT R(CUSTOMER)
```

An alternative approach might require:

```
INSERT  INTO  CUSTOMER  VALUES  (52,  'ADAMS',  '15  ABBEY  RD',
'PLYMOUTH')
```

Deletion

The complex selection expressions possible with relational databases allow for the creation of a set of tuples within the user work area as a result of any one request. It is therefore not surprising that all such tuples can be deleted with a single statement. Thus, deleting all CUSTINV tuples where the customer number is 82:

```
RANGE CUSTINV CI
HOLD (CI) INTO RESULT WHERE CUSTNUM = 82
DELETE RESULT
```

11.10 Tuple-based languages

The two approaches to relational database data manipulation described so far are in marked variation from all data-manipulation approaches that have gone before in this book. They are essentially (relation) file-at-a-time approaches as opposed to the previous record-at-a-time. However, this is not to say that the host-language approach is not possible with the relational database. By referring again to the tables shown in Figure 11.1, it is noticeable that the relations are very similar to conventional files con-

```
01 CUST-REC.
   03 CUST-NO    NUMBER(5).
   03 SURNAME    CHAR(15).
   03 STREET     CHAR(20).
   03 TOWN       CHAR(15).
```

Figure 11.5 Customer relation as a COBOL record

taining six, six and nine records, respectively, with each record containing a number of fields. Thus the CUSTOMER relation could be expressed as in Figure 11.5.

With it defined in such a way there is no reason why a particular record cannot be found using a COBOL search:

```
LOOP.
READ CUSTOMER AT END GO END-FILE.
IF C-TOWN NOT = 'BRADFORD' GO LOOP.
```

and so on. A similar approach could be taken using a language such as C.

Similarly, COBOL or C facilities could be used to create, delete or update records. In this way many essentially non-procedural-language-based relational databases have been extended to cater for procedural languages, sometimes by extending the relational language (see Chapter 13) and sometimes by embedding the relational statements within a host language and then using a special precompiler to generate code.

11.11   Comparison of the three approaches

It must be said that to any reader familiar with COBOL or C but not with relational algebra or calculus, the tuple-based approach might seem easier to understand, but a moment's thought will show that the other two approaches require far less training and time for the casual user to use, and within a matter of hours a user could grasp most of the necessary syntax and semantics. It must also be borne in mind that relational databases are constructed of relations whose relationships are shown only by the commonality of attributes between them. Thus many of COBOL's advantages in allowing complex navigational aids are inappropriate. As has been mentioned many times in this book, nearly all non-relational database philosophies incorporate the 'how and where' of record storage within the schema definition. As a result of this physical data dependence, the COBOL program needs to know how the record is to be accessed (e.g. whether it has a Calc key) and very often where it is to be accessed from (ACCESS IS VIA SET). These combine to make the host language approach very procedural. The algebra approach is partially procedural because the user has to specify how to get the result (though never from where) by using JOIN and PRO-JECT. The calculus approach, however, is entirely non-procedural. Any non-standard extensions required within the tuple-based approach must be dealt with programmatically. Thus if a count of records satisfying a particular condition is required then extra code must be written. Relational calculus, in particular, allows the usage of many library functions to perform these tasks and, with the algebra approach, the creation and storage of user-defined functions and procedures (and abbreviations) is usually possible.

11.12 Summary

This chapter has looked at the theory behind relational databases. In practice, the best features of both the algebra and calculus approaches have been merged to form a common general practice language called SQL (structured query language) and that is described more fully in the next chapter.

12
SQL

12.1 Introduction

SQL has become the standard relational database language, and the majority of relational database systems now use it for data retrieval and update. It is non-procedural in nature and, as will be shown, this is both an advantage and a disadvantage. Many of the larger organizations, while holding on to their wide base of 3GL programs, have adopted relational databases because of their maintainability and flexibility, and they access them through embedded SQL as outlined at the end of the last chapter. The present chapter does not purport to be a complete guide to SQL but rather gives a flavour of the range of statements and functions available.

12.2 Basic constructs

SQL is based on the simple statement:

SELECT [list 1] FROM [list 2] (WHERE [search criteria]);

where

[list 1] is a list of the required attributes delineated by a comma if there are more than one (an asterisk can be used to denote the whole of a table);

[list 2] is a list of the tables in which the required attributes reside, again delineated by a comma if there are more than one;

[search criteria] is an additional clause if the WHERE is used specifying which records are to be retrieved.

Each statement is terminated by a semi-colon. Therefore, since most implementations are command-line-driven, a <RETURN> at the end of a line will not cause the command to be executed. In this way multi-line statements can be constructed. At the end of the final line a semi-colon followed by <RETURN> will cause the entire statement to be syntax-checked and, if error-free, executed. The statement, as entered, will reside in the SQL buffer and will remain there until replaced by the next statement. Thus if a syntax error occurs the error can be edited out in that buffer before re-execution.

If a statement is written but there is a need to delay/prevent execution then a

<RETURN> on a blank line is entered (i.e. no semi-colon). A '\' or 'RUN' can be used to execute the contents of the SQL buffer at any time.

Statements can be saved by:

SAVE name

and are normally stored in the root directory with an appended .SQL. To load them into the buffer use

GET name

SQL data must be enclosed in single quotes if the data type is either character-based or of DATE type (see Section 12.9).

SQL is not case-sensitive in terms of language but it is in terms of data, that is, if the data is stored as 'Green' then WHERE NAME = 'GREEN' will not locate it.

The following sections build SQL as a language with all examples using the data structure shown in Figure 11.1.

12.3   Table creation and deletion

These are carried out by means of the CREATE and DROP verbs.

Field names in SQL can be up to 30 characters long and must comprise alphabetic characters plus _ (underscore), $, # and @. At the simple level the investment table of Figure 11.1 could be described as shown in Figure 12.1.

Notes

1 The data types can be one of the following:

CHAR(size)	the field can contain any characters up to a maximum size of 256
VARCHAR(size)	the field is variable length but only the actual length will be stored
LONG	variable-length field up to 65 535 characters (only one of these is allowed per record type)
NUMBER	numeric data up to 38 digits
NUMBER(X,Y)	numeric data, X digits with Y decimal places
INTEGER	numbers with 10 or fewer digits
SMALLINT	numbers with 5 or fewer digits
DATE	date of the form '30-JUL-97'

```
CREATE TABLE INVESTMENT(
    ACCNO         NUMBER(5) NOT NULL UNIQUE,
    ACCTYPE       NUMBER(1) NOT NULL,
    DATE_OPENED   DATE NOT NULL,
    BALANCE       NUMBER(5,2) NOT NULL,
    BRANCH        NUMBER(3));
```

Figure 12.1 An SQL definition of the Investment data

It is interesting and important to note that while DATE appears to be an alphanumeric type of field, it can be used as a numeric field in calculations, for example, two dates can be subtracted from each other to give a number that would be the number of days between them. The date field types are further explored in Section 12.9.

2 The NULL in SQL is defined as being a non-value, neither numeric nor alphanumeric, and attributes can be stored with null values. The NOT NULL expressions in Figure 12.1 are data integrity checks to ensure that when a new record is created and stored, the NOT NULL fields cannot be left empty but must have data entered.

3 The UNIQUE clause specifies another integrity constraint – that no two records can be stored with the same ACCNO.

In Figure 12.2 the CUSTINV relation is defined to show another feature of integrity maintenance.

```
CREATE TABLE CUSTINV(
     CUSTNUM           NUMBER(3) REFERENCES
                       CUSTOMER(CUSTNO),
     ACCNO             NUMBER(5) REFERENCES
                       INVESTMENT(ACCNO),
     POSITION          NUMBER(1) NOT NULL,
     PRIMARY KEY (CUSTNUM, ACCNO));
```

Figure 12.2 An SQL definition for the Custinv relation

Both CUSTNUM and ACCNO are foreign keys as defined in the last chapter. To ensure that a CUSTINV record cannot be created without there already existing both a customer (CUSTNUM) and an account (ACCNO), the REFERENCES clause is used. If either does not exist in their root tables then the CUSTINV record will not be stored. This is an example of **referential integrity**. This is an important concept because, as a corollary, we could not delete either the customer or the account records if their keys are in existence on a CUSTINV record, which makes a lot of sense in the real world.

Tables can be deleted in their entirety by using:

```
DROP TABLE <name>;
```

Again referential integrity, if defined, will prevent the customer table being dropped before CUSTINV. Thus in a more complex data model the tables have to be both created and dropped in a set order.

Note

An alternative to the CREATE statement shown is to create a new table based on some existing one. For example, if we want to work with a table that is a subset of the investment table where the account type is 1, we could use:

```
CREATE TABLE INV1 AS
  SELECT * FROM INVESTMENT WHERE ACCTYPE = 1;
```

12.4 Simple retrieval

In order to look at the variations on data retrieval, this section gives a variety of examples, introducing new concepts with each one.

1 `SELECT * FROM CUSTOMER;` will select all the data from the customer table.
2 `SELECT ACCNO, BALANCE FROM INVESTMENT;` will select only the account number and balance from all investment records.
3 `SELECT ACCNO, BALANCE FROM INVESTMENT WHERE ACCTYPE = 1;` is the same as (2) but will only select those records where the account type is 1.
4 If we wished to know all the account types available on all investment records then `SELECT ACCTYPE FROM INVESTMENT;` would return one from each row of the table, that is, there would be a great deal of duplication.
5 Instead we therefore use `SELECT DISTINCT ACCTYPE FROM INVESTMENT;` which will only return each value once, in the order in which they appear.
6 If we wanted the output ordering we could use: `SELECT DISTINCT ACCTYPE FROM INVESTMENT ORDER BY ACCTYPE;` The default is ascending order (use `DESC` appended before the semi-colon if descending required).

12.5 Operators

If the `WHERE` clause is used SQL contains a variety of operators that can be used in conjunction with it. Apart from the '=' already used, there are:

!=	not equal to
>	greater than
<	less than
>=	greater than or equal to
<=	less than or equal to

Others are given in the following examples:

1 `SELECT ACCNO FROM INVESTMENT WHERE BALANCE BETWEEN 100 AND 1000;`
The values used are inclusive.
2 `SELECT SURNAME FROM CUSTOMER WHERE SURNAME LIKE 'S%';`
The '%' acts as a wild card such that this query would find all customers whose surnames begin with 'S'.
3 `SELECT SURNAME FROM CUSTOMER WHERE SURNAME LIKE '%S';`
This is as above but finds names that end in 'S'
4 `SELECT SURNAME FROM CUSTOMER WHERE SURNAME LIKE '%LL%';`
The surname contains 'LL'.
5 `SELECT ACCNO FROM INVESTMENT WHERE BRANCH IS NULL;`

Since the branch field can be left null, this statement would find all such occurrences. Note the usage of the word 'IS' rather than '='. The opposite is 'IS NOT NULL'.

More complex search patterns can be written using AND and OR. As with all computer logic, the ANDs are evaluated/actioned before the ORs. If in doubt, parenthesize.

6   `SELECT * FROM INVESTMENT WHERE ACCTYPE = 1 AND BRANCH = 101;`
    is simple but if we want to get all accounts from either branch 101 or 104 where account type is 1:

7   `SELECT * FROM INVESTMENT WHERE ACCTYPE = 1 AND`
      `BRANCH = 101 OR BRANCH = 104;`
    will get type 1s from 101 but will get all account types from 104. It should be written:

8   `SELECT * FROM INVESTMENT WHERE ACCTYPE = 1 AND`
      `(BRANCH = 101 OR BRANCH = 104);`

12.6 Joining tables

What has been shown so far involves retrieval from a single table, but the power of a relational database lies in its ability to extract data efficiently from two or more tables. The ability to JOIN two tables (as defined in Chapter 11) is made possible by there being a common attribute (of the same domain) between them. If normalization was performed correctly then entities related in the real world will be linked by a common attribute in the conceptual model.

The term 'join' is not actually used in SQL. Joining is effected by naming the common attribute as part of the WHERE clause. If the common attribute has the same name in both tables then all occurrences of that name within the SQL statement must be prefixed by the table name. Clearly, in this case, both tables must be named in the FROM clause.

Before an example is given, it is worth noting at this point that SQL allows the usage of abbreviations, much like the RANGE statement in Chapter 11. These are simply appended to the table name in the FROM clause after a space, for example:

  `SELECT * FROM INVESTMENT I;`

This example means nothing as I is not used again within the statement, but consider the next example:

1   How much money has customer 17 got in each of their accounts?

    `SELECT I.ACCNO, BALANCE FROM INVESTMENT I, CUSTINV CI`
    `WHERE CUSTNUM = 17 AND CI.ACCNO = I.ACCNO;`

Note that ACCNO needs qualifying with the table name as the data name is identical in both tables. The first ACCNO after the SELECT in this statement also needs qualifying even though either name would do. BALANCE does not need qualifying because it only appears in one table.

What this statement is saying is simply a representation of the SELECT, PROJECT and JOIN operators of the last chapter:

(a) Select all the CUSTINV records where the customer number is 17.
(b) Extract the account number from all these records.
(c) Go through the investment table and extract balances for these account numbers.

Note that if the join condition is not specified in this example then SQL would simply concatenate the selected CUSTINV records with every single record in the investment table.

2 More than two tables can be joined:
What are the account numbers and balances of Ms Barnard's accounts?

```
SELECT I.ACCNO, BALANCE FROM INVESTMENT I, CUSTINV CI, CUSTOMER C
    WHERE SURNAME = 'BARNARD' AND CUSTNO = CUSTNUM
        AND CI.ACCNO = I.ACCNO;
```

Note that the ordering of the various conditions in the WHERE clause is immaterial.

Joining a table to itself

Find the account numbers and balances for all accounts that have a balance greater than or equal to that of account 13173.

```
SELECT I1.ACCNO, I1.BALANCE FROM INVESTMENT I1, INVESTMENT I2
    WHERE I1.BALANCE >= I2.BALANCE
        AND I2.ACCNO = 13173 AND I1.ACCNO != I2.ACCNO;
```

This will use two copies of the same table. In the second it will find ACCNO = 13173 and the associated balance, and will then read through the first searching for any balances that are greater than or equal to it. In this example the != is necessary, otherwise ACCNO 13173 would also be displayed.

Outer joins

In some instances we may wish to display output from one table even if a specific record is not logically joined to another table. In Figure 11.1 the last customer, Jenkins, has no investment accounts and so does not appear in the CUSTINV table, but if we wished them to be displayed with other customers and their account numbers we could use:

```
SELECT CUSTNO, SURNAME, ACCNO FROM CUSTOMER C, CUSTINV CI
    WHERE C.CUSTNO = CI.CUSTNUM(+);
```

The + acts as an outer join, effectively adding a dummy row for CUSTINV when one does not naturally occur. Only one + is permitted per join and it is placed on the column for the table in which there is not going to be a match.

12.7 Simple functions

SQL contains many functions, a few of which are demonstrated here by example. Because the example of Figure 11.1 is only a limited data set, there will not always be an apparent motive as to why we should want the output.

1 SELECT LOWER(SURNAME) FROM CUSTOMER; will convert all upper-case characters in the surname to lower-case. The use of UPPER would have the opposite effect.

2 `SELECT INITCAP(SURNAME) FROM CUSTOMER;` will convert the first character in a string (or the first character of each word if there are more than one) to upper-case.

3 `SELECT SUBST(STREET,1,2) FROM CUSTOMER;` would select the first two characters from Street, starting at position 1.

4 `SELECT LENGTH(SURNAME) FROM CUSTOMER;` will output the number of characters in each surname.

5 `SELECT MOD(BALANCE, 12) FROM INVESTMENT;` will give the remainder if the balance is divided by 12.

6 `SELECT ROUND(BALANCE,2) FROM INVESTMENT;` will round the balance to two decimal places.

7 `SELECT TRUNC(BALANCE,1) FROM INVESTMENT;` will truncate the balance to one decimal place.

8 `SELECT CEIL(BALANCE) FROM INVESTMENT;` rounds the balance to the nearest integer.

9 `SELECT FLOOR(BALANCE) FROM INVESTMENT;` truncates the balance to the nearest integer.

10 `SELECT TO_CHAR(BALANCE, '$99,999') FROM INVESTMENT;` will display the balance in the given edited format. TO_CHAR is an extremely useful function for converting data from one format to another.

More examples are given in Section 12.9.

12.8 Grouping functions

These are so named because they involve SQL processing groups of records. They are largely self-explanatory, but have the drawback that they cannot be selected together with normal attributes without using a GROUP BY function (see Section 12.10).

At this point we also note that column headings (the default being the attribute name) can be renamed by listing the replacement heading within double quotes after the attribute.

```
SELECT AVG(BALANCE) 'Average' FROM INVESTMENT;
SELECT COUNT(ACCTYPE) FROM INVESTMENT WHERE ACCTYPE = 1;
```

Using COUNT(*) would give the same result.

DISTINCT can also be used to good effect here: for example,

```
SELECT COUNT(DISTINCT ACCTYPE) FROM INVESTMENT;
```

would return the answer 4.

Other functions are MAX, MIN and SUM.

The 'parameter' within the parentheses can be an arithmetic expression: for example,

```
SELECT SUM(BALANCE/12) FROM INVESTMENT;
```

12.9 Date functions

As previously mentioned, DATE fields can be used as numerics in calculations:

1 SELECT DATE_OPENED + 7 FROM INVESTMENT;
   will return a date that is one week after that stored in DATE_OPENED. For example, if the latter is 14-MAY-97 then 21-MAY-97 will be returned. Note that the system date and the system time are available from a dummy table, normally called DUAL, as SYSDATE and SYSTIME. If they are used then it must be noted that results can be obtained with decimal places; e.g. subtract a date field containing yesterday's date from SYSDATE and you might get 1.45 (yesterday started at midnight, so there is a whole day there plus whatever proportion of today has passed).

2 SELECT ADD_MONTHS(DATE_OPENED, 6) FROM INVESTMENT;
   will return a date six months after the DATE_OPENED. Note that negative numbers can be used in these functions.

3 SELECT MONTHS_BETWEEN(I1.DATE_OPENED, I2.DATE_OPENED)
       FROM INVESTMENT I1, INVESTMENT I2 WHERE
           I1.ACCNO = 12745 AND I2.ACCNO = 13852;
   would return an answer of 6.

4 SELECT LAST_DAY(DATE_OPENED) FROM INVESTMENT;
   will move the date forward to the last of the month in question.

5 SELECT ROUND(DATE_OPENED, 'MONTH') FROM INVESTMENT;
   will round the date up or down to the nearest month and display that month. TRUNC would work in a similar way.

The TO_CHAR function is one of the most useful when dealing with dates because it allows conversion from one format to another. Its general form is

    TO_CHAR(date, 'format')

where format can be, among others:

CC	converts the date to the century, e.g. 19
YYYY	extracts the four-digit year from the date, e.g. 1997
YY	extracts the last two digits of the year, e.g. 97
YEAR	returns a date in English, e.g. nineteen ninety-seven
Q	returns the quarter of the year 1–4
WW	returns the week of the year, 1–52
W	gives the week of the month, 1–5
DDD	gives the day of the year, 1–366
DD	extracts the day of the month, 1–31
D	gives the day of the week, 1–7 (Sunday = 1)
MONTH	gives the full month name, e.g. September
MON	extracts the three-letter month name, e.g. Sep
MM	gives the month of the year, 1–12
DAY	gives the day of the week in English, e.g. Monday
DY	gives a three-letter version of the day, e.g. Mon
HH	gives the hour of the day for a 12-hour clock
HH24	as above but for a 24-hour clock

MI   gives the minutes of the hour
SS   gives the seconds

Suffixes can also be used, for example, DDTH will give 29TH.
   One example is given here to show the general usage:
How many accounts were opened on a Saturday?

```
SELECT COUNT(*) FROM INVESTMENT WHERE
   TO_CHAR(DATE_OPENED, 'D') = 6;
```

12.10   The GROUP BY function

Suppose that we wished to find the average balance for each account type:

```
SELECT ACCTYPE, AVG(BALANCE) FROM INVESTMENT
   GROUP BY ACCTYPE;
```

Such functions are useful in themselves but do not answer the question of how we could find who has the highest balance.

```
SELECT ACCNO, MAX(BALANCE) FROM INVESTMENT;
```

is illegal as previously stated. If we used

```
SELECT ACCNO, MAX(BALANCE) FROM INVESTMENT
   GROUP BY ACCNO;
```

we would simply get a list of all account numbers and their balances. The next section will provide the answer.

12.11   Subqueries

A useful extension of the WHERE clause is that part of the condition can itself be a SELECT statement. This **nested subquery** will be executed first and the result fed back to the outer query.

1   ```
    SELECT ACCNO, BALANCE FROM INVESTMENT
       WHERE BALANCE = (SELECT MAX(BALANCE) FROM INVESTMENT);
    ```
    will find the maximum balance and will then search the table looking to see who has it.

2   Find all accounts whose balance is greater than the average balance for branch 101.
    ```
    SELECT ACCNO, BALANCE FROM INVESTMENT
       WHERE BALANCE > (SELECT AVG(BALANCE) FROM INVESTMENT
    WHERE BRANCH = 101);
    ```

Note that the subquery must only return a single value or row otherwise a TOO_MANY_ROWS error will occur. Thus:
    ```

```
SELECT ACCNO, BALANCE FROM INVESTMENT
   WHERE BALANCE > (SELECT BALANCE FROM INVESTMENT
      WHERE BRANCH = 101);
```

will not work because the subquery will return every row from branch 101, and the outer query will not know how to handle them.

This can be avoided by the use of further operators:

```
ALL, ANY, NOT IN
```

For example,

```
SELECT ACCNO, BALANCE FROM INVESTMENT
   WHERE BALANCE > ANY(SELECT BALANCE FROM INVESTMENT
      WHERE BRANCH = 101);
```

This subquery will return many rows but the ANY will effectively turn it into one (the maximum).

```
SELECT CUSTNO FROM CUSTOMER WHERE
   CUSTNO NOT IN (SELECT DISTINCT CUSTNUM FROM CUSTINV);
```

will select all customers that do not appear in the CUSTINV table.

Note that the WHERE clause cannot itself contain a group function because the latter refers to groups of records and the WHERE must apply to individual records. If this kind of function is required then the HAVING clause must be used (replacing the WHERE). For example, to list all the branches where the average balance is greater than the average balance of all accounts:

```
SELECT BRANCH, AVG(BALANCE) FROM INVESTMENT
   GROUP BY BRANCH
   HAVING AVG(BALANCE) > (SELECT AVG(BALANCE) FROM INVESTMENT);
```

Note the GROUP BY which is to calculate the average for all accounts within a branch. This must appear before the HAVING.

The reader will have noted that we have suddenly gone from relatively simple examples to quite complex ones. Because SQL is non-procedural it is not always obvious how to construct a statement to solve a particular problem, nor is it always easy to ascertain why a statement fails to produce the expected results. In a procedural language such as COBOL or C we could construct a program design that could be dry-run to test if it will work, but we cannot always do that here. From experience SQL is very much a heuristic learning exercise, that is, if the user has seen a similar solution that works they can adapt it to the current problem.

For the rest of this chapter we shall return to simpler matters.

12.12 Adding, updating and deleting records

```
1   INSERT INTO CUSTOMER(CUSTNO, SURNAME, STREET, TOWN)
       VALUES(42, 'BROWN', '23 HIGHGATE', 'BURNLEY');
```

If column names are not specified then they are set to null (unless NOT NULL is specified in the table definition, in which case an error will occur). As can be imagined, it is easy to insert a single record but extremely tedious to insert many. For this reason many implementations will allow records to be created in batch mode, by passing parameters, via text files. As the methods vary no examples will be given here. On the subject of parameters, there is nuisance value in having to use:

```
SELECT * FROM CUSTOMER WHERE SURNAME = 'DAVIES';
```

and then having to edit the statement to look for another customer. SQL allows the usage of parameters by means of an ampersand '&'. With this we can construct general queries which, when executed, will prompt the user to enter a value for the parameter which will then be passed into the query. Thus

```
SELECT * FROM CUSTOMER WHERE SURNAME = '&SURNAME';
```

will, when run, produce Enter value for SURNAME and the user can enter a new surname each time they run the query. Note that the identifier after the ampersand need not be the column name because it is this that is displayed in the prompt. Also, if the &SURNAME is enclosed in quotes then the data input does not need to be.

2   UPDATE INVESTMENT
   SET BALANCE = 1125.50
     WHERE ACCNO = 19651;
   will update the account.

3   UPDATE INVESTMENT SET BALANCE = 0;
   would zeroize all accounts.

4   DELETE FROM CUSTOMER WHERE CUSTNO = 29;
   is self-explanatory.

5   DELETE FROM CUSTOMER;
   would delete all customers.

12.13   Restructuring

The ALTER TABLE command allows columns to be added easily, and item types to be changed. To delete columns will require a CREATE TABLE AS, then SELECTing only the required columns.

1   ALTER TABLE INVESTMENT
   ADD(DATE_CLOSED DATE);
2   ALTER TABLE INVESTMENT
   MODIFY(ACCTYPE NUMBER(2));

There are various restrictions here and, for example, you would not be able to make existing data illegal – by changing a column definition to include NOT NULL if there are already rows containing nulls.

12.14 Views

The relational database version of the CODASYL subschema is termed a 'view'. It can be constructed very simply and then password-protected if required.

```
CREATE VIEW VIEW1 AS
        SELECT ACCNO, ACCTYPE, BALANCE FROM INVESTMENT;
```

will give the user access only to the three declared columns, whereas

```
CREATE VIEW VIEW2 AS
        SELECT * FROM INVESTMENT WHERE BRANCH = 101;
```

would give access to all data for branch 101 only.

In these instances, no new data sets are produced, but the views create masks for existing data. They can, however, be used as tables in SELECT statements. For example a user who is using VIEW2 as defined can enter:

```
SELECT BALANCE FROM VIEW2 WHERE ACCNO = 14682;
```

If the same user tried

```
SELECT BALANCE FROM VIEW2 WHERE BRANCH = 104;
```

they would get a NO ROWS SELECTED message because those rows are not defined in VIEW2.

Views can also be constructed as selection from various joined tables. In such cases the data would be presented as a concatenation of data from the chosen tables, for example:

```
CREATE VIEW3 AS
    SELECT CUSTNUM, POSITION, ACCNO, SURNAME
        FROM CUSTINV CI, CUSTOMER C, INVESTMENT I
    WHERE BRANCH = 101 AND I.ACCNO = CI.ACCNO
        AND CUSTNUM = CUSTNO;
```

This would give all the customer names for accounts of branch 101 but no account details. The data would appear as:

```
46      2      14682  WILLIAMS
82      1      14682  DAVIES
46      1      13173  WILLIAMS
```

12.15 Output formatting

The statements shown so far are SQL-based and relate to the SQL buffer. Although they are powerful, the output formatting is weak and outputs of numerics may not be aligned. For example, if three balances for accounts were chosen and displayed, and contained 52.51, 52.50 and 52.00, then the output would appear as:

```
52.51
52.5
52
```

SQL therefore has output formatting capabilities which are defined outside the SQL buffer.

Note that the following examples use the standard SQL prompt SQL> to distinguish those lines that will not appear in the SQL buffer, and therefore do not end with a semi-colon:

COLUMN (column-name [option])
where [option] can be: (among others)

ALI[AS] name	name assigns the specified alias for the column
FOR[MAT]	specifies a display format (see below)
HEA[DING] text	defines a column heading

The format option for numerics could be:

99	the number of 9s specifies the number of displayed digits
0	e.g. 099 displays leading zeros (999 would not)
$	prefixes a currency sign
MI	displays a '-' after a negative number
EEE	displays numerics in scientific notation
DATE	displays a date field as MM/DD/YY
An	displays an alphabetic field as n characters

Note that there are many other options for all of these functions, but only a few common ones have been displayed here, and are used in the examples.

```
SQL>COLUMN BALANCE HEADING 'CURRENT BALANCE' FORMAT 9999.99
```

This and any other defined headings will remain active for all subsequent statements throughout the user's session unless they are changed.

The BREAK command suppresses duplicate values. For example, if you were to

```
SELECT * FROM CUSTINV ORDER BY CUSTNUM;
```

the output would be exactly that shown in Figure 11.1. However, if you used

```
SQL>BREAK ON CUSTNUM
```

prior to the statement above you would get:

12	15214	1
17	19651	1
	12745	2
23	19651	2
46	12745	1
	13173	1
	14682	2
82	14682	1
	13852	1

If subtotals are required one could use the SUM function (this is different to the SQL group function). For example,

```
SQL>COMPUTE SUM OF BALANCE ON ACCTYPE
SQL>SELECT * FROM INVESTMENT ORDER BY ACCTYPE;
```

would display a subtotal for each ACCTYPE.

To produce grand totals one could use:

```
SQL>BREAK ON REPORT
SQL>COMPUTE SUM OF BALANCE ON REPORT
```

The words TTITLE and BTITLE can be used to produce headings and footers respectively, and a final example will show their usage:

```
SQL>SET PAGESIZE = 66
SQL>SET LINESIZE = 45
SQL>BREAK ON ACCTYPE
SQL>COMPUTE SUM OF BALANCE ON ACCTYPE
SQL>TTITLE CENTER 'Balances for Branch 101' SKIP 1 CENTER
   SYSDATE SKIP 2
SQL>COLUMN ACCNO HEADING ACCOUNT
SQL>COLUMN ACCTYPE HEADING TYPE
SQL>COLUMN BALANCE FORMAT 9999.99
SQL>SELECT ACCNO,ACCTYPE,BALANCE FROM INVESTMENT
   WHERE BRANCH = 101;
```

12.16 Summary

It must be stressed that this chapter only presents a brief outline of the SQL language and its constructs. There are many more complete guides on the market, some of which are listed in Appendix B.

SQL is easy to use, in fact for simple queries it could be used by almost anyone with very little training. Its weakness lies in its non-procedurality and its inability to deal with two basic programming constructs, the conditional (IF) and the iterative (LOOP). Both of these are considered in the next chapter.

13
PL/SQL

13.1 Introduction

PL/SQL was introduced as a procedural extension to SQL by the Oracle Corporation with the release of Oracle 6. Its main functions were to allow for the provision of a procedural language available to Oracle programs without the need to pass control back to the user after the execution of every SQL statement (one of the weaknesses of SQL being that the user can only execute a single statement at one time).

PL/SQL can be used to implement the following three types of program:

- 4GL procedures and functions which are executed within application triggers,
- packaged procedures and functions,
- database triggers which are executed whenever one of the SQL operations INSERT, UPDATE or DELETE is carried out.

It is beyond the scope of this book to study all the applications (see Appendix B for further reading). This chapter, therefore, looks at PL/SQL as a language in terms of its constructs and functions, with examples again based on Figure 11.1.

13.2 PL/SQL blocks

PL/SQL statements are terminated by a semi-colon. Comments can be inserted by means of a double hyphen '--' for a single line, or by '/*' (beginning) and '*/' (end) for multi-line statements.

PL/SQL blocks (as defined below) may themselves contain blocks such that an application program may contain sets of contiguous and/or nested blocks. Each PL/SQL block consists of (usually) three components:

- A declarative part in which all the variables, constants, cursors (see next section) and user exceptions are defined. This part will begin with the word DECLARE.
- The executable part containing the actual coding of the procedure including SQL statements, conditional clauses and loop constructs.
- The exception-handling part where the errors concerned are either explicitly defined by the user or implicitly defined by the system. When an error occurs within the executable part, control is passed to the appropriate exception-handling code. If there is none then the program will terminate.

If all three components are defined within a PL/SQL block then the executable part will start with the word BEGIN and the entire block will terminate with END;. Each of the components will be studied in turn following the next section.

13.3 Cursors

When an SQL statement is processed PL/SQL opens a work area called a **context area** in which all the information required to process the statement is stored. This area is referenced by means of a **cursor** which can be one of two types:

- **implicit cursors** which are generated by the Oracle server,
- **explicit cursors** which must be user-defined whenever an SQL statement is going to return more than one row of data (if such a cursor is not defined then the exception TOO_MANY_ROWS will be generated).

An explicit cursor must be defined within the DECLARE part and must comprise two elements:

- a cursor name which follows the SQL rules for identifiers (see Section 12.3),
- a SELECT statement to which the cursor is assigned.

A third optional element is the inclusion of one or more input parameters.

An example of a simple cursor using the data of Figure 11.1 might be:

```
CURSOR BRANCH101 IS
   SELECT ACCNO, BALANCE FROM INVESTMENT
      WHERE BRANCH = 101;
```

A similar example using a parameter would be:

```
CURSOR BRANCH101(BCODE NUMBER(3)) IS
SELECT ACCNO, BALANCE FROM INVESTMENT
      WHERE BRANCH = BCODE;
```

In the second example the same procedure could be used for any branch by entering the code at run time. Other examples are given in Section 13.5.

13.4 Declarations

Variables declared within a block are considered local to that block, but global to any blocks nested within it. All variables must be declared before they are used.

The data types available include all those referenced in Section 12.3, plus some other types such as BOOLEAN (which can only be 'true' or 'false').

A very useful feature is the ability to inherit data types from the parent data resident in the data tables. This is achieved by appending %TYPE after the table identifier, for example:

```
DECLARE
V_BALANCE    INVESTMENT.BALANCE%TYPE;
```

Here PL/SQL will extract the data type from the table balance and use it for the variable V_BALANCE.

It is also possible to inherit a whole row definition on to a set of implicitly defined variables. Thus:

```
DECLARE
INV_REC    INVESTMENT%ROWTYPE;
```

will generate five variables which can be referenced by:

```
        INV_REC.ACCNO
        INV_REC.ACCTYPE
        INV_REC.DATE_OPENED
        INV_REC.BALANCE
        INV_REC.BRANCH
```

Values can be assigned to variables using the 'becomes equal to' sign, ':='. Thus to initialize variables:

```
DECLARE
        V_ACCUM NUMBER(6,2)  := 0;
        V_TYPE BOOLEAN := FALSE;
```

The right-hand sides of assignment expressions can also be complex expressions (within the executable code), for example:

```
INTEREST_PAID    :=    (SYSDATE  -  DATE_OPENED)   *   BALANCE   *
RATE_PER_DAY;
```

Alternatively, variables can be filled by SELECT statements, such as

```
SELECT (SYSDATE - DATE_OPENED) INTO V_DAYS
   FROM INVESTMENT WHERE ACCNO = 13852;
```

or

```
SELECT ACCNO, BALANCE, BRANCH INTO V_ACCNO, V_BALANCE,
   V_BRANCH FROM INVESTMENT WHERE ACCNO = 13852;
```

13.5   Executable statements

The executable part of a PL/SQL block can contain a series of one or more SQL and/or PL/SQL statements, and it is here that the procedurality becomes evident.

Labels

As with any procedural language, PL/SQL allows labels to be inserted into the code as points to which control can be passed by means of a GOTO. Because labels are normally referenced within loops (though it is illegal to transfer into a loop) or conditional statements, examples will be given later.

Conditionals

The simplest form involves IF … THEN … END IF, for example:

```
IF V_BRANCH = 101 THEN
  V_ACCUM := V_ACCUM + V_BALANCE;
END IF;
```

Further to these are the ELSE which corresponds to statements to be executed if the original statement is false, for example

```
IF V_BALANCE > 500 THEN
    V_TOTAL1 := V_TOTAL1 + V_BALANCE;
  ELSE
    V_TOTAL2 := V_TOTAL2 + V_BALANCE;
END IF;
```

There is also an ELSIF which applies a further conditional test if the original statement is false, for example:

```
IF V_ACCTYPE = 1 THEN
    V_ACCUM1 := V_ACCUM1 + V_BALANCE;
  ELSIF V_ACCTYPE = 4 THEN
    V_ACCUM4 := V_ACCUM4 + V_BALANCE;
  ELSIF V_ACCTYPE = 5 THEN
    V_ACCUM5 := V_ACCUM5 + V_BALANCE;
  ELSE
    V_ACCUM6 := V_ACCUM6 + V_BALANCE;
  END IF;
  END IF;
END IF;
```

PL/SQL can use any of the conditional operators shown in Section 12.5.

Loops

The controlling keywords within a PL/SQL loop function are LOOP … END LOOP. There are two constructs for controlling the loop: WHILE and FOR. The following examples show the use of many of the PL/SQL constructs described so far.

1   Suppose that we wished to find how many account balances fall within certain bands, such as 0 to 499, 500 to 999, the results being put in a table called TEMP.

```
DECLARE
  V_LOW NUMBER (4) := 0;
  V_HIGH NUMBER (4) := 499;
  V_COUNT NUMBER (4);
BEGIN
  WHILE V_HIGH <= 2500 LOOP
    SELECT COUNT(*) INTO V_COUNT FROM INVESTMENT
      WHERE BALANCE > V_LOW AND BALANCE <= V_HIGH;
    INSERT INTO TEMP (LOW, HIGH, COUNTER)
      VALUES(V_LOW, V_HIGH, V_COUNT);
```

```
        V_LOW := VC_LOW + 500;
        V_HIGH := V_HIGH + 500;
    END LOOP;
END;
```

In this example we know the maximum balance so we can define the loop ending condition, namely

```
WHILE V_HIGH <= 2500
```

These is no reason, however, why the end condition cannot be a variable: for example, by adding:

```
        V_MAX NUMBER(4);
BEGIN
    SELECT MAX(BALANCE) INTO V_MAX FROM INVESTMENT;
    WHILE V_HIGH <= (V_MAX + 500) LOOP
```

2   The FOR loop could be used to the same effect, using the same variables:

```
BEGIN
    FOR I IN 1..5 LOOP
        SELECT COUNT(*) INTO V_COUNT FROM INVESTMENT
            WHERE BALANCE > V_LOW AND V_BALANCE <= V_HIGH;
        ...
    END LOOP;
END
```

In this instance I is implicitly defined (in fact I can be any variable name), and the 5 could be replaced by a variable name.

If we wished to leave the LOOP before the natural termination we could use EXIT, for example:

```
LOOP
    ...
    IF <condition> THEN EXIT;
END LOOP:
```

in which case control would be passed to the first statement after the END LOOP. A similar effect could be obtained by labelling the first statement after END LOOP and then using a GOTO label instead of EXIT.

3   The main function of the cursor as defined in Section 13.3 is to be able to process one record at a time when more than one would be returned by a SELECT statement.

Cursors must be opened before they are used, and closed afterwards. Thus, expanding the example of Section 13.3 we have:

```
DECLARE
    V_ACCNO INVESTMENT.ACCNO%TYPE;
    V_BALANCE INVESTMENT.BALANCE%TYPE;
    CURSOR BRANCH101 IS
        SELECT ACCNO, BALANCE FROM INVESTMENT
            WHERE BRANCH = 101;
```

```
BEGIN
  OPEN BRANCH101;
  LOOP
    FETCH BRANCH101 INTO V_ACCNO, V_BALANCE;
    EXIT WHEN BRANCH101%NOTFOUND;
    ... process data ...
  END LOOP;
  CLOSE BRANCH101;
END;
```

Notes

1   The EXIT condition should be when we run out of records belonging to branch 101. A cursor attribute of %NOTFOUND set to true or false facilitates this and the statement above sends control out of the loop when %NOTFOUND is true. Other cursor attributes are:

%FOUND	self-explanatory
%ISOPEN	true if the cursor is open when evaluated
%ROWCOUNT	gives the number of rows FETCHed so far

2   Implicit cursors are opened by PL/SQL every time an SQL statement is executed within a block. Although the cursors themselves are not accessible by the user, the cursor attributes, as defined above, can be used with an SQL prefix instead of the cursor name, for example:

```
IF SQL%NOTFOUND THEN ...
```

However, normally if an SQL statement finds no data then a NO_DATA_FOUND exception is raised which will pass control to the exception processing part of the block.

13.6   Exception processing

PL/SQL allows errors in processing to be handled by the EXCEPTION part of the block. If the appropriate error-handling code is not specified then the program will terminate. In many cases an error such as NO_DATA_FOUND is to be expected when all records have already been processed so it is important that such an error be trapped. In this instance we may not wish to actually do anything, in which case a NULL statement can be used, for example:

```
DECLARE
    various variables
    CURSOR C1 ...
BEGIN
  OPEN C1
  LOOP
    FETCH C1 . ... ...
    process
```

```
    END LOOP;
EXCEPTION
    WHEN NO_DATA_FOUND THEN NULL;
END;
```

A keyword OTHERS can be used to trap all other errors, for example:

```
WHEN OTHERS THEN …
```

Other program exception handlers include:

PROGRAM_ERROR   (used for internal errors)
TOO_MANY_ROWS   (used if select statements return more than one row,
                      i.e. cursors were not used)
ZERO_DIVIDE   (self-explanatory)

and there are many others.

Such errors are implicitly RAISEd by the PL/SQL processor. The user can, however, define their own exceptions, for example:

```
DECLARE
    V_BRANCH INVESTMENTS.BRANCH%TYPE;
    V_ACCNO INVESTMENTS.ACCNO%TYPE;
    V_BALANCE INVESTMENTS.BALANCE%TYPE;
    CURSOR B1 AS SELECT ACCNO, BALANCE, BRANCH FROM INVESTMENT;
    NO_BRANCH EXCEPTION;
BEGIN
    OPEN B1
    LOOP
      FETCH B1 INTO V_ACCNO, V_BALANCE, V_BRANCH;
      IF BRANCH IS NULL THEN
        RAISE NO_BRANCH;
      END IF;
      … processing …
    END LOOP;
EXCEPTION
    WHEN NO_BRANCH THEN …
END;
```

If no exception handler is located within a block then the enclosing block is searched (if the first block was embedded). If a handler is located then control passes to the block containing the block containing the handler. If no handler is located then the program is terminated.

13.7 Forms and triggers

Oracle Forms will not be looked at in any depth here except to note that it is an applications generator allowing the user to view data from tables on screen. The latest version is Windows-based and allows the construction of forms by a 'drag and drop' process. Each form may comprise one or more blocks (on one or more screen pages) each of which may relate to one table of data. The reason for highlighting such a facility here is in reference to the fact that this representation of stored data allows records to be created, amended and deleted. To maintain integrity, Oracle has defined three types of trigger (a trigger being a piece of code that is executed when a certain event occurs):

- key triggers – these are actioned when the user presses one of the keyboard keys, for example, the F6 key might be depressed to clear the screen data and create a new record (which keys do what will vary from installation to installation);
- navigational triggers – which are actioned as the user moves about the screen (in forms) usually by means of the 'tab' key, for example PRE-FIELD, POST-BLOCK;
- transactional triggers – which are actioned whenever data on the form is changed.

All of the triggers are written in PL/SQL. In the case of the key triggers, these are generated by the system when the form is created but can be accessed and amended by the developer. Certain transactional triggers are also generated to match the integrity constraints as specified in the database definition. For example, if a field is declared as NOT NULL then forms will generate an ON-VALIDATE-FIELD trigger which will prevent the user from leaving that field empty.

Since all triggers are code-accessible the form can be customized to meet the user requirements and a full range of integrity checks can be applied interactively while the user is creating, amending or deleting data, and this itself necessitates further extensions to PL/SQL: the MESSAGE function allows messages to be shown on the message bar at the foot of the screen, for example:

```
IF :BALANCE < 0 THEN
   MESSAGE ('AMOUNT CANNOT BE LESS THAN 0');
   RAISE FORM_TRIGGER_FAILURE;
END IF;
EXCEPTION
   WHEN FORM_TRIGGER_FAILURE THEN NULL;
```

Notes

1   The colon in front of BALANCE decrees that the field concerned is on the screen as opposed to the one in the base table (investment). If there are two identically named fields on the screen then the block name is used as a prefix to the variable, for example:

```
:INVBLOCK.BALANCE
```

2   The RAISE FORM_TRIGGER_FAILURE is one of many predefined exception handlers. This one will keep the screen cursor in the current form field, essentially until the user gets the input correct.

Also associated with forms are a set of packaged procedures, again generated by the system, which are used to perform queries, insertions and deletions and which can be called from the triggers.

See Appendix B for further reading in this area.

13.8 PL/SQL and recovery

From what has gone before in this and the previous chapter, it can be seen that both SQL and PL/SQL facilitate the creation, amendment and deletion of data, but what happens if something goes wrong? Can an error leave the data in a non-integral state where consistency is unknown?

All SQL and PL/SQL updates are performed on a 'temporary' basis until a COMMIT statement is actioned. After a COMMIT the changes become permanent and cannot be undone by the single user (although there are still options for the DBA to initiate a database rollback as outlined in Chapter 7).

If a PL/SQL program goes wrong prior to a COMMIT then the updates carried out since the last COMMIT can be undone by using a ROLLBACK statement. Not surprisingly ROLLBACK statements are often found in exception handlers.

If there is a need to ROLLBACK, but not as far as the last COMMIT, then the programmer can then use the ROLLBACK TO option.

Thus if, for example, a customer wished to pay money into their account (as a cheque) and then immediately draw some out (as cash), then it is possible that until the cheque clears they may not have enough in the balance to withdraw the required amount. If both events occur as a single database transaction then we certainly would not want to undo the deposit if the withdrawal fails. In this case we could use:

```
DECLARE
  NOT_ENOUGH EXCEPTION;
BEGIN
  process deposit
  update account
  create transaction
  SAVEPOINT WITHDRAW;
  create transaction record
  IF AMT_REQUIRED > BALANCE THEN
  RAISE NOT_ENOUGH;
  END IF;
EXCEPTION
  WHEN NOT_ENOUGH THEN
  ROLLBACK TO WITHDRAW;
END;
```

13.9 Summary

To describe any database system thoroughly would require an entire book, and the reader is encouraged to read further (some bibliographical references are given in Appendix B). The purpose of this chapter has been to show that most of the original weaknesses of relational database languages have been removed by extending those languages into procedural approaches without losing any of the power of the original language.

When the first edition of this book was written, relational databases were being developed rapidly and most database research was being channelled into this area.

Ten years on and improvements are still being made, but new database types – those of object orientation – are emerging. For that reason the remainder of this book looks at current developments.

Part Four
Advanced Database Systems

14

Distributed and multi-media databases

14.1 Introduction

Although distributed and multi-media databases are grouped together in this chapter, they are really only related by being recent developments in database technology. They arise from the increased physical separation of computer users (of the same system) from each other and the attendant need to communicate material other then simple text.

Distributed multi-media databases do exist, however, although there is no reason why you cannot have a non-distributed multi-media database or a non-multi-media distributed database. We will therefore first discuss the problems of distribution and then discuss the problems of multi-media data.

14.2 Distribution in databases

There are many degrees of distribution possible in database systems. It is helpful to separate the concept of distribution into data distribution and DBMS distribution. In both cases, the distribution takes the form of splitting the data or DBMS between a number of different computers that may be geographically separated but interconnected by a network.

It is generally accepted that a database is only a distributed database if its data is distributed. It is not sufficient to simply operate the DBMS over a number of different machines and still refer to it as 'distributed'.

To introduce distributed databases we need to consider a range of database architectures that lead to full distribution, starting with the antithesis of distributed databases – centralized databases.

Complete centralization

This is the architecture that is associated historically with database systems. It comprises a single central computer running the DBMS with a number of 'dumb' terminals connected directly to it.

A centralized database system is shown in Figure 14.1. The terminals may be connected to the central computer using a modem to provide remote access to the system. The central computer would typically be a mini-computer or a mainframe. The

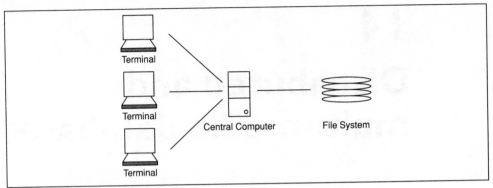

Figure 14.1 The architecture of a centralized database system.

terminals would at one time have been completely processor-less devices, originally teletypes and later 'dumb' terminals. These days, a personal computer (PC) running terminal-emulation software is probably the most common form of terminal.

Systems like this are becoming rarer as technology has shifted away from the use of single large computers towards the use of networks of personal computers. Centralized systems are in some respects easier to maintain since both the data and the DBMS reside on the same single machine.

The disadvantages of this system lie in the limitations imposed by the communication between the terminals and the central computer and by the need for the central computer to carry out all the processing. All the user-interface processing for each terminal must be carried out by the central computer. By making more use of the processing power available at each terminal, we can move to an architecture called 'client–server'.

Client–server

A **client–server database system** is shown in Figure 14.2. Such systems rely on a network. The network is a group of computers that may for instance be spread over a building and are connected together such that any one of them can send data to or receive data from any of the other computers in the network.

In client–server systems, the DBMS is split into two parts; the DBMS client and the DBMS server. The DBMS server is installed on one of the computers in the network and receives messages from the DBMS clients installed on the other machines in the network.

These client computers provide all the necessary user interface processing for the system, communicating with the server database and its associated computer. This is important because networks can only carry a finite amount of information and so, by only communicating data and by handling all user interface processing locally at the client, the performance of the system is less likely to be limited by the network.

In this situation, the database processing has been distributed between a number of machines in a network. This is still not an example of a distributed database since all the data still reside with the server computer.

The use of client–server databases has made it possible to provide superior interfaces to the database, moving beyond the text-based query or primitive form-based

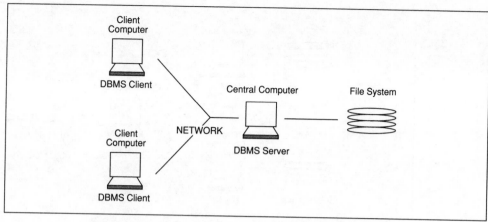

Figure 14.2 The architecture of a client–server database system

interface to the use of advanced graphical interfaces. It lends itself well to applications where the user interface is as important to the application as the data management. For instance, in a geographical information system (GIS) the client user interface appears as a map but the data that is used to draw the map is kept in the server part of the system.

Down-loading systems

The client–server architecture allows distribution of the processing in a DBMS. Some databases allow a degree of distribution of data without handling all the concurrency control problems usually associated with a distributed database.

For instance, under certain circumstances, a copy of the data can be down-loaded from the server database to a client that can then use the data. At some point in the future the data used locally must be copied back to the server database. If the data that was originally down-loaded has not been modified, then there is no need to copy it back to the master database.

This is acceptable as long as any data that the client changes will not be changed by other users. Such a situation could be found in a retail outlet that is part of a chain and supplied by a central warehouse as shown in Figure 14.3.

Data for the current head-office stock list could be down-loaded at the beginning of the day. This information would be used to handle customer enquiries about availability of products. Since the data is read-only, and will not be modified, there is no need to up-load the data. Similarly, the sales for the shop could be recorded locally and up-loaded to the central computer at the end of the day.

In the example of Figure 14.4, the same data structure is used to record the data both at the headquarters and at each branch. The data has a composite primary key on the branch and the product. It is assumed that a second sale of a product will result in the UnitsSold attribute being incremented rather than a new record being added.

Since every sales record has the branch as part of its key, there will be no conflicts when the data are merged.

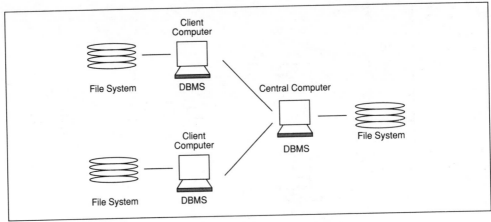

Figure 14.3 Architecture of a down-loading database system

SALES (Local copy)

BranchID	ProductID	Date	UnitsSold
BHAM	7246C	23/9/96	1
BHAM	7253D	23/9/96	2
BHAM	7546A	23/9/96	1

SALES (Headquarters)

BranchID	ProductID	Date	UnitsSold
BHAM	7246C	23/9/96	1
BHAM	7253D	23/9/96	2
BHAM	7546A	23/9/96	1
RDNG	6745C	23/9/96	3
RDNG	7451H	23/9/96	1
RDNG	7546A	23/9/96	1

Figure 14.4 Down-loading database tables

14.3   Distributed databases

Although the down-loading system we examined in the previous section is distributed, it does not fully embrace the ideal of a distributed database: that is, that the data may be anywhere in the system and the user need not be aware of its exact location. This concept is called **location transparency** and is one of the key goals of distributed databases.

Figure 14.5 shows a distributed database. In this arrangement, the DBMS is distributed across all the computers in the system. All the computers or 'nodes' in the network are running the same DBMS. There is no separation into client and server DBMSs.

In Figure 14.5, the data within the system are given letters. We can see that node 3 contains a complete set of the data, whereas nodes 1, 2 and 4 only contain some of the data. This means that some of the data is replicated at more than one of the

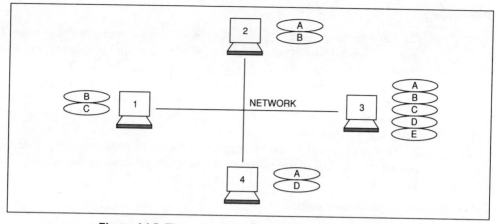

Figure 14.5 The architecture of a distributed database system

nodes. Such replication of data makes the job of ensuring consistency within the distributed databases all the more difficult.

The goals of a distributed database have been summarized by Kroenke (see Appendix B) as providing a number of transparencies from the user's point of view. These are paraphrased here.

- **Location transparency** – when the user needs to access a piece of data, the user should not have to specify on which node the data resides. So, if for instance there is not a copy of the data required at the present node, then the DMBS is responsible for retrieving the information from another node, without the user being aware of this.
- **Replication transparency** – the user should not have to be aware of how many copies there are of a piece of data. The problem of keeping multiple copies consistent in the face of user updates to the data is a function that the DBMS must perform.
- **Concurrency transparency** – duplicated and distributed data must respond to simultaneous user access in the same way as for a non-distributed system.
- **Failure transparency** – any failure in the system should behave as you would expect with a non-distributed system. Atomic transactions should either complete or fail and the database should remain in a consistent state.

All of these transparencies can be summarized as saying that from the user's perspective, a distributed database should behave in exactly the same way as a non-distributed one.

14.4   Concurrency control in distributed databases

Since there is no longer a single copy of the data the control of concurrent access can no longer be the responsibility of one computer. The nodes in the system must co-operate in order to ensure the consistency of the data. There are two approaches to managing this.

Primary site

In this approach, one of the nodes (sites) has the special responsibility for maintaining a master copy of all the data and for controlling concurrency. This node (the primary site) receives requests from the other nodes to lock items of data. Superficially, this seems very similar to the client–server architecture described in Section 14.2. However, there is a very important difference – namely, that the physical computer used as the primary site can be replaced by a different machine in the event of a failure.

This approach does rather go against the spirit of the distributed architecture in so far as the primary site is different from the other nodes in the system.

Fully distributed concurrency control

The alternative to the use of a primary site is for every request for a lock to be broadcast to every node in the system that holds a copy of the data. Any nodes objecting to the lock can then have their chance to veto the lock.

Distributed database management systems are becoming more widely incorporated into the philosophy of the large DBMS providers. What were once true client–server systems are starting to become multi-client–multi-server systems where there can be more than one server active within the system. From this state of affairs, it is only a short step to distribution.

14.5   Multi-media databases

Traditionally, the data held in a database have been textual and numeric. In recent years there has been a demand to store other media such as sound, video and still digital images. The advent of good user interfaces, made possible by the client–server and distributed architectures, has made it feasible to support the storage of all these media types within a database.

Applications of multi-media

Most existing multi-media systems can benefit from the database facilities of persistent storage and shared access. This leads to a wide range of uses for multi-media databases, a few of which are outlined in the following sections.

Digitized document retrieval

It is becoming more and more common for organizations to digitize paper documents. For instance, some insurance companies now routinely scan into digital form all correspondence with customers. This is particularly useful in insured-loss claim forms. Claim forms frequently contain sketches and other free-form comments to indicate the nature or circumstances of a loss: for instance, a photograph of damage to a car or a sketch of the position of a car in the road prior to a car accident. Such images are lodged in a database and associated with more usual structured data, such as names and addresses. The images and associated information can then be retrieved from anywhere in the company's computer network. This may be in offices all over the country.

Other uses of this kind of approach are in design applications, where design documents are either digitized or are already in electronic form and are catalogued in a database. Such systems are usually based on recording file names and do not therefore demand very much of the DBMS.

Image databases

There are a growing number of applications whose primary type of data is digitized still images. These may be satellite images of the Earth, medical images (e.g. X-ray photographs) or simply photographs for use by advertisers and magazines. The retrieval of images from such databases can be accomplished in one of two ways.

- By keyword – each image has associated with it a number of keywords that the user associates with the image at the time it was added to the database. Retrieving images is then simply a matter of searching on the keywords.
- By image content – in this case, images are retrieved using image processing techniques to find out something of the content of the image. This technique has been used with some success for medical and satellite images, though it relies on working within a specific field, where likely image content is predetermined.

In querying by content, it also becomes possible to query images by similarity to other images.

Interactive multi-media

Many multi-media applications are concerned with training, or what has become known as 'edutainment'. Such systems do not as yet make much use of database technology. Indeed, appropriate database technology is largely still in the research phase. In the future, true multi-media databases will be able to handle large-scale concurrent access of distributed multi-media, perhaps having direct control of the playback of continuous media such as sound and video.

Implementation

A simple technique used in many databases to accomplish the storage of multi-media objects is to place file names for the media items in the database. A database of digitized images might be a catalogue that associates records in the database with files containing the images. Many DBMSs allow such images to be displayed within the user interface of the DBMS without actually storing the images themselves. A similar approach can be used for video and sound, sometimes invoking external helper programs to play the media.

This technique, whilst acceptable for many applications, suffers from a number of difficulties.

- Organization of the potentially large number of media files. An extremely large number of files may impose practical problems for the underlying operating system. A case in point is the DOS operating system which only allows 11-character file names. Meaningful file names are almost impossible and even machine-generated file names may need to be partitioned into a number of directories.

- Controlling access to the serial media such as video and sound: for example, accessing on a frame-by-frame basis for video.

To address these problems, some new DBMS products, particularly OODBMSs, are providing support for what are called 'BLOBs' or 'binary large objects'. This allows multi-media data to be stored in the database rather than simply referenced as files.

14.6   Summary

In this chapter, we have looked at two interesting new areas of database technology. Both distributed databases and multi-media databases impose new requirements on database management systems.

We have explored the full range of distribution of databases, from the more traditional centralized systems to fully distributed systems, with a number of useful intermediate solutions along the way.

We have explored the trend towards storing media other than text in databases and explored some existing examples of the use of multi-media databases, such as digitized document retrieval and image databases. At present, most of the uses of databases in multi-media are concerned with fairly static data such as images. Other more difficult continuous media such as video and sound are still very much in the research domain in their use of database technology.

Both of these areas are stimulating a great deal of research that will shape the future face of database technology.

15
Advanced data modelling

15.1 Introduction

In this chapter, we examine some of the new developments in data modelling. In particular we will set the scene for the following chapter on the object-oriented database (OODB) model and discuss how it is establishing itself as the heir apparent to the relational model.

We will lay the foundations for understanding OODBs by looking at the various data models that have shaped object-oriented database management systems (OODBMSs). In introducing these new concepts we will continue with the example developed in the earlier sections of the book.

15.2 Basic concepts

Starting from the beginning, we need to re-examine how we model data: that is, how we represent the type of relationships that exist between entities, and even what we mean by 'entities'.

There are a number of important concepts common to all these data models that we consider in this chapter. These are:

- types (or classes) and instances,
- aggregation,
- inheritance,
- identification,
- methods,
- versions.

We will now explain each of these concepts in turn.

15.3 Types and instances

The idea of a type is that it represents a template for the construction of actual instances of the data. Thus the definition below defines the attributes or fields that an entity of type CUSTOMER should possess:

```
CUSTOMER
   Account number
   Name
   Address
```

An instance of the type represents the actual data in the database. So, for our example, a single item of data may appear as below:

```
CUSTOMER
   Account number : 45588987766
   Name: Adrian Barnes
   Address: 12 Carlisle St, Dewsbury
```

Clearly there will normally be many instances of any particular type. In the relational model, for instance, it is usual to represent types as relations and instances as rows in a table:

CUSTOMER

Account number	Name	Address
45588987766	Adrian Barnes	12 Carlisle St, Dewsbury
45588987768	Evelyn Farmer	112 Grebe Cl, Harrow
45588987775	George Harris	45 Ingleton Rd, Preston

The term 'class' is sometimes used to mean exactly the same thing as 'type'. However, we favour the more useful definition that a class is a type definition plus the set of instances that belong to that type. That is, a type defines the structure of the instances but does not, itself, know of the existence of any instances, whereas a class keeps a record of all its instances.

15.4 Aggregation

Aggregation is about grouping together information that is related. A type uses aggregation to collect together attributes that belong to a particular entity. This can be taken a step further if we decide that, in our example, we need to represent the component parts of an address separately, as shown below:

```
CUSTOMER
   Account number
   Name
   Address
         Street number
         Street name
         Town
```

What aggregation really means is that something is to be considered as part of another thing. Thus `Street number`, `Street name` and `Town` should each be considered to be a part of `Address`. This has particular implications on the way in which any DBMS handles aggregate items. For instance, in deleting an `Address` from a database, `Street number`, `Street name` and `Town` should all be deleted too.

15.5 Inheritance

Inheritance is an extremely useful concept that has come along with object orientation but has its roots much further back in artificial intelligence. It allows a database to represent natural hierarchies of types. Arranging types in an inheritance hierarchy removes the need to define attributes in many different places for similar data types. It is called inheritance because types lower down the hierarchy are said to inherit attributes higher up the tree.

Consider a database (based on our mortgage example) that contains the following types.

```
CUSTOMER                AGENT
   Account number          Name
   Name                    Address
   Address
```

Clearly, both these types have the attributes `Name` and `Address` in common. By using inheritance, we define a new type which we can call PERSON which contains the attributes that are common to both types. These attributes can then be removed from the original types. The result is the inheritance hierarchy shown in Figure 15.1.

At first sight, this may seem to offer little advantage over simply declaring `Name` and `Address` within both CUSTOMER and AGENT. In fact, there are several advantages to this approach, which are described below.

Every attribute has a domain (or type), string or integer for instance; sometimes the size of this domain is also included in the definition, thus `string20` may indicate a string of maximum size 20 characters. One advantage of using inheritance is that since attributes will have a domain (for instance, `Name : String20`), you will, by using inheritance, standardize this domain for the attribute. In our example, name is defined in the class PERSON, thus both CUSTOMER and AGENT will inherit the same definition of `Name`. If the attributes were defined separately there would be the possibility that they would be defined with different sizes. This could lead to problems if, for instance, the name of a CUSTOMER were being copied on to a new AGENT instance and the sizes were different. For example, if a CUSTOMER used 10 characters to record

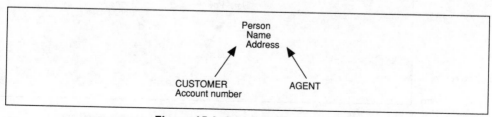

Figure. 15.1 An inheritance hierarchy

a `Name` and `AGENT` used only 7, then if a `CUSTOMER` called 'Jayaratna' were to become an `AGENT`, then either their name would become abbreviated to 'Jayarat' or a system error would occur.

This can be taken a step further if you associate constraints or triggers with the attributes (see Chapter 13). All this has the advantage that any changes to the attribute definition only need to be made at the superclass.

A second advantage of using inheritance is that any instances of `CUSTOMER` or `AGENT` are also instances of `PERSON`. Thus if you wanted to find any `CUSTOMER` or `AGENT` whose name was John, you could simply query the `PERSON` class rather than have to query both `CUSTOMER` and `AGENT` separately and then combine the two results.

In deciding to merge `CUSTOMER` and `AGENT`, as we did above, we are carrying out a process called **generalization**. That is, we are taking a number of classes and producing what is called a **generalized superclass**. This is perhaps the approach you would take when thinking in relational terms during the design of an OODB schema. If you start from the object-oriented viewpoint, it is likely that you would also use a technique called **specialization**.

In **specialization**, you start with a general concept, say `PERSON`, and then **specialize** it into subclasses such as `CUSTOMER` and `AGENT`. These subclasses are identified by you as special cases of the superclass and therefore may have additional attributes.

Any subclass must inherit all the attributes of its parent class. If you find yourself in the position of wanting to create a subclass with fewer attributes than its parent, it is likely that the class you are creating should appear higher in the inheritance hierarchy, as having fewer attributes makes it a simpler and therefore more general class.

What we have described above is termed **single inheritance**, since a class can only have one superclass. Some systems allow **multiple inheritance**, where a class can inherit from more than one parent class at a time. An example of this is shown in Figure 15.2.

A hovercraft has properties of both a land vehicle and a boat. In this case we wish the class `HOVERCRAFT` to inherit the attributes of both the `LANDVEHICLE` and `BOAT` classes.

One problem with multiple inheritance is that under some circumstances a conflict can arise between inherited attributes of the same name. If, for instance, there are two paths up through the inheritance hierarchy, and the attribute `Name` is present in both paths, which `Name` should be inherited? One `Name` could have the domain `String(20)`, the other `String(10)`. This means that systems using multiple inheritance must be able to resolve such conflicts. In practice, instances of multiple inheritance are rare and for this reason some implemented data models do not support it.

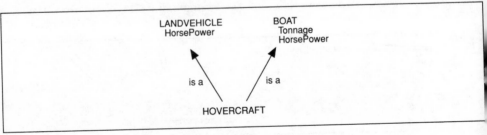

Figure 15.2 An example of multiple inheritance

15.6 Identification

Central to the whole database concept is the ability to refer to one part of the database from another part. For instance, a database containing two types, CUSTOMER and INVESTMENT, will need to be able to associate CUSTOMERs with a particular INVESTMENT because, at some point, a user is going to ask for a list of INVESTMENTs held by a particular CUSTOMER. In a relational database, we can refer from one record to another because every record has a unique primary key. When one record refers to another, it is by recording the value of the other record's primary key in one or more of its attributes. This type of reference is called **reference by value** and it is not the only way of referring from one record to another. Indeed, reference by value has a number of problems associated with it. Not least, there is the problem of inconsistencies appearing if the value of the primary key is changed.

A second disadvantage becomes apparent when, in designing a relational database, a decision has to be made as to whether to use a complex composite primary key (perhaps using three attributes) or to create a new attribute just to act as a primary key. An example of this might be to choose between

```
AGENT
   *Name
   *Town
   Address
   Client list
```

and

```
AGENT
   *AgentNumber
   Name
   Town
   Address
   Client list
```

Both solutions have minor drawbacks. The first solution has the disadvantage that any other relation wishing to refer to a particular agent will have to have two attributes, Name and Town, to be used as foreign keys. The second solution results in a new attribute, AgentNumber, whose only purpose is to serve as an identifier for a record. This identifier will usually be a meaningless number, or possibly an identifying string. This is not really something that the end-user should have to see and deal with since it is not a part of the real world that the database is trying to model.

An alternative to referring to things by value is to refer to them by identity. By this, we mean that every entity within the system has an identity that is independent of the values contained in its attributes. This is a slightly difficult concept to get hold of; one way is to imagine that every record in the database is on a piece of card. You can change anything that is written on the card, and it does not matter because it is still the same card. On the other hand, reference by value (the relational way) relies on some values on the card to identify it.

If you like, you can think of reference by identity as a sort of system-generated primary key that the user never has to see. Any references to an entity uses this key and it has the following properties:

- It cannot be changed.
- It cannot be reassigned to another entity after its original owner has been deleted.
- It is unique throughout the whole database.

In an OODB, such identifiers are called OIDs (object identifiers), pronounced as in aden*oids*, and we will discuss these further in the next chapter.

15.7 Methods

Traditionally, databases have been solely about storing data. When it was necessary to do more complex things with the data, a program was written in an ordinary programming language. This program would contain commands to query the DBMS through its external query interface. In many of the next-generation DBMSs it has become common to store associated pieces of program in the database too.

To some extent, the constraints and triggers of relational databases are a similar idea. However, 'methods' are an altogether more powerful mechanism. A method can contain a mixture of programming commands (often based on a programming language such as C) and queries to retrieve information from other parts of the database.

Methods can be inherited in exactly the same way as attributes, adding greatly to their power. We will discuss methods further in Chapter 16 when discussing OODBs.

15.8 Versions

Relational and older-generation databases provide little support for representing the changing of data over time. Especially in the design process, it is useful for old versions of data to be retained after the data has been changed. In this way a history is kept of previous values for attributes. This can for instance allow the database user to explore different scenarios; for instance, changing some values, knowing that they can always revert to an earlier version with the old values intact.

Versions can be categorized as either **alternatives** or **derivatives**. A number of alternative versions may exist in a system, where alternative options are being considered at the same time. One of these alternatives could then be chosen to be used to create a derivative version, moving things forward.

An example of the use of versions is given in Figure 15.3. In this example, we are considering the process of house buying. Initially, three offers are received for the house (Offer1 to Offer3). These are alternatives. Of these, Offer2 is chosen and Offer2.1 is said to be a derivative of Offer2. In Offer2.1, the value of the Notes attribute has been changed to indicate provisional acceptance of the offer. Two alternatives (Offer2.1.1 and Offer2.1.2) then become apparent – one offer includes fixtures and fittings in the price, the other does not. Finally, Offer2.1.2.1 is derived from Offer2.1.2, producing an accepted offer.

An important property of versions is that it is possible to backtrack to earlier versions: if, for instance, Smith should withdraw from the sale it is possible to revert to Offer1 or Offer3 and derive another version tree from there.

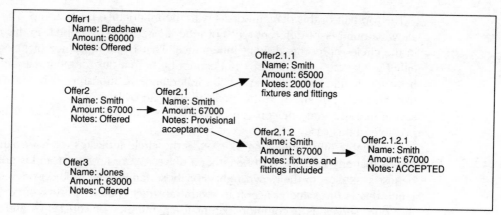

Figure 15.3 An example of versioning

15.9 Enhanced entity–relationship model

In Chapter 4 we introduced the idea of entity–relationship or ER diagrams as a useful technique for data modelling. The ER model has in recent years been extended to include concepts such as inheritance. The enhanced (or extended) entity–relationship model (EER) is, like the ER model, not the technology for a database, but rather a way of modelling data abstractly before mapping it onto an actual database model such as the relational or object model. In the main the EER model is to OODBs what the ER model is to relational databases.

Figure 15.4 shows an EER diagram. Entities are enclosed in rectangles and relationships in diamonds. Attributes are also shown on the diagram as ovals.

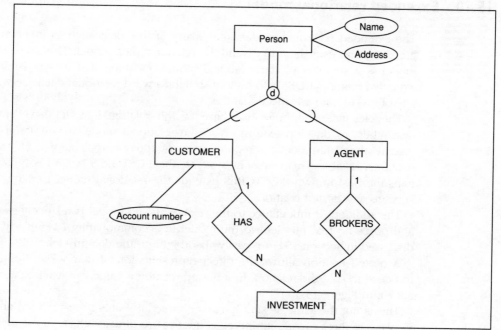

Figure 15.4 An extended entity–relationship (EER) diagram

The top half of this diagram deals with the inheritance relationship. The EER model allows a number of different types of inheritance to be described. In this case, the 'd' in the circle represents disjoint inheritance. That is, any instance of PERSON must be either a CUSTOMER or an AGENT but cannot be both a CUSTOMER and an AGENT. This is how you would normally expect the inheritance relationship to be, however, if you like, you can put an 'o' in the circle to indicate overlapping, in which case you are saying that the same person can be both an AGENT and a CUSTOMER. This is after all possible in this case.

The double line connecting PERSON to the circle indicates total specialization. This means that any PERSON must be either a CUSTOMER or an AGENT and is not allowed to be just a PERSON in their own right. For those familiar with object-oriented programming, this is the same concept as a pure abstract class. A pure abstract class is one that only serves as a common parent for a number of subclasses and is not itself allowed to be instantiated (instances of it cannot be created).

If the double line were replaced by a single line, it would indicate that it is permissible to have instances of PERSON that are neither AGENTs nor CUSTOMERs. Such instances would have the attributes Name and Address.

The remainder of the diagram shows the relationships between the CUSTOMER, AGENT and INVESTMENT entities. The relationships are named and the type of relationship (one-to-many etc.) indicated by a 1 and N on each side of the relationship. Many-to-many relationships are indicated by an M and N on each side of the relationship.

Having looked at the concepts, we can now go on to see how they are applied in a number of data models.

15.10   Extended relational model

The extended relational model takes many of the ideas such as inheritance and aggregation and uses them to extend the relational data model. The extended relational model is a superset of the relational model, meaning that it is possible to use an extended relational DBMS to build a straightforward relational database without using any of these more advanced features.

The elegance and huge user-base of the relational model have spurred some researchers to develop extensions to the relational model in an attempt to accommodate the data-modelling requirements of today's applications. Of the extended relational database management systems, the POSTGRES system is typical, and perhaps the best known. POSTGRES extends the relational model to allow inheritance, versions and nested relations.

The addition of inheritance to the relational data model is relatively straightforward and poses no real problem to the model in accommodating it. Similarly, versions as discussed in Section 15.8 are easily absorbed into the data model.

A nested relation allows the direct representation of composite attributes without the need to split the relation. In a nested relation a value can itself be a relation, as is shown in Figure 15.5.

This is not the same as simply having three attributes Street, Town and PostCode in place of the Address attribute, as queries are directed through the nested relation, for example:

PERSON				
Name	Address			Age
	Street	Town	PostCode	
Fred	10 Queen St	Lancaster	LA1	56

Figure 15.5 Nested relations in the extended relationship data model

```
SELECT Address.Town from Person
```

In this case, the dot notation is used to indicate that Town is a part of a composite attribute Address. The POSTGRES system has demonstrated that much can be accomplished by extending the relational database and hence retaining compatibility with the large body of existing relational expertise. One problem with adapting relational technology is that the elegance of relational calculus queries is, to some extent, corrupted to handle these extra facilities.

15.11 Semantic data model

The semantic data model (SDM) attempts to provide a data model that includes as many useful ways of getting semantic information (meaning) into the structure of the database as possible. Part of the development of SDM was the analysis of the inadequacies of existing data models. SDM is really a data description language (DDL) and can be used to describe schemas of proposed or existing databases. Many of SDM's features have been implemented in OODBs and the influence that SDM has exerted on the data models used in OODBs is readily apparent in the terminology used in SDM.

The SDM is based on classes that comprise sets of objects that all need to represent the same attributes. An SDM schema consists of a number of definitions for such classes. An example is shown below:

```
PERSON
    member attributes:
        Name value class : PERSON_NAMES
        Address value class : ADDRESS
    class attributes :
        Number_of_people value class : INTEGER
    identifiers :
        Name
```

Each class definition has up to three parts: member attributes, class attributes and identifiers. Member attributes are attributes for which every instance of the class will have its own value. Class attributes are associated with the class as a whole and not individual instances, and so only one value is stored for these attributes no matter how many instances there are of the class.

In both cases, the domain of the attribute may be either a primitive type such as STRING or INTEGER or a class name such as PERSON_NAMES or ADDRESS in the example above. Attributes may also be multi-valued, that is, their value is a set of values rather than a single value.

The identifier section of a definition declares attributes that may be used to identify individual instances. Such attributes must have values that are unique within the class.

The SDM also supports inheritance. So our example schema could be written in SDM as:

```
PERSON
    member attributes:
        Name value class : PERSON_NAMES
        Address value class : ADDRESS
    class attributes :
        Number_of_people value class : INTEGER
    identifiers :
        Name

CUSTOMER
    interclass connection: subclass of PERSON
    member attributes:
        Account number
            value class : ACCOUNT_NUMBERS
    identifiers :
        Account number
Agent
    interclass connection: subclass of PERSON
```

The SDM is very powerful and, as well as inheritance, allows relationships to be expressed between classes. We can extend the example above to include the extra class INVESTMENT and the two relationships that link it to CUSTOMER and AGENT. In doing so, we can illustrate another aspect of the SDM, namely inverse relationships, as illustrated in the example below.

```
PERSON
    member attributes:
        Name value class : PERSON_NAMES
        Address value class : ADDRESS
    class attributes :
        Number_of_people value class : INTEGER
    identifiers :
        Name

CUSTOMER
    interclass connection: subclass of PERSON
    member attributes:
        Account number
            value class : ACCOUNT_NUMBERS
    Investments
            value class: INVESTMENT
            inverse: Customers
            multivalued
    identifiers :
        Account number
```

```
AGENT
    interclass connection: subclass of PERSON
    member attributes:
            Investments
                    value class: INVESTMENT
                    inverse: Agents
                    multivalued

INVESTMENT
    member attributes:
            Customer
                    value class: CUSTOMER
                    inverse: Investments
            Agent
                    value class: AGENT
                    inverse: Agents
```

By defining the inverse relationships, we are declaring that should a CUSTOMER add an investment to their attribute Investments, then the Customer attribute of that INVESTMENT must automatically be set to the CUSTOMER to which the investment was added. This process ensures that consistency is maintained between class instances involved in one-to-many and many-to-many relationships.

15.12 Summary

In this chapter, we have looked at a number of key concepts that are important to the understanding of the next generation of advanced database systems and in particular of the object-oriented database management systems that we will meet in the next chapter.

These concepts are:

- types (or classes) and instances,
- aggregation,
- inheritance,
- identification,
- methods,
- versions.

In addition, we have looked at how these ideas are applied in a number of advanced database models that have all contributed to the object-oriented database model.

16
Object-oriented databases

16.1 Introduction

In this chapter, we explore the object-oriented data model which incorporates many of the ideas described in the previous chapter on advanced data models. This object-oriented data model is used as the basis for a number of object-oriented database management systems (OODBMSs). We describe the characteristics of such systems and explore the use of object-oriented databases.

16.2 From relations to objects

The relational database has been found cumbersome and not altogether suited to some new applications such as CAD (computer-aided design), CASE (computer-aided software engineering) tools, GIS (geographical information systems), telecommunications and financial systems.

This unsuitability stems from the rigid and restrictive constraints of normalized relations. It is not that the relational database cannot represent the information, it is just that it becomes unwieldy to represent such things as multi-valued and composite attributes. With the complicated data usually found in such applications this can also lead to prohibitively poor performance.

There is no problem in occasionally representing multi-valued attributes in a relational database by using two tables, but if the applications you are developing mostly use multi-valued attributes, this becomes unwieldy and difficult to manage.

OODBMS standards and maturity

There is no doubt that relational databases are still in the ascendancy commercially. Most new database applications are being built using relational technology. OODBs have now been around as research prototypes for ten years or more and as commercial products for about five years. The technology is still relatively immature and until recently there was very little standardization.

With the advent of the ODMG (Object Database Management Group (Cattell, 1993), a standard set of features and a query language (OQL) have been developed. This standard looks likely to become universally adopted as it is supported by most of the OODBMS vendors and many of the large computer companies such as Hewlett-Packard, SUN and Texas Instruments.

16.3 The object-oriented data model

A data model is the abstract model used by a database to represent data. For a relational database it is the relational data model. For the OODB it is the object-oriented data model.

The elements of the object-oriented data model are classes, instances, attributes, relationships and methods. Of these, a class roughly corresponds to the table of a relational database, instances correspond to a record, and attributes are similar in both models. Relationships and methods are specific to the object-oriented model. Each of these things is now described in more detail.

Classes

A class or class definition defines the type of the data, that is, it specifies the attributes, relationships and methods that data belonging to that class (instances of the class) will possess. A database will comprise a number of class definitions arranged in an inheritance hierarchy as shown in Figure 16.1.

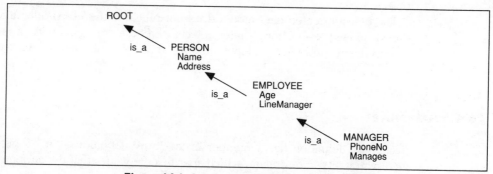

Figure 16.1 An inheritance hierarchy in an OODB

In this figure, all the classes spring from one class at the top of the tree that in this case we have called ROOT, but is sometimes called CLASS or OBJECT. PERSON is a subclass of ROOT. ROOT does not have any attributes for PERSON to inherit. However, EMPLOYEE inherits the Name and Address attributes of PERSON as does MANAGER which also inherits the attributes of PERSON. For more information about inheritance, see Chapter 15.

Instances

What we have described so far is the structure of the data rather than the actual data itself. The actual data is held in what are called instances of the class. Thus Figure 16.2a shows the class definition for EMPLOYEE (inherited attributes shown in italics) and Figure 16.2b shows two instances of EMPLOYEE.

Crucial to the object-oriented data model is the concept of object identity. Every instance has associated with it a unique **object identifier** or OID. This OID stays with the object for the whole of its life and cannot be changed. See Chapter 15 for more information on this subject of reference by identity. In Figure 16.2b, the Line Manager attribute is shown as an arrow indicating a reference to some other object not in the diagram.

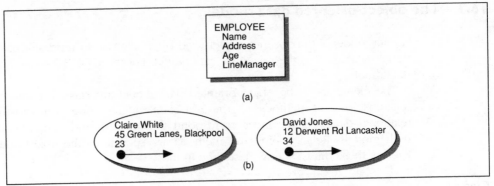

Figure 16.2 Classes and instances in an OODB

Although the data model is called the object-oriented data model, we usually only talk in terms of classes and instances. In the object-oriented data model, both classes and instances are said to be **objects**. In fact, anything that has identity (an OID) is an object.

The object-oriented data model does not preclude the use of identifying attributes (keys). Indeed, even though inter-object references are by identity, it is useful to be able to define attributes as identifying for the purpose of queries from within a class.

16.4 Attributes

Each class definition has a number of **attribute** definitions. An attribute has associated with it a type or domain which specifies the values that the attribute can have.

A major difference between attributes in the object-oriented and relational data models is that in the object-oriented data model attributes can be multi-valued. That is, the value of an attribute can be a set of values rather than just a single value. For instance, a CUSTOMER may have a number of phone numbers, as in the definition below.

```
CUSTOMER
   Name : String
   Phone : SET OF String
```

The availability of multi-valued attributes is particularly valuable where references are from one attribute to another. In this case, the multi-valued attributes are used to represent one-to-many and many-to-many relationships between instances. In some OODBMSs such relationships are simply represented as attributes; however, in the ODMG's object-oriented data model, relationships are represented separately.

16.5 Relationships

If, for instance, a manager manages many employees but each employee is only managed by one manager then there is a one-to-many relationship between the manager and the employee.

In the relational data model this would be represented using primary and foreign keys as shown below:

```
MANAGER
ManagerNumber Name Address

EMPLOYEE
EmployeeNumber Name Address ManagerNumber
```

In the example above, the relationship is only recorded in the EMPLOYEE end of the relationship. In the object-oriented data model this relationship would be represented at both ends of the relationship. The EMPLOYEE would, as in the relational example, record a link to the manager that manages the employee. In addition, though, the MANAGER would record a list of all EMPLOYEEs that they manage. This is represented diagrammatically in Figure 16.3.

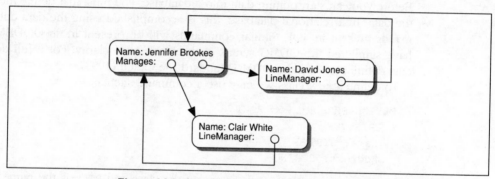

Figure 16.3 References between objects in an OODB

In the example of Figure 16.3, the relationship is recorded in the attributes Manages and LineManager. The use of attributes in this way often entails the use of a special keyword that indicates that a relationship is being recorded. This can also be used to indicate that the relationship is an inverse relationship (see Section 15.11) and should a new EMPLOYEE be added, then when the LineManager attribute is given a value, the object identifier of the new EMPLOYEE is recorded automatically in the Manages attribute of the manager. Similarly, adding a new employee to the list of employees managed by a manager would automatically result in the LineManager attribute of the employee being set to the manager.

16.6 Methods

Methods are pieces of code associated with a class definition and available to all instances of the class. The method can be used to simply calculate and return a value and is convenient if it appears to the user of the database as simply an attribute that calculates a value rather than stores it.

For instance, if an employee has a pay increment every year, then the date of the next increment can be calculated from the date of the last increment and does not therefore need to be stored in the database but can be calculated instead. The example below shows how a method may be defined:

```
EMPLOYEE
   Name
   DateOfLastAppraisal
   NextAppraisal : METHOD DateOfLastAppraisal + 1 Year
```

The code contained in methods may be much more complicated and comprise both query language commands for the database and procedural programming language constructs.

16.7   Data definition

Before you can start putting data into a database, you must first define the structure of the data. In a relational database, this is accomplished using the data definition commands present in SQL. Similar commands will be present in an OODBMS. Here we have simplified the ODMG syntax in the interests of clarity. For a full description of data definition using the ODMG standard see Cattell (1993).

To define a new class we may use a command such as:

```
DEFINE PERSON FROM ROOT
ATTRIBUTES
   Name: STRING
   Address: STRING
```

In this example, PERSON is the name of the class and ROOT is the name of its parent class. In this case we use the class ROOT to represent the top of the inheritance hierarchy. From PERSON we can then define EMPLOYEE:

```
DEFINE EMPLOYEE FROM PERSON
ATTRIBUTES
   Age: NUMBER
```

We can now define a class MANAGER that is a specialization (that is to say, a subclass) of EMPLOYEE. MANAGER will have a relationship with EMPLOYEE whereby any employee is managed by a manager and any manager can manage zero or more employees. This one-to-many relationship can be represented as an inverse relationship by adding a relationship to each class, giving the two classes below:

```
DEFINE EMPLOYEE FROM PERSON
ATTRIBUTES
   Age: NUMBER
RELATIONSHIPS
   LineManager: MANAGER INVERSE OF MANAGER Manages

DEFINE MANAGER FROM EMPLOYEE
ATTRIBUTES
   PhoneNo: STRING
RELATIONSHIPS
   Manages: SET OF EMPLOYEE INVERSE OF EMPLOYEE LineManager
```

The presence of the inverse relationship will ensure that should, for instance, a new instance of EMPLOYEE be created, and its LineManager be set to a MANAGER instance that already exists, then that instance will automatically be added to the set of employees recorded in the Manages attribute.

The ODBMG has developed a standard object-oriented data model that provides explicitly for the collection of the instances of a particular class. So rather than assume that the class itself will keep a record of all its instances, a separate variable is used to hold the set of instances for a class. Thus in defining a new class, it is usual to also state the name of the variable that will hold the set of instances of the class using the EXTENT keyword thus:

```
DEFINE EMPLOYEE FROM PERSON
EXTENT Employees
ATTRIBUTES
    Age: NUMBER
```

It is then possible to carry out queries on all the instances of a class using this EXTENT variable.

16.8 Data manipulation

The standard query language for relational databases is SQL or structured query language. Until recently, there was no standard equivalent for OODBs. Each OODBMS had its own query language, often called OSQL. However, with the advent of the ODMG standards group, a query language has been defined called OQL (object query language) and this seems likely to be universally adopted.

Like SQL, OQL is declarative; that is, queries are expressed in terms of what you want rather than how to get it. The OQL has the virtue that as a standard it is somewhat flexible about its syntax, providing an abstract set of functions for querying and holding results that lends itself to being actually implemented either as a stand-alone query language (like SQL) or with a syntax based on the C++ or Smalltalk language. In the remainder of this section we discuss the OQL in terms of the stand-alone query language; that is, as an object-oriented equivalent of SQL.

The OQL assumes that the OODBMS's variant of the object-oriented data model is being used. This model is just as described in the previous sections. The basic syntax of OQL is very similar to SQL, being centred on the SELECT FROM WHERE expression. To find all the ages of all managers under 40, we could write:

```
SELECT x.age
FROM x IN Managers
WHERE x.age <= 40
```

If there are only two managers in the database then the result of this query might be:

```
(40 32)
```

Note that Managers is an extent variable for the class MANAGER and not actually a class. The query variable x is used to represent any instance of the class.

In a command-line interface to an OODB, this would cause the query result to be displayed, listing all the ages of managers under 40. A result would also be returned, and this could for instance be assigned to a variable.

So, an OQL expression will return one of the following:

- a single primitive (literal) value such as 23 or "Rosie",
- a collection of primitive values (as in the example above),
- a single object (usually an instance),
- a collection of objects.

Thus, if we were to carry out a query to find the name as well as the age of all managers under 45, we would write:

```
SELECT STRUCT(n: x.name, a: x.age)
FROM x IN Managers
WHERE x.age < 45
```

The result of this is that for each manager under 45, a structure containing the name and age of that manager will be constructed and added to the collection. Finally, this collection will be returned and printed out, as shown in the text below.

```
((n: Jennifer Brookes a: 40) (n: Andrew Smith a: 32))
```

From the examples above, it is clear that the OQL has a collection and structuring functionality built in. In fact, OSQL supports structures, sets, lists (ordered sets), bags (sets with repeated elements) and arrays. For a full explanation of the features of OQL see Cattell (1993).

In returning values, queries can be nested, so that the result of one query forms part of another query. Thus, if we wished to find all the employees whose salary is greater than £15,000, together with their manager, but grouped by the manager, we could write:

```
SELECT STRUCT (mgrName: x.name, subords:
    (SELECT y.Name FROM y in x.Manages WHERE y.Salary > 15000))
FROM x in Managers
```

This would return the following:

```
((mgrName: Jennifer Brookes subords: (Andrew Smith, Claire White,
David Jones))
(mgrName: Andrew Smith subords: (Beryl James)))
```

16.9 Language bindings

Just as many applications that use relational databases comprise both a DBMS and external clients, the OODBMS also has programs containing embedded query language commands that allow development outside of the OODBMS.

Figure 16.4 shows the relationship between the various components of an OODBMS. As well as a command-line query language equivalent to the SQL of a relational database, there are language bindings that allow external programs to act on the database. These language bindings may be similar to the embedded SQL found in relational databases. However, in an OODB the binding may be much closer. That is

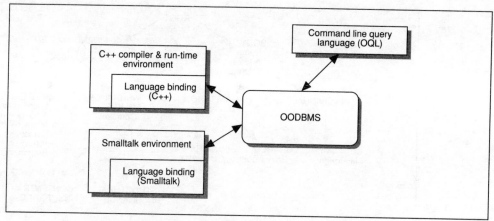

Figure 16.4 Ways of interacting with an OODBMS

to say, rather than simply embedding OQL commands, it is often possible to use the built-in data structures of the programming language directly, by allowing them to mirror the corresponding data in the database. The ODMG's definition of OQL allows OQL to use the syntax of other programming languages.

16.10 An example

In this example, we will develop a database structure, populate it with some data and then carry out a number of queries on it. We start with the entity–relationship diagram of Figure 4.3 repeated and extended in Figure 16.5.

From the entities of Figure 16.5, we can derive two inheritance hierarchies: one concerned with individuals and organizations such as CUSTOMER, BRANCH and INSURANCE_COMPANY and a second concerned with the financial entities MORTGAGE and INSURANCE. These hierarchies are shown in Figure 16.6. Note that we have also specialised INSURANCE into CONTENTS_INSURANCE and STRUCTURAL_INSURANCE.

The classes for this database are now defined:

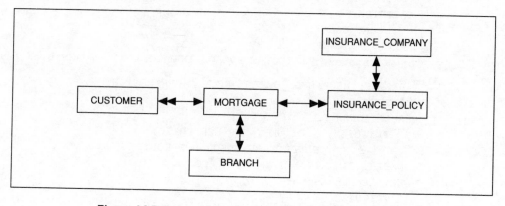

Figure 16.5 Entity–relationship diagram for a mortgage example

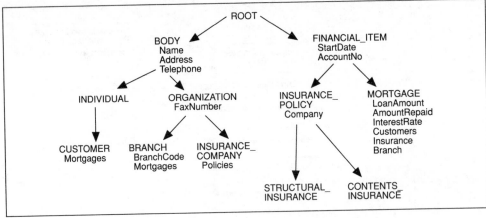

Figure 16.6 Inheritance hierarchy for mortgage example

```
DEFINE BODY FROM ROOT
KEY Name
ATTRIBUTES
  Name : STRING
  Address : STRING
  Telephone : STRING

DEFINE INDIVIDUAL FROM BODY

DEFINE CUSTOMER FROM INDIVIDUAL
EXTENT Customers
RELATIONSHIPS
  Mortgage : MORTGAGE
           INVERSE OF MORTGAGE Customers

DEFINE ORGANIZATION FROM BODY
ATTRIBUTES
  FaxNumber : STRING

DEFINE BRANCH FROM ORGANIZATION
EXTENT Branches
ATTRIBUTES
  BranchCode : STRING
RELATIONSHIPS
  Mortgages : SET OF MORTGAGE INVERSE OF MORTGAGE Branch

DEFINE INSURANCE_COMPANY FROM ORGANIZATION
EXTENT Insurance_Companies
RELATIONSHIPS
  Policies : SET OF INSURANCE_POLICY
           INVERSE OF INSURANCE_POLICY Company
DEFINE FINANCIAL_ITEM FROM ROOT
KEY AccountNumber
ATTRIBUTES
  StartDate : DATE
```

```
    AccountNumber : STRING

DEFINE INSURANCE_POLICY FROM FINANCIAL_ITEM
EXTENT Insurance_Policies
RELATIONSHIPS
   Company : INSURANCE_COMPANY

DEFINE CONTENTS_INSURANCE FROM INSURANCE_POLICY

DEFINE STRUCTURAL_INSURANCE FROM INSURANCE_POLICY

DEFINE MORTGAGE FROM FINANCIAL_ITEM
EXTENT Mortgages
ATTRIBUTES
   LoanAmount : CURRENCY
   AmountRepaid : CURRENCY
   InterestRate : NUMBER
RELATIONSHIPS
   Customers : SET OF CUSTOMER INVERSE OF CUSTOMER Mortgages
   Insurance: SET OF INSURANCE INVERSE OF INSURANCE Mortgage
   Branch : BRANCH INVERSE OF BRANCH Mortgage
```

Having defined the classes for this example, we can now add some data:

```
CUSTOMER (Name : 'Jennifer Brookes', Address : '56 Mansell
Court, Reading', Phone : '27946')
CUSTOMER (Name : 'Claire White', Address: '45 Green lane,
Blackpool', Phone : '732954')
CUSTOMER (Name: 'David Jones', Address : '12 Derwent Rd,
Lancaster', Phone : '325469')
```

Note that the relationship Mortgage is not given a value here. This will not take place until the Mortgage is created. Similarly, we can now create some branches and some insurance companies.

```
BRANCH (Name : 'Preston Central', Address : 'Market Square,
Preston', BranchCode: 'PRES1')

BRANCH (Name : 'Reading Central', Address : 'Church St,
Reading', BranchCode: 'READ1')
INSURANCE_COMPANY (Name: 'Happy Accident')
INSURANCE_COMPANY (Name: 'Wisdom')
```

Having now created instances of CUSTOMER, BRANCH and INSURANCE_COMPANY without providing any relationship values, we can now accomplish this by creating an instance of MORTGAGE.

```
MORTGAGE (StartDate: 15/12/96, AccountNumber: 7235419,
LoanAmount: 30000, AmountRepaid: 750, InterestRate: 7.75,
Customer: SET (SELECT x FROM x IN Customers WHERE x.name =
'Claire White')
Insurance: (CONTENTS_INSURANCE (StartDate: 15/12/96,
   Company: (SELECT x FROM x IN Insurance_Companies
                  WHERE x.name = 'Happy Accident')))
```

```
Branch: (SELECT x FROM x IN Branches WHERE x.name = 'Preston
Central'))
```

In creating an instance of MORTGAGE in this way, the inverse relationships Customers, Insurance and Branch will all result in references being added to the other side of the reference.

Note the creation of an insurance instance from within the mortgage creation statement. Another interesting aspect of this statement is the use of a query to retrieve the appropriate customer to assign to the mortgage. In practice, such an assignment is more likely to come about as the result of direct manipulation of a user interface.

Having created our database, we can now give some example queries.

Find the names of all customers.

```
SELECT x.Name FROM x IN Customers
-> ('Jennifer Brookes', 'Claire White', 'David Jones')
```

Find the name of the branch where Claire White's mortgage is held.

```
SELECT x.Mortgage.Branch.Name
FROM x IN Customers WHERE x.Name = 'Claire White'
-> 'Preston Central'
```

Find the names of the insurance companies used in mortgage transactions broken down by branch.

```
SELECT STRUCT (B: x.Name, Ins:
    (SELECT y.Company.Name FROM x.Mortgage.Insurance)
FROM Branches
-> ((B: 'Preston Central' Ins: ('Happy Accident')) (B: 'Reading
Central' Ins: ()))
```

16.11 Summary

In this chapter we have examined the concepts that make up the object-oriented data model. We have compared the relational and object models and seen how the limitations of the relational model are addressed by object orientation. The development of the ODMG standard for OODBs has been explained and examples given of data definition and manipulation using this standard.

17

The design of object-oriented databases

17.1 Introduction

The design of object-oriented database schemas is fraught with difficulty. On the one hand, the close relationship between object-oriented databases and programming languages makes the object-oriented design methodologies such as HOOD and OMT appropriate. On the other hand, the data models traditionally used for data model design, such as entity–relationship (ER), extended entity–relationship (EER) and semantic objects could be equally valuable.

The choice of design methodology depends largely on the application being developed. An application that is very closely tied to a programming language might best be designed using HOOD or OMT, whereas an application that is very database-centred may be more suited to being designed using EER or semantic object model (SOM) techniques.

Since the use of object-oriented methodologies is well documented elsewhere (Sommerville, 1993) we will concentrate on the use of EER and SOM for designing the data model of the system.

17.2 Extended entity–relationship modelling

The EER model (described in Chapter 15) extends the ER model which was originally devised in the 1970s to aid the design of relational databases. The EER adds inheritance to the ER model, making for a close relationship between the EER and object-oriented database data models. In general, an EER can be directly mapped onto an object-oriented database schema, as shown in Figure 17.1. Figure 17.1a shows an EER diagram and (b) the corresponding OODB schema definition commands.

Each entity type is mapped onto exactly one class and all the attributes of the entity transferred to the class. The inheritance hierarchy is declared in the subclasses. That is, when CUSTOMER is declared, it is declared as a subclass of PERSON, using the ISA keyword.

Relationships are modelled in the object-oriented data model using attributes. Thus, the one-to-many relationship between CUSTOMER and INVESTMENT is represented in the object-oriented data model using an attribute Customer in the INVESTMENT class and a set-valued attribute (Investments) in the CUSTOMER class. The relationship between AGENT and INVESTMENT is modelled in a similar way.

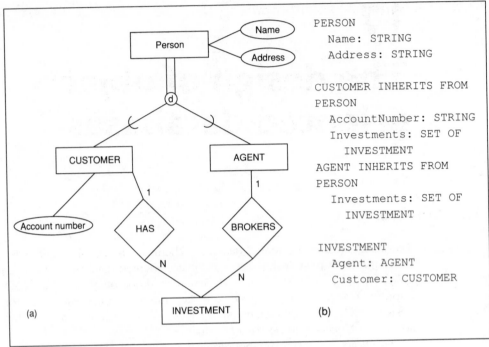

Figure 17.1 Mapping an EER data model onto an OODB schema

The EER and object-oriented database data models each have some features that the other does not represent. These are shown in Figure 17.2, where EER concepts that have an object-oriented equivalent are connected by arrows and concepts that have no counterpart in the other model are shown disconnected.

The fact that some concepts that are present in the EER model are not present in the OODB model and vice versa means that in designing a data model using the EER approach, some information in the EER model will not be used when the EER diagram is converted into an object-oriented database schema. Similarly information not directly represented in the EER will have to be added to the final schema.

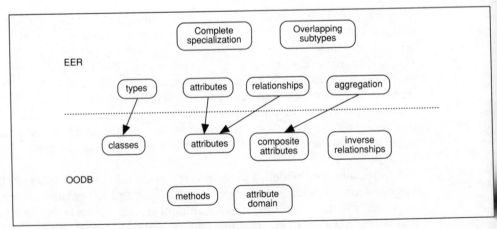

Figure 17.2 The relationship between the EER and OODB concepts

17.3 The semantic object model

The semantic object model (SOM) is a recent development from the semantic data model (SDM) which was described in Chapter 15. The SOM is very closely related to the object-oriented database model and is arguably a much more suitable technique for designing object-oriented database schemas.

The main building block of the SOM is the **semantic object** (SO) which corresponds very closely to the class definition. The SOM represents inheritance and aggregation directly and represents all relationships as attributes. All relationships are inverse and are represented as attributes in the SOs on both sides of the relationship.

All attributes (and hence relationships) have a minimum and a maximum cardinality. This allows one-to-many relationships to be represented by two attributes, one with cardinality 1:1 and the other with 1:n as shown in Figure 17.3. In the example of Figure 17.3, the attribute CUSTOMER of the semantic object MORTGAGE must have exactly one value and that value will be a CUSTOMER. Similarly, CUSTOMER has an attribute called MORTGAGE whose value must be zero or more mortgages.

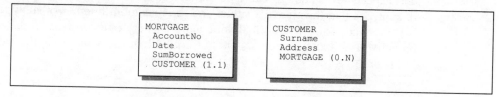

Figure 17.3 A one-to-many relationship in the SOM

Multi-valued attributes are represented directly in the SOM using the same cardinality notation as for relationships. In addition, it is also possible to define composite attributes that are made up of a number of atomic attributes. These composite attributes can also be multi-valued. Thus in Figure 17.4, there may be up to two addresses for a customer, each address comprising Line1, Line2, Town and PostCode. There may also be up to three phone numbers for an individual.

Representing inheritance

Clearly, if it is to be of any use in designing OODBs, the SOM must allow specialization and generalization to be represented. The SOM represents specialization and generalization (inheritance) in a similar way to other relationships. For example, the inheritance relationship between CUSTOMER, AGENT and PERSON might be that PERSON is an abstract class with attributes Name and Address, and CUSTOMER and AGENT are

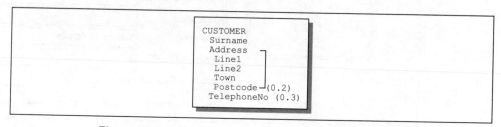

Figure 17.4 Composite and multi-valued attributes in the SOM

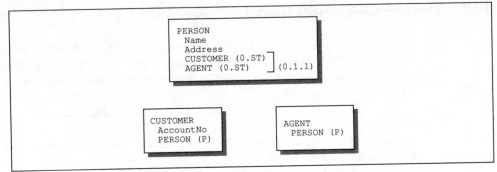

Figure 17.5 Inheritance in the SOM

both specializations (subclasses) of PERSON. The SOM notation for this is shown in Figure 17.5.

The three numbers separated by dots (0.1.1) in the definition of PERSON represent respectively whether a subtype is required or not (0 or 1), the minimum number of subtypes that must have a value, and the maximum number of subtypes that must have a value. Thus, for 'normal' inheritance, where one particular instance may only be either a CUSTOMER or an AGENT but not both at the same time, the values will be (0.1.1).

Representing design information

The SOM diagrams that we have looked at so far do not provide much information about the domain (type) of the attributes defined. Nor is there any place to record more detailed information about what that attribute or SOM means. Computer-aided software engineering (CASE) tools that support the SOM, such as SALSA, provide facilities for recording this type of information that is useful in the design process. Figure 17.6 shows a window from the SALSA design tool that allows this type of information to be recorded.

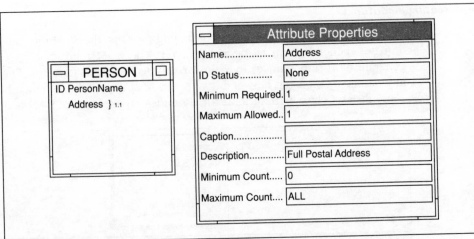

Figure 17.6 Representing additional design information using SALSA

17.4   Translating an SOM design into an OODB schema

Since there is such a close relationship between the SOM and the object-oriented data model, the translation is very straightforward. We can look at each of the elements of the SOM and how it translates to the object-oriented data model.

Semantic objects

Each semantic object will translate into a class definition. Where an semantic object has subtypes, those subtypes will become subclasses in the OODB. Thus the SOM of Figure 17.5 can be translated into the following data definition code:

```
DEFINE PERSON FROM ROOT
KEY NAME
ATTRIBUTES
   Name : STRING
   Address : STRING

DEFINE CUSTOMER FROM PERSON
ATTRIBUTES
   CustomerNo : NUMBER

DEFINE AGENT FROM PERSON
```

Attributes

Simple attributes translate directly between models. Multi-valued attributes that are defined in the SOM will become multi-valued set attributes in the OODB schema. For instance, the `TelephoneNo` attribute of Figure 17.4 will become:

```
TelephoneNo SET OF STRING
```

Or, if the OODB supports arrays, the maximum cardinality of 3 could be enforced by a statement such as:

```
TelephoneNo ARRAY[3] OF STRING
```

Composite attributes will make use of the structure construct of the OODB. Figure 17.7 shows an example of such a composite attribute, as well as the multi-valued attribute described earlier, and shows how they would both be represented in the OODB.

```
CUSTOMER
  Surname
  Address
   Line1
   Line2
   Town
   PostCode ┐(0.2)
  TelephoneNo (0.3)
```

```
DEFINE CUSTOMER FROM PERSON
ATTRIBUTES
   Surname: STRING
   Address: STRUCT (Line1 : STRING,
     Line2: STRING, Town: STRING,
     PostCode: STRING)
   TelephoneNo: SET OF STRING
```

Figure 17.7 Composite and multi-valued attributes

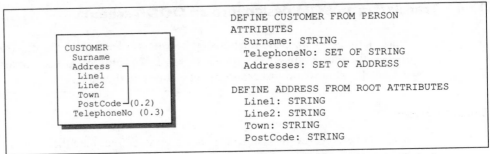

Figure 17.8 Composite and multi-valued attributes (alternative representation)

An alternative implementation of this would be to use a separate database class to represent the address. This might be necessary if the OODBMS used did not support structures and is in any case probably a more object-oriented way to implement such composite attributes. The result of choosing this implementation route is shown in Figure 17.8.

Note that, in this case, there is no need for a relationship from ADDRESS to CUSTOMER, since it can be assumed that it will never be necessary to retrieve the CUSTOMER from an ADDRESS. If it were thought necessary to do that, then the design would have made ADDRESS a separate semantic object in the first place.

Relationships

Relationships are mapped onto the object-oriented data model in a very similar way to attributes. The relationship shown in Figure 17.3 would result in the following data definition commands:

```
DEFINE MORTGAGE FROM ROOT
RELATIONSHIPS
   Customer : CUSTOMER

DEFINE CUSTOMER FROM PERSON
RELATIONSHIPS
   Mortgages : SET OF MORTGAGE
```

The class MORTGAGE has a relationship Customer whose value will be an instance of Customer. At the other end of the relationship, CUSTOMER has a relationship Mortgage which will have a set of instances of MORTGAGE as its value.

17.5   A case study

As an example we will first of all derive a semantic object model for a much simplified motor insurance system. In this system, we can assume that the following semantic objects are of interest: CUSTOMER, POLICY, DRIVER, ADDRESS, CAR and MOTORCYCLE. These objects have been identified as having the attributes shown in the table below:

CUSTOMER	Name	Address	Policies		
POLICY	PolicyNumber	Customer	Vehicles	Drivers	ExpiryDate
DRIVER	Policy	Name	Address	Age	
ADDRESS	Line1	Line2	City	PostalCode	
CAR	Make	Model	EngineSize		
MOTORCYCLE	Make	Model	EngineSize		

It is clear that we have used attributes to implicitly define what in the ER model would be called 'relationships'. CUSTOMER has the relationship Policies which associates a number of policies with a CUSTOMER. Similarly, POLICY has an attribute Vehicles which denotes the motorcycles and cars covered by a particular policy. POLICY also has an attribute (Drivers) that lists the drivers insured to use the vehicle under the policy.

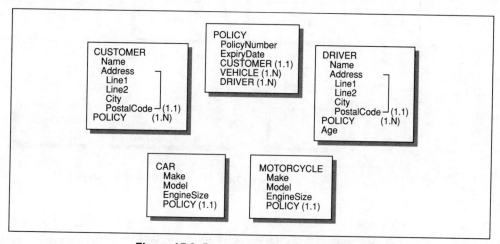

Figure 17.9 Example SOM without inheritance

This information can be taken and used to create the SOM shown in Figure 17.9. Note that we have chosen to represent addresses in both CUSTOMER and DRIVER as composite attributes. We could instead have chosen to represent the address as a separate semantic object. A separate semantic object allows the same address instance to be used by, for instance, two customers who live at the same address. However, this does mean that should one of those customers move to a different address, then the system would have to arrange for a new instance of address to be created rather than simply modify the existing address, as this would result in the wrong address being recorded for the customer who did not move. The down-side of this is that should both customers change address simultaneously, then two addresses will need updating rather than one.

The fact that some of the semantic objects we have identified have attributes in common hints that there is call for some use of inheritance. Clearly, MOTORCYCLE and

CAR have the same attributes and can thus be generalized to VEHICLE. We will retain the two subtypes MOTORCYCLE and CAR as it may be useful to be able to query them separately – for example, to report solely on policies concerning motorcycles. They can of course always be retrieved together by querying the VEHICLE semantic object. An alternative solution would be to have the single semantic object VEHICLE but to use another attribute as a flag to indicate the type of the vehicle (i.e. CAR or MOTORCYCLE).

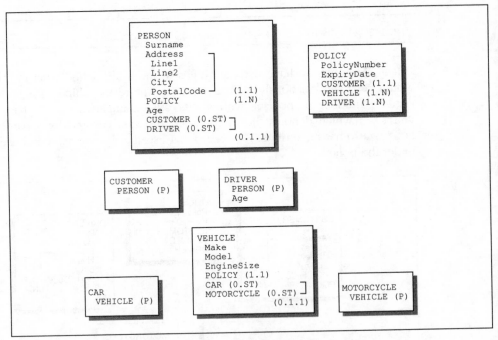

Figure 17.10 Example SOM with inheritance

The resulting SOM is shown in Figure 17.10. This can simply be transformed into a set of data definition commands for the OODB shown below:

```
DEFINE PERSON FROM ROOT
EXTENT Persons
ATTRIBUTES
    Name : STRING
    Address : (
          Line1 : STRING
          Line2 : STRING
          City : STRING
          PostalCode : STRING)

DEFINE CUSTOMER FROM PERSON
EXTENT Customers
RELATIONSHIPS
    Policies : SET OF POLICY INVERSE OF POLICY Customer

DEFINE DRIVER FROM PERSON
```

```
EXTENT Drivers
ATTRIBUTES
   Age : Number
RELATIONSHIPS
   Policy : POLICY INVERSE OF POLICY Drivers

DEFINE POLICY FROM ROOT
KEY PolicyNumber
EXTENT Policies
ATRIBUTES
   PolicyNumber : INTEGER
   ExpiryDate : DATE
RELATIONSHIPS
   Vehicles : SET OF VEHICLE INVERSE OF VEHICLE Policy
   Drivers : SET OF DRIVER INVERSE OF DRIVER Policy
   Customer : CUSTOMER INVERSE OF CUSTOMER Policy

DEFINE VEHICLE FROM ROOT
EXTENT Vehicles
ATTRIBUTES
   Make : STRING
   Model : STRING
RELATIONSHIPS
   Policy : POLICY INVERSE OF POLICY Vehicles

DEFINE CAR FROM VEHICLE
EXTENT Cars

DEFINE MOTORCYCLE FROM VEHICLE
EXTENT MotorCycles
```

The translation is straightforward (see Chapter 16 for more information) and there are only a few points to note:

- The structure syntax is used to define the composite attribute Address. This attribute will therefore be considered a part of any instances of CUSTOMER or DRIVER. Deleting an instance of either of these attributes will result in the address being deleted too.
- CAR and MOTORCYCLE are both defined, even though they have the same attributes. This allows retrieval of instances of the two classes independently.
- Inverse relationships are used for all the relationships between classes.

This example shows how a set of semantic objects can be identified for a system and used to define an object-oriented database schema. It is worth observing that it is not in reality much more difficult to go straight to the object-oriented schema definition. The advantage of using the SOM becomes apparent when the methodology is supported by a CASE tool. This allows the recording of documentary information about the usage of attributes and semantic objects that is useful for design and maintenance, but is not included in the final schema definition statements. In addition, a graphical notation is easier to understand and can be more easily browsed.

17.6 Summary

In this chapter we have looked briefly at the EER data model as a means to designing OODB schemas. We have also considered in much more detail the use of the SOM for such a purpose.

It is by no means certain that the use of such techniques is always the best technology for the design of OODBs. The close coupling between OODBMS and programming language may make the use of a more programming-language-oriented approach such as HOOD or OMT more appropriate for some types of system.

The consensus on how to design OODBs is by no means as mature as for relational databases and is still undergoing a process of discovery.

APPENDIX A
Data storage and access methods

A.1 Introduction

Much of this book refers to standard computer-based access and storage mechanisms, and perhaps not all readers will be overly familiar with them. This appendix therefore sets out to redress that deficiency, but it can also be used to refresh the memory of other readers.

At the most basic level, files consist of groups of related records which each consist of a set of data items. The records can be stored physically in blocks (called 'pages' on some machines) such that several records can be read into memory (or written from memory) with a single physical I/O. The remainder of this appendix will look at each of the different methods of physically storing those records (in a non-database sense) on backup storage, and at how to access them.

The actual syntax for each method varies from manufacturer to manufacturer and for that reason none is given here. Readers who wish to follow this book in a practical sense are recommended to refer to their own user manuals.

A.2 Serial access

This is the simplest form of file organization. Records are written to the file purely in the order in which they are created, the physical address of the next available record being kept usually in a 'header block' at the start of the file. The advantages lie in its simplicity. The disadvantages are that a specific record cannot be located without a serial (linear) search through the file and that any deletions (if permitted) will leave holes in the file. The general usage for such files is for work files where the ordering is unimportant.

A.3 Sequential access

These are similar to serial files except that the records are presorted into some defined sequence based on one of the constituent data items. Clearly, this sorting means high processor overheads which must be repeated every time new records are added. The result of this is that sequential files are in practice usually used for fixed files with little record creation. Advantages over serial files are that, for the latter, to establish whether or not a record exists will take n reads if the record does not exist, whereas, with sequential files, the average number of reads necessary will be $n/2$, where n is the number of records on the file.

A.4 Indexed files

The essential ingredients of indexed files are that the records themselves are kept in arbitrary order, but an index of the records' keys is maintained separately in key order with each index owning a pointer (a physical disc address) to the associated record/block. The index can be one of three forms.

Implicit

All possible keys are maintained in sequence. As a result a dichotomizing (binary) search can be used to locate the required entry (whereby the index is split in two, the file management system decides whether the required record's key is greater or less than the mid-index value, the other half is discarded and the remaining half is split again and the process continues until the relevant entry is found). The advantage of this method is that target records can be found quickly without block searching (see the next two sections following). The disadvantages are several.

First, if there are a great many entries in the index, the binary search may be slow. The answer to this would be to have levels of indexes as shown in Figure A.1. Here the index is split into a number of tables, each having a fixed maximum number of entries. To find the record whose key is 73, the file system first looks to the coarse table (sub-subindex) and ascertains that the required subtable is 2. This is then read into memory and from it the file system determines that the fine table required is 10. This is in turn read into memory, the key for record 73 is found, and hence the physical address of record 73.

In practice, the number of entries in a table is far greater than eight, which lessens the number of I/Os, but in general if m is the number of entries in a table, then if m is exceeded a new subindex will be required, if the number of records exceeds $m \times m$ then a sub-subindex will be required, and so on. Thus in general the number of levels of tables required will be k where:

$$m^{k-1} < n < m^k \ (n = \text{population of the file}).$$

This in turn implies $k + 1$ reads are required to access a particular record – a high overhead. Another disadvantage is that, in reality, the keys are rarely numbered 1, 2, 3, ..., 8, and so on, so that the tables have to be maintained with any m discrete (but not contiguous) values. Thus, if a table contained the following values, with $m = 8$:

10386
10402
10407
10413
10483
10489
10491
10523

INDEX

KEY			
1	address	1	TABLE 1
2	..	2	
4	..	4	
7	..	7	
9	..	9	TABLE 2
10	..	10	
15	..	15	
17	..	17	TABLE 3
20	..	20	
21	..	21	
23	..	23	
24	..	24	
etc.			

SUBINDEX

TABLE NO	HIGHEST VALUE	
1	7	SUB TABLE 1
2	15	
3	24	
..	..	
..	..	
8	63	
9	72	SUB TABLE 2
..	..	
..	..	
16	128	
etc.		

SUB-SUBINDEX

SUB TABLE NO	HIGHEST VALUE
1	63
2	128
..	..
etc.	

Figure A.1 Levels of tables within an implicit index

if we now wished to create an entry for value 10437, then it would not fit into the above table. Rather than shuffle all existing entries around from table to table to create room for the new value, the file system would create an overflow table (here containing the entry 10523) with a physical pointer to it from the above table and a physical pointer from it to the next logical table. Since the overflow table is likely to be situated elsewhere on disc, a large number of overflow tables will give expensive I/O costs and a loss of efficiency.

Basic

These tables are used to support index-random files. An index might appear as shown in Figure A.2.

In this methodology, the ordering of the index is random but, should sequential reading be required, a set of chain pointers allows access to the next highest key value. Thus for entry 1, key 1 the chain points to entry 3 as containing the next highest key value. Entry 5 has a chain value of zero because the next highest value is also

ENTRY NO ADDRESS	KEY	PHYSICAL	CHAIN
1	1	0	3
2	3	12	5
3	2	42	2
4	6	79	0
5	4	84	0
6	5	29	4

Figure A.2 Example index of basic type

the next physical entry. This method has the advantage of never needing overflow tables (because new entries are simply added at the end with the relevant pointers being 'fixed up'). Also multiple levels of indexing are not required, but the disadvantage is that for large files a sequential read will involve many head movements in following the chains. This type of file organization is not supported by COBOL but is found in certain database systems.

Limit

This type of file organization is a compromise between the above two types. The records are grouped in blocks, each block having an exclusive range of keys, the highest of which is stored in an index (similar in principle to the subindex of Figure A.1). The file management system can thus find out from the index which block to search for a given record. Because not every record has a key entry, the number of tables is reduced. Within each block the records are chained as in the basic index filing described above, to cut down on linear searching.

Note

The definitions of index random and index sequential here are generalized definitions. Some manufacturers have evolved their own forms of indexing which are idiosyncratically labelled 'index random' or 'index sequential'. For the purposes of this book, the general definitions will suffice.

A.5 Direct files

Again, the definitions vary from manufacturer to manufacturer. In particular, the following are two fairly common forms.

1 The records are grouped into blocks with no indexes. Instead, the user provides a hashing or address-generating algorithm to calculate the block address from the key, and once the block is found a serial search locates the desired record. The user must also provide means for dealing with overflow records.

   Unfortunately, it is difficult to design an algorithm that allows for future insertions and overflow situations. In addition, sequential processing is not possible, and so direct files (of this definition) are limited to online files for which fast random accessing is required. In many ways they are similar to random files (see following), but not as fast.

2   Perhaps the more common definition of direct files is where the records are ordered (beginning at 1) with the record key corresponding to the position on the file. Thus a record with key 236 will be the 236th record on the file. Knowing the size of each record, the system can quickly calculate the offset down the file and locate the record. Thus it is extremely quick and sequential processing is possible. The disadvantage is that the file may have no natural keys of 1, 2, 3, and so on, and if, for example, it actually contains four records whose values are 1, 236, 467 and 1045 then space is allocated for all of the missing records with the resulting file being 1045 physical records long.

A.6   Random files

These are a special case of (1) in the previous section where the hashing function is supplied by the manufacturer (as are the means to overcome overflow problems). The user (file manager) must usually state how many records will exist in the file and the system will calculate a suitable block size and generate a hashing function which will minimize overflow problems. This will probably mean that, at initial creation time, each block may only be half-filled, leaving room for further creations at a later date, although the user can often specify the volatility of the file which, clearly, has some bearing on this. Given a key value, the system will use the hashing function to calculate the disc address at which the record is to be stored. Retrieval involves exactly the same procedure. Clearly, the hashing function must be 'clever enough' to fill the blocks roughly equally, though, as they are 'randomly' stored, there is always the chance that some blocks will be more full than others. To this end there are several types of hashing function, but all are beyond the scope of this book.

The advantages of random files are therefore that very quick accessing is afforded (a single I/O unless there is overflow), but the disadvantage is that sequential reading is impossible.

A.7   Inverted files

The files mentioned so far have been simple in terms of their all having (at most) a single key. Accessing a record by multiple keys involves the inverted file approach. This can take one of three forms.

Fully inverted

Every data item is a key and an index is maintained for all their values. As all the data items of each record are stored within the index table, there is no need to store the data record in the usual way.

Partially inverted

Records are stored in the usual way, as well as in the index table, and therefore not all the data items need be keys.

Secondary file indexing

This is frequently seen in normal file-management systems whereby one key is designated as a primary key and any others are secondary keys (the number of secondary keys permissible varies from system to system). Each key type is maintained within its own index. In general, the prime key must be unique, but the secondary keys need not be necessarily so.

A.8 List, chain and ring files

These all refer to similar types of file. Related records are connected by pointers, either in a forward direction or a backward direction, or both. If the last record in a chain has a pointer back to the first then we have a chain or ring.

In the conventional filing-system sense, these are used for available space tables. Suppose that we have a file from which several records have been deleted, leaving holes. If we now wish to create new records it would be more space-efficient to be able to reuse these holes. Good file management systems will therefore keep a linked list of pointers to the various holes such that new records can be directed to the next available gap. If a record is deleted then its address is added to the end of the chain. Usually, but not always, the oldest space is filled first. Examples are shown extensively in Chapter 6.

Other uses of these structure types are common within database management systems (as in index random files, see above, and throughout the CODASYL database philosophy).

APPENDIX B
Bibliography

Parts 1 and 2

C. J. Date, *An Introduction to Database Systems*, 6th edn, Addison-Wesley,1995.
R. Elmasri and S. Navathe, *Fundamentals of Database Systems*, Benjamin Cummings, 1989.
F. R. McFadden and J. A. Hoffer, *Database Management*, Benjamin Cummings, 1985.
L. A. Maciaszek, *Database Design and Implementation*, Prentice-Hall, 1990.
H. Robinson, *Database Analysis and Design*, Chartwell-Bratt, 1981.

Part 3

U. Gupta and W. Gietz, *SQL Programmers Guide*, Que, 1989.
M. Krohn, *Using the Oracle Toolset*, Addison-Wesley, 1993.
G. Sturner, *Oracle 7*, ITT Publishing, 1995.
R. F. Van der Lans, *Introduction to SQL*, Addison-Wesley, 1988.

Part 4

D. B. Bock and T. Ryan, Accuracy in Modelling with Extended Entity Relationship and Object Orientated Data Models, *Journal of Database Management*, 4(4), 30–9, 1993.
R. Cattell, *The Object Database Standard: ODMG-93*, Morgan Kaufmann.
M. Hammer and D. McLeod, Database Description with SDM: A Semantic Database Model, *ACM Trans. Database Systems*, 6(3), 351–86, 1981.
W. Kim, *Introduction to Object-Oriented Databases*, MIT Press, 1990.
D. M. Kroenke, *Database Processing: Fundamentals, Design, Implementation*, 4th edn, Macmillan: New York, 1992.
S. R. Monk, Schema Evolution in Object-Oriented Databases Using Class Versioning, *SIGMOD Record*, 22(3), 16–22, 1993.
I. Sommerville, *Software Engineering*, 4th edn, Addison-Wesley, 1993.
M. Stonebraker and G. Kemnitz, The POSTGRES Next-Generation Database Management System, *Comm. of ACM*, 34(10), 78–92, 1991.
G. Vossen, Bibliography on Object-Oriented Database Management, *SIGMOD Record*, 20(1), 24–46, 1991.

Index